In this time of a red-hot economy, pressures to attract and retain employees could cause a leader to lose sight of the need to make tough and unpopular decisions. Scott's book is a reminder for leaders to lean into the uncomfortable.

—John Schroeder, Chairman and CEO at MapR

Great teams are built around purpose and vision. Through *The Power of Mandate*, Scott brings together the stories and learnings of great leaders who have been unwavering in their vision and purpose and clearly demonstrates how you can empower and unleash these great teams toward your own mandate.

—Rob Chapple, Chief Revenue Officer at Civis Analytics

Members of high-performing organizations develop mutual respect and admiration and give one another the benefit of the doubt marching together to conquer the impossible. In *The Power of Mandate*, Scott Stawski gets it right. Working together to craft a shared vision builds buy-in and commitment. Once the mandate is accepted and embraced, the human locomotive barrels forward at full speed—all at once powerful and virtually unstoppable. Well done, Mr. Stawski, well done.

—H. Neil Matkin, EdD, District President at Collin College

The digital disruption we are seeing in the marketplace is only accelerating. It necessitates that businesses operate faster and more agile than ever. While many books have been written about the technology, *The Power of Mandate* addresses the necessary leadership skills and traits needed to succeed in today's disruptive environment.

—Sid Nair, EVP & Chief Sales & Marketing Officer
at Cox Automotive

This is a book about business and yet transcends the parameters of contemporary thinking. It is a book about creativity, vision, daring, and those who would see their ideas to success. I highly recommend it for any entrepreneur, thinker, or artist in all walks of life. The survival of any idea, company, invention, or conception is not dependent on groupthink, it comes from bold leadership. Feeling stagnant and want to find a way forward, read Scott Stawski's *The Power of Mandate.*

—Steven Young, Associate Professor
at Texas Woman's University

Despite the ever increasing focus on collaborative business models, this book commands C-Suite executives to remain decisive. Top leaders build great companies by establishing and executing a bold vision to outpace the competition.

—Anthony Erickson, EVP & COO at Cenergistic

Work, and the way work is done, is undergoing massive change, disruptions under sail, and necessary. Scott gets it, and offers working insights into a new leadership paradigm, a leadership mindset that challenges the status quo.

—Stephen Percoco, Vice President, Sales Strategy
and Innovation at Quickbase

This journey into the world of leadership underlines the process of transforming a creative vision to a business-oriented success. It perfectly shows how leaders exceed the eternal burden of consensus. A Must-Read.

—Salaheddine Mezouar, Chairman of General Confederation
of Moroccan Enterprises. Former Moroccan Minister
of Foreign Affairs, Economy and Finance

A reminder of how unrelenting focus with a clear goal is key to driving impactful transformations. *The Power of Mandate* is a great guide in helping any leader drive real change.

—Mahesh Shah, Chief Product and
Technology Officer at CDK Global

A blueprint for success in this fast moving, disruptive business.

—Tom Ament, General Manager Global
Alliances at Micro Focus

Scott draws out what we all knew but didn't have the courage to accept. In our increasingly conflict averse, "safe" zone work places, his book is a reminder and a good playbook to break the mold and increase the chances of innovation blossoming. Scott weaves in pragmatic advice based on his years in the corporate world, a fresh practitioner's view as opposed to a professorial framework.

—Elango R, President HP/DXC SBU at Mphasis

A very insightful book in which Scott Stawski shows how worthy it is to develop your own leadership style driven by a vision and not by a consensus. A must-read for all leaders and managers, especially those who evolve in a fast changing, challenging environment.

—Yassine Haddaoui, Executive Vice President of
Strategy and Investments at CDG Capital

THE POWER OF
MANDATE

THE POWER OF
MANDATE

HOW VISIONARY LEADERS KEEP
THEIR ORGANIZATION FOCUSED ON
WHAT MATTERS MOST

SCOTT STAWSKI

with Jimmy Brown, PhD

New York Chicago San Francisco Athens London Madrid
Mexico City Milan New Delhi Singapore Sydney Toronto

1 2 3 4 5 6 7 8 9   QVS   24 23 22 21 20 19

ISBN   978-1-260-45440-6
MHID   1-260-45440-1

e-ISBN   978-1-260-45441-3
e-MHID   1-260-45441-X

Library of Congress Cataloging-in-Publication Data

Names: Stawski, Scott, author. | Brown, Jimmy, author.
Title: The power of mandate : how visionary leaders keep their organization focused on what matters most / Scott Stawski, with Jimmy Brown, Ph.D.
Description: New York : McGraw-Hill, [2019] | Includes bibliographical references and index.
Identifiers: LCCN 2019017063 (print) | LCCN 2019018951 (ebook) | ISBN 9781260454413 | ISBN 126045441X | ISBN 9781260454406 (alk. paper) | ISBN 1260454401
Subjects: LCSH: Leadership. | Chief executive officers--Case studies.
Classification: LCC HD57.7 (ebook) | LCC HD57.7 .S7248 2019 (print) | DDC 658.4/092--dc23
LC record available at https://lccn.loc.gov/2019017063

McGraw-Hill Education books are available at special quantity discounts to use as premiums and sales promotions or for use in corporate training programs. To contact a representative, please visit the Contact Us pages at www.mhprofessional.com.

Dedicated to my mentors and coworkers.
Over a 25-year career, I have had numerous mentors that
have guided my career. And for the past 10 years,
my coworkers at DXC Technology and Hewlett Packard
have provided me invaluable learnings.
To them, I am grateful.

CONTENTS

ACKNOWLEDGMENTS

To family, friends, coworkers, and academics who have assisted me in numerous ways, I wish to express gratitude. To my wife, Hope, and son, Henry, who have tolerated my many late nights and weekends of research and writing, their support and encouragement have been never-ending. Jimmy Brown, PhD, has been more than a contributor to this book. Over the years there have been many evenings with Jimmy discussing leadership and management concepts and their practical applications. To my researcher Robin Smith, without whom this project would not have reached completion. His thorough research was key to building the foundation of the subject matter.

To my editor Donya Dickerson at McGraw-Hill who expressed faith and encouragement from the onset. She epitomizes the value that publishing houses bring to these endeavors. Jeanne Levine at Pub Zone Consulting who helped move this project from concept to reality. Don Ostrowski, research advisor in the social sciences and lecturer at the Harvard University Extension School, who has provided me invaluable guidance on writing techniques over the years. Richard Adamonis, director of communication at DXC Technology, for both encouragement and content suggestions.

To the numerous current and former employees of Amazon, Apple, Netflix, Airbnb, Facebook, DXC Technology, and Microsoft. Your candor both on the record and off the record provided the data that led to the hypothesis key to this project. Lastly, I wish to thank the myriad number of friends who have always been a constant source of encouragement and inspiration, with a special shout-out to the Dritschler, McConnell, Klaus, Young, and Chapple families.

CHAPTER 1

INTRODUCING THE MANDATE DRIVEN LEADER

Good business leaders create a vision, articulate the vision, passionately own the vision, and relentlessly drive it to completion.
—JACK WELCH, former Chairman and CEO, General Electric

Teaching leadership skills and principles in itself is a large business. And most consultants and business schools teach consensus building and management as the core foundation of leadership. In fact, in many companies, the concept of achieving consensus has achieved a sacrosanct status. But truth be told, consensus-driven leadership is, in fact, a root cause of many a failed business.

Consensus can be defined a number of different ways. The broadest definition is "general agreement." The synonyms we find in *Roget's Thesaurus* are terms along the lines of *concur, assent,* or *popular opinion.* When we start digging through MBA texts, we find terms like "a decision reached by a group, not through the mandate of an individual, but through agreement of all the participants." In other words, it means the decision was reached by the overall opinion of the group. It does not necessarily mean the decision was reached easily or that there were not widely differing views or active group discussion. It simply means that it was a group decision and/or action. Given that there had to be debate and discussion, it is clear that reaching consensus requires negotiation and compromise. The question that must be addressed especially in today's disruptive business environment is whether this is always the best approach.

Many scholars and business leaders have praised the virtues of consensus management. In a 1990 *Harvard Business Review* article, "Consensus, Continuity, and Common Sense," Rod Canion, cofounder and CEO of Compaq Computer, stated: "Our management process is based on the concept of consensus management. The real benefit of the process is not that you get the answer but all the things you go through to get the answer. You get a lot of facts, you get a lot of people thinking, and the result is that everybody owns the decision when you get through."[1] The assumption here is that groups always make the right decision. *Really?* I know some very charismatic individuals who are great at consensus building, right to the point where the consensus-driven programs they implemented failed miserably. As for Compaq Computer and its much-hailed consensus management approach of the late 1980s, after many turbulent years Compaq was acquired by Hewlett Packard in 2002, and the Compaq brand was discontinued in 2014.

The case we will make in this book is that while consensus-based decision making is very popular and does tend to make people *feel good*, it is not necessarily the best approach. And it is rarely the right approach for C-level executives—especially during a time when technology is driving real business disruption.

Being Popular Is Not the Same Thing as Being Effective

Peter Drucker, the legendary management consultant, educator, and author, once remarked, "Leadership is not magnetic personality; that can just as well be a glib tongue. It is not 'making friends and influencing people,' that is flattery. Leadership is lifting a person's vision to higher sights, the raising of a person's performance to a higher standard, the building of a personality beyond its normal limitations."[2] Drucker's comment helps crystalize the fact that visionary leaders establish objectives higher than the status quo—or, completely outside the box of the status quo. Frankly, these visionary and disruptive leaders eschew the status quo, and they realize that consensus management techniques epitomize status quo thinking.

In today's business world, too many senior leaders practice consensus management in a business environment that demands a different approach. Today, companies using harmony of decision making can be on a fast track to failure for the simple reason that consensus is not necessarily about what is best for the company. Nor is it about establishing and moving toward a vision that lifts everyone's performance. It is about finding the outcome that is least objectionable to everyone involved. Quite often in that approach innovation gives way to harmony and good behavior. And similar to the saying about well-behaved people rarely making history, comfortable organizations rarely change the world.

When we consider the facts at hand, it becomes painfully apparent that too many businesses and their leaders have moved too far down the path of consensus-driven management. They strive for congruity to the detriment of company success. While this point may always have been true throughout business history, it is being amplified by the inflection point and resulting business disruption we are at today.

Today much of our economy, the digital economy, is now driven by technology. This technological innovation is resulting in real, long-lasting business disruption. New markets and channels are being created, entire business paradigms rethought, supply and demand channels upended. Nothing is sacrosanct.

Think about it—the winners in today's digital economy are the disrupters—the absolute antithesis of consensus.

So how do we have all these amazing technological innovations that power our world and allow us to do things that only a few years ago were the stuff of science fiction? Simply put, these disruptive companies are propelled forward by Mandate Driven Leadership. And as we'll learn through the course of this book, these leaders are not consensus driven, and they really don't care who agrees with them when it concerns achieving their vision.

So why study these troublemakers, who sometimes are equally hated as loved? Because in today's disruptive business environment, we have too many executives who seek and are rewarded more by successful consensus management than by mandating a vision to reality. However, it is the Mandate Driven Leaders who are the true effective leaders, and their companies are not just disrupters; they are making lasting change to the world around us. Leaders that epitomize Mandate Driven Leadership have created or redefined entire industries: Jeff Bezos of Amazon, Steve Jobs of Apple, Mark Zuckerberg of Facebook, Reed Hastings of Netflix, Brian Chesky of Airbnb, Mike Lawrie of DXC Technology, and, of course, Bill Gates of Microsoft. In this book, we will discuss the theory of Mandate Driven Leadership and review practical learnings from these disruptors.

What Is Leadership?

Leadership is a very popular topic. There are articles, classes, and even entire degree programs devoted to it. Walk into any bookstore, and you'll find many stocked shelves to browse. Type the word *leadership* into Amazon's search function, and you'll get more than 60,000 books. Google will pull up even more articles and studies. Obviously, there is no shortage of opinions and perspectives on the subject. That, of course, is part of the problem. Even if we set aside the discussion of whether a leader should be mandate or consensus driven, there are so many different views on what it takes to be a good leader that it can be hard to muddle through them all.

We could look for theoretical guidance from people like Warren Bennis in his *On Becoming a Leader* (1989). Bennis interviews some exceptional leaders including director Sydney Pollack, author Betty Friedan, and A&M Records founder Herb Alpert. The premise of his book is that leadership is a learned trait and it takes work to make it a personal habit. Then there are the practical recommendations of people like Mike Thompson in *The Anywhere Leader* (2011) and Jeffrey Fox in *How to Become CEO* (1998). Both of these works provide exceptional guidance. Thompson relates how great leaders tend to have three characteristics. They are driven by progress, sensationally curious, and vastly resourceful. Fox provides even more practical advice for upcoming leaders: avoid writing a nasty memo, overpay your employees, and skip all office parties. Each of these works has valuable insight; in particular for those beginning their management career. However, from a leadership perspective, these are not the works that address what traits and models are needed for a leader to be effective in today's disruptive environment. For example, what type of leader is needed at the traditional broadcast networks if they are to compete, even survive, against Netflix?

There are even the borderline sociopathic approaches recommended by Robert Greene in *The 48 Laws of Power* (1998). In this book, Greene puts forth 48 essential laws that will propel leaders to success in their objective; more aptly, Greene would say to domination of their environment. He draws support for these laws from philosophers, Machiavelli and Sun Tzu among others, and historical figures as diverse as Henry Kissinger, Julius Caesar, and P. T. Barnum. The *Los Angeles Times* referred to Greene as a "cult hero with the hip-hop set, Hollywood elite and prison inmates alike."[3] Even though some of Greene's advice might be handy for some Mandate Driven Leaders, for karma's sake we're going to leave this one alone.

In 2016, Patrick Lencioni wrote the bestselling leadership book *The Ideal Team Player: How to Recognize and Cultivate the Three Essential Virtues*. The book traces a fictional leader who is trying to turn around a company by reestablishing its culture of teamwork. Notice that we said it is fiction, not a biography.

Despite all these different efforts to address the topic, no one seems to be able to answer the question—what does it really take to be an effective leader in today's disruptive business environment? As important, what is the definition of an effective leader? With skyrocketing executive compensation, some would say that statement has become a multimillion-dollar question. When we consider the impact a leader can have on the outcomes of an organization, it is actually more like a multibillion-dollar question. Nowhere is this more apparent than when we consider leaders who are driving innovations that are changing our world and propelling the digital economy. Given the littered landscape of failed companies built on great ideas, it is obvious that having the right leader at the helm is critical.

What differentiates a good leader from a bad one? What makes someone able to drive a group to a desired set of outcomes? How do leaders keep their organizations focused on what truly matters most? There are a lot of different ways to ask it, but at the end of the day, it is all about driving not just desirable but visionary outcomes for the organization and the people in it.

It seems like every author who has ever typed a single word about leadership is determined to put his or her own spin on what it takes to be an effective leader. A fairly detailed qualitative meta-analysis of the leading literature suggests that leadership traits and characteristics can be grouped into three common themes of what it takes to be an effective leader. Those themes are represented in Figure 1.1.

However, in today's disruptive environment it is not enough for an effective leader to solely draw from these three themes. For today's leader to be effective, these themes must be superimposed on an environment where the leader has defined a vision for the company and through directive management mandates that vision to execution each and every day. The leadership traits summarized in these three themes are critical, but they cannot exist in a vacuum without this visionary mandate.

The first theme is that *leaders expect the best from themselves and from others*. This may sound like something from a basic Boy Scout credo, but a leader's performance can really only be evaluated in terms of the performance of the group. Thus, if leaders want to succeed, they need everyone doing

FIGURE 1.1   Three Themes of Effective Leadership

things right. Some advocates of "servant leadership" approaches suggest that true leaders focus on the success of the team, not on making themselves look good. William Cohen wrote in *The Stuff of Heroes: The Eight Universal Laws of Leadership*, "My research debunks the myth that many people seem to have . . . that you become a leader by fighting your way to the top. Rather, you become a leader by helping others to the top. Helping your employees is as important as, and many times more so than, trying to get the most work out of them."[4] While this isn't necessarily always the case, at the end of the day all good leaders know the only path for them to success is for the team to succeed. Team success is sometimes mistaken to be solely the realm of consensus management. Not true. Mandate Driven Leaders also drive teams to success. In fact, they absolutely require it.

Regardless of what a leader's motive is, leaders *stay motivated and motivate others*. This is our second common theme, and it is quite an important leadership characteristic. Why is it so important? Let's answer that question with another question. Have you ever seen someone who was unmotivated effectively lead a successful team or organization? Probably not. Have you ever seen an exceptional leader who was not pushing the team to achieve even higher goals? Didn't think so. Good leaders know how to get a team to do more than they think they can do. We'll debate about whether it is better for a leader to motivate through inspiration or anxiety in a later discussion, but at the end of the day great leaders push individuals and teams to a higher goal than they could ever imagine for themselves.

In addition to motivating their teams, leaders are also *not shy about letting the world know about their accomplishments.* The great ones are even less shy about letting the world know *about their team's accomplishments,* which is our third theme. When broadcasting their successes, they talk about "we" much more than "I." Servant leaders do this out of a commitment to their team's well-being. Narcissistic leaders do it because they recognize that people like being recognized for their hard work and really dislike it when others take credit for their work. Mandate Driven Leaders understand that recognition drives outcomes and helps teams drive toward the vision set by the leader. Effective leaders understand this and leverage this knowledge in how they interact with their teams.

As discussed earlier, the literature to date includes outstanding works delving further into these three themes and all the learned leadership characteristics, traits, and some would say rules that compose the themes. Missing is the realization that no company today can afford to be led within a status quo environment. Organizations cannot be led by those who excel at consensus management and propel themselves to the forefront through a path of least resistance. Organizations led by the qualified yet ordinary are setting themselves up for failure.

Today we need leaders who can push organizations in directions they may not want to go, in part because they don't realize they need to. These leaders have a vision, and they command the organization to take a certain course of action to achieve that vision. These visionary leaders have a belief, idea, strategy, or tactic that is so compelling that they do not accept no for an answer. Through mandate, they drive the vision from concept to implementation. Through this leadership willpower, organizations are propelled toward the vision. Once on that path, management and the employee base of these companies can increase the depth, breadth, and velocity of that forward motion. A leader that possesses the traits within these three themes who has also established an environment where the vision of the future is clear and is being mandated to execution is the effective leader needed for today.

What is effective leadership? Effective leadership is about maximizing the performance of teams, groups, and organizations, and this definition is fairly consistent with most experts. Effective leadership promotes effective team and group performance and drives the desired outcomes. The key is the desired outcomes. Mandate Driven Leaders rarely use consensus to uncover the desired outcomes. They have a vision, and they dictate the desired business outcomes required by the organization to achieve that vision. Ideally, the resulting vision will enhance the well-being of the people being led, even if they don't realize it at the time. And if those outcomes aren't beneficial? Well, that particular leader won't be in that spot very long.

Being an effective leader and being an effective manager are not necessarily the same thing. This debate often devolves into an analysis of the differences between leadership and management. This debate is very tricky as the two terms are often used interchangeably, and the difference can be a matter of degrees and perspective. Even when people do recognize that there is a difference, the delineation can be quite nuanced. Ask 10 different people the difference between leadership and management, and you might get 11 different responses. While the details may vary, the commonalities usually break down into something about leaders being strategic, charismatic, and admired and managers being organizational taskmasters with a whip in one hand and a bullhorn in the other. While Mandate Driven Leaders prefer to be inspiring and revered, it doesn't bother them one bit to be seen as autocratic and prescriptive. And most important, they know when to be which.

It is important to note here that we use the word *effective* rather than *good* or *liked* as the definition of what a leader needs to be. It is great if you can do both at the same time, but it is not always the case. Sometimes the most effective leaders are not necessarily what we would consider "likable" people. Steve Jobs, founder and former CEO of Apple, once said, "I don't want people to dislike me. I'm indifferent to whether they dislike me." That being said, he was disliked by many within Apple, in part because his leadership style was anything but consensus driven. He also revolutionized several industries and created to this day one of the most valuable companies in the world.

Jobs himself admits that he was a better leader and a better change agent than he was a manager. And for every Apple employee, stockholder, or iPhone user—that is just fine. Many people, myself included, consider Steve Jobs to be one of the great technological visionaries and Mandate Driven Leaders of the modern age. What is often forgotten, however, is that he had a well-deserved reputation of being a difficult and demanding individual. Read the stories of people who worked for him, particularly early in his career, and you'll see a picture of someone who was impatient and arrogant, and who really didn't play well with others unless they wanted to play his game.

Steve Jobs's official biographer, Walter Isaacson, in *Steve Jobs: The Exclusive Biography* relates how Jobs was both inspiring and intimidating at the same time. In 1981 Xerox was introducing the Xerox Star computer. Steve and his team of managers were given a preview. They were less than impressed. Steve Jobs later called Bob Belleville, the chief Xerox Star designer, and said, "Everything you've ever done in your life is shit . . . so why don't you come work for me?" He did. Throughout Jobs's career, people were intimidated by him, but they wanted to work for him. However, in 1985 his leadership style did catch up with him, and he left Apple, the very company he founded. Jobs learned a thing or two, however, by the time Apple's board of directors brought him back in 1997. He had learned how to lead with more than just a technical vision, but a vision to change consumer habits. He sought to embrace others in the pursuit of his vision: to change the way we work, play, and interact. He then took an active role in championing how those products could make the world a better place. The result, of course, is the whole Apple ecosystem that includes iPhones, iPads, and i-everything that pervades everything we do. By the time Steve Jobs stepped down from his role at Apple in 2011, two months before his death, Apple was valued at $347 billion, making it the second most valuable company in the world.

Whenever I talk about the concept of Mandate Driven Leadership or directive stewardship, I often get asked for examples. The late Steve Jobs is one of the more visible examples of someone who exhibited this model. Jeff Bezos, the founder of Amazon, is another who is also profiled in this book. Like Jobs, Bezos has a reputation for being obstinate, at times mean-spirited, and to this day he is said to be a very difficult and challenging person. All that being said, in January 2019 Amazon became the world's most valuable company in terms of market capitalization.

Mandate Driven Leaders' clear priority is to be effective over being liked. However, this is not an either/or discussion. A critical understanding that will be discussed throughout the book is that individuals bring their own persona into their Mandate Driven Leadership model. When you look at all the various personas of disruptive Mandate Driven Leaders, it becomes obvious that leaders don't necessarily have to choose between being effective and being liked. Yes, some leaders like Jobs and Bezos have reputations for being disliked. However many other Mandate Driven Leaders are much admired by their employees. Brian Chesky, the CEO and cofounder of Airbnb, is profiled in this book. In 2016 Airbnb was named the "Best Place to Work" by Glassdoor, having dethroned Google. Larry Page, the cofounder of Google, would easily be characterized as a Mandate Driven Leader but has a well-deserved reputation for not only being visionary, aggressive, and ambitious, but also collaborative and fun.

Mandate Driven Leaders who are successfully leading innovative organizations that create new value in the market focus first on *being impactful* using the persona and traits at hand.

Mike Lawrie, chairman and CEO of DXC Technology, is one of the leaders interviewed for this book. For transparency, the author is an executive for the same company. As an author and academic, it was important to maintain objectivity. So, the natural question—why profile your own corporate leader? In researching this project, it was important to profile disruptive, Mandate Driven Leaders both in start-up environments as well as individuals leading established companies that are being impacted by the digital economy. Each month, we are seeing the previous titans of various industries being disrupted right out of business. During the final edits for this book perhaps the most well-known retailer of all time, Sears & Roebuck, has filed for bankruptcy with probable liquidation—one of many companies that could not survive today's inflection point. Two good examples of companies that have been severely impacted by this disruption are Computer Sciences Corporation and Hewlett Packard Enterprise Services (formerly EDS). Both of these Fortune 50 companies were struggling to merely survive until a Mandate Driven Leader, Mike Lawrie, took the helm. Since they were merged to create DXC Technology, the company has delivered outstanding results, moving from victim to disrupter. DXC, employing more than 125,000 people, is a case study worthy of discussion.

Interestingly, Mike Lawrie stresses that the use of directive leadership must be situational, not absolute. Rightfully, he does not advocate Mandate Driven Leadership in all situations. In the end, Lawrie believes that is far more important for leaders to understand what a particular situation requires and to act appropriately, instead of relying solely on either mandates or consensus. In other words, leaders need to understand what the circumstances demand and what the people around them need to achieve success. The most important thing for leaders to do is to have a diverse leadership toolbox that includes an understanding of when it is most appropriate to use varying leadership styles to accomplish organizational objectives.

"In some cases, a consensus-based leadership style is fine," Lawrie states. "Others, a much more directive or mandate-based leadership style is appropriate. The leader has to have a very good understanding of the environment within which they are thrust and the challenges of the organization. That dictates the leadership style, not the other way around. As a matter of fact, a leadership style that is misapplied to a given situation can be a disaster."[5]

Steve Jobs and the other leaders profiled in this book have changed our world. And make no mistake, in each case that change was a result of a vision. That vision became a mandate, and the mandate drove the organization forward. Not everyone is always comfortable working in these kinds of organizations, and the stories of people who left Apple during Jobs's tenure are many. Of course, for every one that left, Jobs had 10 resumes of others who were ready to take their place. And this is the difference between a Mandate Driven Leader and someone who is just a big jerk. Jerks are hard to work with because that is just who they are, and they are going to be that way all the time. Mandate Driven Leaders have an innovative vision that will disrupt a market and may make the world a better place. They have a passion for achieving the vision that may overwhelm some people. However, they don't worry that others don't see their vision yet. They aren't worried about pushing others out of their comfort zone for the greater good. And most important, they realize that sometimes crowds are not all that wise.

In today's disruptive business environment that demands innovation, companies must have Mandate Driven Leaders in their leadership positions. Vision, strategy, and even aspects of implementation and daily management that are driven by consensus management are more apt to fail. Entire industries are being disrupted and disintermediated by the digital economy. Whether an established company or a start-up, the companies that will survive and thrive will be driven by executive leaders who have a clear vision of their company's future and drive that vision down throughout the company to implement. They do not take no for an answer. They don't surround themselves with executives or employees that are "half in." They don't tolerate questions or problems without answers. "It can't be done" and "That is not possible" are comments that will be quickly rebuked.

These Mandate Driven Leaders have a vision, and they simply demand that vision be turned into a reality.

CHAPTER 2

STEVE JOBS OF APPLE: REALITY DISTORTION FIELD

Here's to the crazy ones. The misfits. The rebels. The troublemak-
ers. The round pegs in the square holes. The ones who see things
differently. They're not fond of rules. And they have no respect for
the status quo. You can quote them, disagree with them, glorify
or vilify them. About the only thing you can't do is ignore them.
Because they change things. They push the human race forward.
And while some may see them as the crazy ones, we see genius.
Because the people who are crazy enough to think they can
change the world are the ones who do.

—APPLE INC. MOTTO

Steve Jobs pulled the blinds to hide the sun in order to capture fully the darkness of his expulsion the previous day from the company that he had built from a precarious and precocious seed to an untamed mammoth of a tree. Initially, he wept in his unfurnished 14-bedroom Woodside mansion as he contemplated the complex collision that had become his existence, and then he sat around for months as he attempted to come to terms with his dismissal. He was humbled, for sure, which was not a characteristic commonly found on Jobs's list of personality traits. In a 2005 commencement speech at Stanford University, Jobs reflected upon those dark days in the spring of 1985.

"I felt that I had let the previous generation of entrepreneurs down," Jobs said, "that I had dropped the baton as it was being passed to me."[1]

13

Jobs had cofounded Apple, a technology company worth $750 billion today, at the age of 21 and was a millionaire by the time he was 23. In his late twenties, he created the Macintosh computer, which his team released to the public in 1984. This desktop computer was a technological marvel; for the first time, consumers had access to a user-friendly way to interact with a computer. The Macintosh was congenial, affordable, and flawlessly marketed. Jobs immediately started a personal computing revolution and became a star.

However, his fall from stardom came quickly. After Macintosh sales failed to manifest fully, an ongoing and contentious battle with Apple's CEO followed, and the war ended with the Apple board of directors removing Jobs as the Macintosh team leader. The directors gave him a ceremonial position as a board chairperson with no real mission before him and sent him off to an isolated corner of the Apple campus.

"I was out; and very publicly out," he recalled. "What had been the focus of my entire adult life was gone, and it was devastating."[2] Instead of staying at Apple, Steve Jobs quit. However, he was far from done.

Inside of his lonely and cavernous home, the Apple figurehead watched the film *Patton*, the biography of the controversial and hard-driving World War II commander. He also listened to Bob Dylan tapes, "for the times they are a-changin'," while worried friends visited in an effort to help him stabilize his wavering mental health. It didn't look good for Jobs at the time, but he would later say that being forced out of Apple was the best thing that could have ever happened to him. "The heaviness of being successful was replaced by the lightness of being a beginner again, less sure about everything," he said. "It freed me to enter one of the most creative periods of my life."[3]

By sheer will and focus, Jobs had crafted Apple into a pop culture company, becoming a technology icon along the way. He threw tantrums, he regularly cried when things didn't go his way, he distorted reality, he drained people as he pushed them to meet impossible deadlines.

And he seldom allowed his visions to be clouded by the guidance of those around him.

For Jobs, individuals would have to follow his lead or be left behind, because he wasn't sticking around to pick them up, and through these means, he succeeded at the highest level. He chose to lead through mandates, or it chose him. Seldom did he pursue any vision in his life through consensus.

Even though it all came crashing down for him in the spring of 1985, he would later be called back to command the company that had ousted him. Jobs's reclamation and legendary comeback made him a worldwide folk hero and a global legend when he returned to Apple to pull his company from the grips of bankruptcy by inventing the iPod, iPhone, iPad, and other radical breakthroughs in technology, before dying young from cancer in 2011.

Yes, the late Steve Jobs is truly the epitome of a Mandate Driven Leader.

The Early Life of the Man Who Would Build an Empire

Although Jobs's adoptive parents never kept from him that he was adopted, he never knew his biological parents until he searched for them as an adult. His welcoming lower-middle-class parents counted themselves lucky to have the energetic baby as their own, and they adored him. Steve's adoptive dad, Paul, was a high school dropout and worked in repossessions for a finance company early in Jobs's life, and his mother, Clara, was a bookkeeper. In his spare time, Paul, a solid mechanic, fixed up used cars and sold them.

Jobs recalled crying as a child when a neighborhood kid speculated that his parents didn't want him, and he often told his friends that he felt conflict and pain because his biological family had abandoned him. He consistently went to his parents for security on the matter, and they told him endlessly while looking straight into his eyes, "We. Specifically. Picked. You."

Many people with a personal familiarization with Jobs believe that his adoption drove him to regulate all situations and outcomes throughout his life. Colleague Delbert Yocam said in the definitive biography *Steve Jobs* by Walter Isaacson, "I think his desire for complete control of whatever he makes derives directly from his personality and the fact that he was abandoned at birth."[4]

Jobs grew up in Silicon Valley before it became the Silicon Valley, in a town called Mountain View, California, right outside of Palo Alto. At the time of his upbringing, numerous US defense contractors had planted offices in the area where he lived, and the technology company Hewlett Packard was down the road and growing fast. Stanford had completed a 700-acre industrial park, which encouraged private companies to use the space to commercialize their students' ideas, and Fairchild Semiconductor, the silicon pioneer of the community, which built transistors with silicon instead of the typical germanium, employed 12,000 people.

This technological populace of varying types of engineers surrounded Jobs as he grew up in the Valley, and that influence eventually led him to become a member of the Hewlett Packard Explorers Club. The young teenagers in the group learned about the ongoing HP projects through the eyes of actual engineers, and the club of a dozen students was encouraged to create projects of their own.

When Jobs needed a few parts for his project, in typical Jobs fashion, he pulled out the phone book and called the HP CEO, who not only sent him the parts but also gave him a job on an HP assembly line. Jobs also had a paper route and worked as a clerk at an electronics store. Early in his life, he was ambitious and hardworking, and he soaked up all of the information he could from the HP engineers in the break room when he wasn't working the assembly line, and he explored the bins and shelves of the electronics store, which were full of electrical components.

When he entered Homestead High School, he took an electronics class taught by John McCollum. The retired US Navy pilot was an authoritarian who dressed in white button-down shirts and ties, and Jobs was a growing rebel child with a dislike for institutions. Their personalities were not a match, and while McCollum willingly nurtured the talents of all his students with detailed knowledge of electronics in his well-equipped lab, he never fully embraced Jobs. One of McCollum's star students was Stephen Wozniak, who was five years older than Jobs. After Wozniak graduated from high school, the two met through a mutual friend, and Jobs immediately attached himself to Wozniak.

"He was the first person I met who knew more about electronics than I did at that point," Jobs told *Playboy* magazine in 1985. "We became good friends because we shared an interest in computers and we had a sense of humor. We pulled all kinds of pranks together."

Jobs said that Wozniak was in a world that nobody understood. "No one shared his interests, and he was a little ahead of his time," he said. "It was very lonely for him. He's driven from inner sights rather than external expectations of him."[5]

The two became inseparable, and Wozniak would become Jobs's business partner for many years; in fact, they would create history together. There would be no Apple without "Woz."

"Woz and I are different in most ways, but there are some ways in which we're the same, and we're very close in those ways," Jobs continued. "We're sort of like two planets in their own orbits that every so often intersect."[6]

After Jobs graduated high school in 1972 with a 2.65 GPA, a B and C student, he went to Reed College in Portland, Oregon. However, the pace wasn't fast enough for him there, and he couldn't find inspiration, so he dropped out in the first semester. He began searching for a job and casually walked into Atari one afternoon and demanded a position. The budding video game manufacturer hired Jobs as a technician for $5 an hour.

After only a year, a young and still unsettled Jobs left Atari to take a seven-month sabbatical to India, where he hoped to find enlightenment. While traveling around India from New Delhi to the Himalayas, he contracted dysentery, lost 40 pounds, got his head shaved by a guru, and lived minimally under an umbrella of self-deprivation. He also learned a few things about society, if not enlightenment, and upon returning, he surmised that Western rational thought is not an innate human trait, but a learned one. He appreciated this notion and thought it was important, but he also clung to another particular idea that he found in India: he told Isaacson that he learned to appreciate the power of instinctive feeling.

"The people in the Indian countryside don't use their intellect like we do," Jobs said. "They use their intuition instead, and their intuition is far more developed than in the rest of the world. Intuition is a very powerful thing, more powerful than intellect, in my opinion. That's had a big impact on my work."

After Jobs returned from India in 1975, he went back to work at Atari. His first big project for the company was to design the video game Breakout, and he would receive a bonus if he could create the game with fewer than 50 computer chips. He called his friend Wozniak, who worked at HP, to give him a hand and offered to split the fee with him. Jobs convinced Woz that the two could create the game in four days.

"A game like this might take most engineers a few months," Wozniak recalled in *Steve Jobs*. "I thought there was no way I could do it, but Steve made me sure that I could."[7]

Wozniak completed the work in four days, working day and night, and the two split the fee; but there is a discrepancy in the historical details. Jobs said he split the additional bonus with Woz, who did most of the work and created the game using only 45 chips. Woz doesn't recall ever receiving the bonus, and years later, after the two were worth millions of dollars, he still couldn't come to terms with the fact that the nominal bonus was not shared.

"Ethics always mattered to me," Wozniak told Isaacson, "and I still don't understand why he would've gotten paid one thing and told me he'd gotten paid another, but, you know people are different."[8]

The reality distortion field was beginning to take root.

The Reality Distortion Field Disrupts the Consumer Technology Market

According to Bud Tribble, a software designer on the original Macintosh team, Jobs had an almost mystical, unseen technology that he used to create what his colleagues called the reality distortion machine, a term used to describe Jobs's ability to spin a version of reality that no one else could see until it was processed through him. The processed information, done at light speed, would then be presented to his team through a distortion field, becoming truth, and thereby transferring impossible ideas into tangible reality.

Jobs's dynamic personality, his magical ability to motivate people in various ways to get the best out of them, or in some ways to drain them, to do exactly as his plans dictated in impossible time frames is presented in two ways. Either he had created within himself a monster, a maleficent and oppressive tyrant who was smarter than anyone on his path, or he was a genius storyteller who created a splendiferous tale of man conquering beasts to get the most out of his people and propel them to greatness.

"In his presence, reality is malleable," Tribble said in *Steve Jobs*. "He can convince anyone of practically anything."[9]

He also said that Jobs would not accept any facts contrary to those translated through his distortion field, and Andy Hertzfeld, a computer scientist on the same team, agreed, saying, "The reality distortion machine was a confounding mélange of a charismatic rhetorical style, indomitable will, and eagerness to bend any fact to fit the purpose at hand."[10]

A member of the Macintosh team made "Reality Distortion Field" T-shirts, so the entire team was aware of Jobs's illusion technology, but the technology still accomplished its mission. Those who worked for him were powerless in the presence of the field.

"We would often discuss potential techniques for grounding it," Hertzfeld said, "but after a while, most of us gave up, accepting it as a force of nature."

They came to terms with everything Jobs presented to them: more could be done with limited resources in less time, and the truth was nothing more than an option; and if the truth didn't fit into Jobs's schedule and final destination, then half-truths or complete lies would fill the space until they actually became truth. The record shows, and people detail, that it happened all the time. New realities were continually born under the wing of Jobs, and it empowered and upset his crew. To a person, the distortion became self-fulfilling, and the impossible routinely became possible.

While implementing the reality distortion field, Jobs was notoriously brusque. Reports are rampant that Jobs wasn't the type to coddle those around him. He pushed hard to get the most out of his innovative ideas and the people on his team who built his inventions to completion. Isaacson recalls the last time he saw Jobs before he died in an article he wrote for the *Harvard Business Review*. Isaacson was in the finishing stages of the Jobs book when he asked him about his tendency to be rough on the people who worked with him, and Jobs's reply was simple: "Look at the results." Jobs continued, "These are all smart people I work with, and any of them could get a top job at another place if they were truly feeling brutalized. But they don't." He paused, a long pause, and one could only wonder about the gamut of ideas that pushed and pulled through his mind as he examined the collective history of all that he and his teammates had created, before saying (as Isaacson recalls, "wistfully"),

"And we got some amazing things done."

Apple I

In the bedroom of Steve Wozniak's home in Los Altos, California, Apple was born through its first product, Apple I. The partnership between Jobs and Wozniak that created the Apple I was clearly a strange animal.

"I never wanted to deal with people and step on toes, but Steve could call up people he didn't know and make them do things," Wozniak says, as quoted in *Steve Jobs*. "He could be rough on people he didn't think were smart, but he never treated me rudely." Wozniak needed Jobs, who astonished him with his driven personality that opened every needed door.

The Apple I prototype (Figure 2.1) was a fully assembled motherboard driven by software created by Wozniak in the late hours after he finished his work at HP. The invention was funded by the sale of Wozniak's $500 scientific calculator and Jobs's $200 Volkswagen Bus. The prototype ended up being a monumental achievement. The Apple I used a keyboard to input information and a screen to present the output, which was a brand-new concept.

"I typed a few keys on the keyboard and I was shocked!" Wozniak recalls in his memoir *iWoz*. "It was the first time in history anyone had typed a character on a keyboard and seen it show up on the screen right in front of them."[11]

FIGURE 2.1   Apple I Prototype   Photo: Chris Brown

    The two Steves presented the Apple I to the Homebrew Computer Club, a computer hobbyist group in the area. There was little interest from those who had gathered except from one person, Paul Terrell, the owner of the Byte Shop, the only computer shop in the town. Terrell eventually agreed to buy 50 of the assembled boards and pay $500 apiece for them, a $25,000 order. Jobs and Wozniak were thrilled; however, the pair would need $15,000 worth of parts to fill the order, and they had no money.

    Jobs would not allow his venture to fail, and he set off to find funding. While Wozniak was unquestionably the technological mastermind of the operation, Jobs was the fuel that accelerated Apple down the road to the finish, from the very beginning. Even as Jobs marched around without shoes—described by all who saw him as scruffy and unpleasantly odorous— he was able to get what he needed. He dominated rooms with fire from the pit of him, but his appearance spelled indifference and a certain kind of sincerity born outside of an institution, a physical constitution that people believed was harmless. The combination of a bohemian outsider and aggressive pitchman worked for him. He was an enigma, but a believable one.

He borrowed $5,000 from a friend, but the Los Altos bank declined to loan him money, so he was still short of the needed funds. He headed to the electronics shop where he had worked in high school, but they would not give him the parts for equity in the company. Atari wouldn't help either. Finally, a company called Cramer Electronics extended Jobs 30 days' credit for the parts the pair needed after the store confirmed through a phone call that there was a deal on the table.

Inside the Jobs's home, a crew of family and friends soldered boards for the order, using the garage, a spare bedroom, and the kitchen table as an assembly plant. The impromptu assembly team completed the 50 mother-boards two days before their loan deadline, and Jobs delivered the first Apple order for payment. They would create 200 boards in total, and after those sales, Apple was profitable.

The Apple I became the first personal computing motherboard of the modern age, as we understand them today. This board was innovative because it worked with a regular television set to view the computer activity instead of relying on paper tape and printouts, and it used a typewriter-like keyboard instead of the toggle switches, punch cards, and LED lights of the few personal microcomputers before it. It changed technology forever, and the way that everyone would interact with computers to this very day, but Wozniak wasn't looking to make a universal impact.

"When I built this Apple I . . . it wasn't really to show the world here is the direction the world should go," he told NPR. "It was to really show the people around me, to boast, to be clever, to get acknowledgment for having designed a very inexpensive computer."

The Apple II

In order to get the money to manufacture the Apple II, Jobs and Wozniak needed an investor, and after shopping their merchandise around Silicon Valley, they found their best bet, a guy named Mike Markkula. The retired 33-year-old had made millions of dollars through the stock options he had earned as an employee at Intel after the microchip maker went public, and he was looking for an investment.

Markkula was excited by what he was presented with that day, and the three wrote a business plan together and incorporated Apple. Jobs and Wozniak agreed to give Markkula one-third of the company's equity for a

$250,000 line of credit. In the end, Jobs and Woz would each own 26 percent of the stock in the company, and they would reserve the remaining stock for future investors.

The first West Coast Computer Faire was held in 1977 in San Francisco, and it is often referred to as the birthplace of the personal computer. A 21-year-old Steve Jobs debuted the newly incorporated Apple Computer Co., and the Apple II there.

The machine was a complete package with end-to-end integration from its power source to its embedded software. The groundbreaking machine had a built-in keyboard, color graphics, tape-based storage, expansion slots for other hardware, and a lightweight and sophisticated plastic case that sheltered its wires and boards, making it look like something anyone could use, and "anyone" did. The original Apple II and its upgraded models sold nearly 6 million units and were on the market until Apple ended the model's production in 1993.

Before the launch of Apple II, Apple was worth $5,309, and by the end of 1980, as the company prepared to go public, Apple was valued at $1.7 billion. Many gave Wozniak all the credit for the Apple II creation and the company's rapid rise, but Regis McKenna, a publicist for Apple who worked on the Apple II brochure, said that it was unfair to downplay the impact of Jobs.

"Woz designed a great machine," McKenna said in *Steve Jobs*, "but it would be sitting in hobby shops today were it not for Steve Jobs."[12]

Apple III and LISA

The company expanded rapidly due to the success of the Apple II. Multiple project teams began working on the next big product introduction, with Steve Jobs's time being spent with the Apple III and the LISA product design teams. It is here that Jobs received his first lessons in failure. Both computers were to be designed and marketed to the business marketplace. Jobs delegated much of the responsibility of the Apple III project to the project leader, Dr. Wendell Sander, and Apple's marketing department was heavily involved in the product design. In his 2006 book *iWoz: From Computer Geek to Cult Icon: How I Invented the Personal Computer, Co-founded Apple, and Had Fun Doing It*, Wozniak believed that the primary failure of the Apple III was that the product was designed more by the marketing department than Apple's traditional engineering-driven projects. Introduced in 1980, the product had to be recalled due to stability issues. It was reintroduced in 1981 but eventually discontinued in 1984, selling less than 75,000 units.

Without doubt, this failure would have an impact on solidifying Jobs's belief in a Mandate Driven Leadership model. From his earlier success at Atari and then with the Apple I, Jobs was turning *his* vision into reality and succeeding. Yet, when he relinquished his Apple III vision to the collaborative, consensus-management approach of a marketing department—he experienced failure. This was his first lesson in the potential harms of groupthink.

Jobs was much more involved with the LISA project. However, Jobs's desire to greatly move technology forward along with his well-known penchant for perfection ran into practical and internal roadblocks. Jobs's continual prodding of the product team to make improvements before LISA's release eventually led to him being removed from the LISA project toward its end. While many of the computer's features were revolutionary, the computer processor unit the LISA team chose after Jobs's removal could not keep up with the technology, resulting in sluggish performance. And with a price tag of $9,995, Apple sold less than 100,000 units.

Jobs learned several key things during this time frame. He was less involved with the design of the Apple III, allowing his marketing department to dictate product features that could correspond with a certain price point. This proved disastrous. Jobs had pushed the LISA team for revolutionary product improvements. However, he did not see the project through to completion. These mistakes coupled with high price tags and production miscalculations resulted in the failure of both endeavors. He would not make those mistakes again.

Another key learning for Jobs during these days was to use the learnings and ideas of others to rapidly improve Apple's next generation of products. This reputation for "borrowing" technology is reinforced by the often-repeated but inaccurate story that Steve Jobs stole ideas from Xerox to create the LISA and subsequently the Mac. This tale stems from the true story of a 1979 visit by Jobs and his team to Xerox's Palo Alto Research Center (PARC) for three days. During that visit, the Apple team saw cutting-edge technology like bit-mapped screens, graphical user interfaces with desktop icons like folders and trash cans, Ethernet, printers, and of course the now ubiquitous mouse. Four years after that visit, Apple shipped the LISA, and a year after that, the Macintosh. Both devices are notable for being some of the first publicly available computers to utilize concepts the Apple team had first seen at the PARC.

Jobs and his team didn't steal anything from Xerox; however, they did legally pick up concepts from the visit that were brought to reality by Apple engineers. At the time of the visit, Apple was still pre-IPO, and Xerox offered those three days of access for an option to buy 100,000 shares of Apple stock for $10 per share after it went public. When Apple did finally go public a year later, the value of that stock had grown to $17.6 million. The logic then is that essentially Apple paid Xerox $17.6 million for Xerox to show its research to Jobs and his team.

Xerox did not necessarily agree with this logic. It brought suit against Apple in 1989. While the case was dismissed, it showed that not everyone was happy with Jobs's aggressiveness. It also had the lasting impact of Apple's focus on aggressively patenting and defending anything it felt was proprietary and of value in its products. One of the clear signs of leaders like this is that while they might be seen as aggressive toward others, they do not like that aggressiveness being turned toward them.

In reflection, Jobs could see the bigger picture that comes with missteps and seldom looked back with regret. In 2001, during an Apple employee question-and-answer discussion, Jobs said that he had very little interest in riches and wasn't driven by the buck, while adding a caveat to that idea: "Going to bed at night saying we've done something wonderful, that's what matters to me," he said. "Sometimes when you innovate, you make mistakes. It is best to admit them quickly, and get on with improving your other innovations."

The Macintosh

Jef Raskin, the thirty-first Apple employee, started the project to develop the Macintosh computer in 1979 and even came up with the machine's moniker in the early stages of development because the McIntosh was his favorite apple. Essentially, the machine that would propel Jobs to celebrity status was not his idea, and he wasn't even on the initial development team.

Through the mind of Raskin, the Macintosh was envisioned as a small "appliance" with all current peripherals built into the machine at the cost of $1,000. During the development of the Macintosh, Jobs's notorious bad behavior evolved to an acute and obtrusive level in order to gain control of the project. The conflict began over cost and components. Jobs did not believe in cutting corners to reduce expenditure, but Raskin wouldn't budge from his proposal to get cheaper parts for the Mac. Raskin says he was unimpressed by Jobs's thoughts on how computers should work, but there were deeper issues that went to a personal level.

"I think that he likes people to jump when he says jump," Raskin told *Ubiquity* magazine in 2003. "I felt that he was untrustworthy and that he does not take kindly to being found wanting. He doesn't seem to like people who see him without a halo."

The edge was where Jobs kept people, and it was clearly written in an Apple internal memo that an engineer sent to Raskin, "Jobs seems to introduce tension, politics, and hassles rather than enjoying a buffer from the distractions," the memo read. "I thoroughly enjoy talking with him, and I admire his ideas, practical perspective, and energy. But I just don't feel that he provides the trusting, supportive, relaxed environment that I need."[13]

Raskin's loathing of Jobs grew, and ongoing complaints from other employees implored him to take the matter to the top. In a memo to Apple CEO Mike Scott, he blasted Jobs and his leadership skills. Raskin expanded on the memo and his overall feelings about Jobs in the manuscript for a documentary called "The Mac and Me," which never made it to production.[14]

"The memo reflected the running joke that the way to get Jobs to agree to something was to tell him about it, let him reject it, and then wait a week until he came running to tell you about his new idea at which point you'd exclaim, great idea Steve, we'll do it right away!" he said. "In the memo, I also made what was to prove a perfect prophecy; Jobs was wrong on his Apple III schedule, wrong on the LISA schedule, wrong on the cost and price estimates, and he will be wrong on Macintosh. He is a prime example of a manager who takes the credit for his optimistic schedules and then blames the workers when deadlines are not met."

It is important to note that this is a somewhat unfair description of Jobs, and Raskin was clearly upset by Jobs's poor treatment of him as an individual, there is certainly admissible evidence in that department. What Raskin would say were poor estimates on cost and schedules, others would say was Jobs's Reality Distortion Field at work. Jobs could get people to move in impossible directions for the sake of the company's mission. Isaacson explains in his book that the improbable was often accomplished by Jobs through esprit de corps.

After the Raskin memo, Scott set up a meeting to include both Jobs and Raskin. Jobs cried during the meeting. In the biography *Steve Jobs*, there are more than a dozen instances when Jobs weeps, and his meltdowns are over a myriad of things. Most of the time, Jobs cried when he didn't get his way, and he used it to show how serious he was about the matter, whether as a manipulative tactic or without self-control. However, Jobs also cried when his team created things he considered beautiful in design or concept. Regardless of varying perspectives on his emotions, they carried him and controlled how he interacted with the world. He had to have control, or genuine sorrow ripped him to pieces.

Well, Jobs won the battle against Raskin and gained control of the leadership of the Mac development team. It is possible that Jobs's tears assisted with the decision, but others speculate that it was Scott's way to get Jobs focused on other things outside of the feud, and additionally, get him off the main campus. At the time, Apple considered the Macintosh a minor project, and a team was developing it in a building away from the core complex. Regardless of why, Jobs and his Mandate Driven Leadership and vision for the Mac won out. As for Raskin, he was asked to take a leave of absence.

The Macintosh progressed through development and went on sale in 1984. Its graphics were state of the art, and it did not require DOS prompts to operate it, unlike earlier computers. It had folders, fonts, icons, and a mouse. It was the archetype for all that was to come on the personal computing platform, but it had its issues: the initial model was underpowered and lacked adequate memory, which made it incredibly slow. Its price of $2,495 was quite high for the time. The Commodore 64, technological inferior to the Macintosh, was introduced in 1982 targeting the home computer user and priced at $595. IBM introduced its Personal Computer in late 1981 targeting the enterprise marketplace and priced at $1,565.

The Macintosh sold 72,000 units in its first 100 days, and by the end of 1984, Apple had sold 250,000 units. However, the initial sales performance was much less than anticipated and was not enough to compensate for the continual internal infighting between Jobs and Apple's CEO and board of directors.

Change was coming.

Steve Jobs Leaves Apple, the Company He Cofounded

The passion that led Jobs to help create such innovative products was great for a small, growing company. But, as Apple moved from a start-up to a public company, it had to instill more traditional corporate processes. After going public, Apple had to implement normal control structures like a board of directors and corporate governance. Recognizing that he needed someone with more experience in these matters, Jobs recruited John Sculley from Pepsi-Cola. Reportedly Jobs told Sculley, "Do you want to sell sugar water for the rest of your life, or do you want to come with me and change the world?"

Sculley took over as Apple's CEO in 1983. While their partnership was initially great, Sculley's focus on things like profit margin and cost controls grew thin with Jobs, and their relationship quickly deteriorated. However, Sculley often protected Jobs from the dissatisfaction other executives had with Jobs's management style. Yet, through all of this—it is a corporate myth that Jobs was fired from Apple by Sculley.

The initial Apple Macintosh sales for 1984, while good, were not great. Steve Jobs was adamant that certain technology enhancements sacrificed in the original Raskin design must be done and that Apple must sacrifice margin to create volume. He was also adamant in his belief that ultimately consumers would pay a premium for a product that was clearly not just better technologically, but would ultimately be viewed as enhancing the life of its users.

Jobs had a vision and went on one of his no compromise, no consensus crusades. However, he was unable to convince the product design team to immediately do certain upgrades to the Macintosh. He was also unable to convince product marketing or CEO Sculley to lower the price of the Macintosh to compete with the IBM Personal Computer. Having given up day-to-day management control of the company to Sculley, Jobs could no longer mandate these decisions. In one last attempt, Steve Jobs went to the board of directors to try to convince them that Apple should pursue a high-quality, lower but still premium price, higher volume strategy for the Macintosh.

His appeal to the board was not successful.

The board and Sculley believed that keeping Steve on the Macintosh project would be too disruptive. They removed him from the project but retained Steve as chairman of the company with the ability to pursue other assignments. Rather than compromise, Steve officially took a leave of absence from Apple Computer while retaining his role as chairman.

While on official leave, Steve started NeXt Computer with the initial support of Sculley and the board of directors. Ultimately, a combination of internal politics at Apple and within the board as well as perception in the marketplace became too complex. Jobs officially resigned from Apple on September 17, 1985, writing "I am but 30 and want still to contribute and achieve. After what we have accomplished together, I would wish our parting to be both amicable and dignified. Yours sincerely, Steven P. Jobs."

While officially Jobs resigned from the company he cofounded and propelled to tremendous success, he paid a heavy price for sticking with his vision for the Apple MacIntosh and his Mandate Driven Leadership style, albeit for a very short time. After market research, focus groups, market and customer feedback, and months and months of consensus building and groupthink, Apple eventually implemented the technology enhancements and marketing programs previously mandated by Jobs. By 1987 Apple was selling more than 1 million MacIntosh units each year at a 50 percent profit.

Today, Apple Macintosh is considered to be one of the most revolutionary advances in personal computing as well as one of the bestselling, most profitable product lines of all time.

Pixar

The troublemaker quickly moved on from Apple. He met with the executives of Pixar, the Lucasfilm computer division, in the fall of 1985 to acquire it. George Lucas was attempting to unload the property, which created software and hardware to enable computer-guided animation, but it was a work in progress. Lucas didn't find it of great value. A meeting with the Lucasfilm CFO was scheduled to figure out a financial plan going forward. When the CFO didn't arrive on time, Jobs took control of the meeting and started it without him to the dismay of the CFO, who was hoping to come in after everyone had settled and establish himself atop the chain of command, according to Steve Jobs. Let's be honest, in Jobs's world, like many Mandate Driven Leaders, he is at the top of every hierarchy, with title or official chain of command meaning very little. In the end, Jobs agreed to purchase 70 percent of the company for $10 million in January 1986.

Pixar stumbled when it initially tried to be nothing more than a computer hardware and software company that sold its technology. Lawrence Levy, Jobs's newly hired CFO for Pixar, at this time feared that his initial concerns about Steve's management style and abrasive nature were coming to fruition, and he was troubled by it. "Although Steve and I were getting along great so far, his mercurial reputation had made most people I knew caution me against working with him," Levy wrote in his book. "Even more problematic was the company itself. Pixar had been in business for ten years and had made almost no impact."

At this point, Jobs had invested more than $50 million and was unwilling to invest more. He recognized that he either needed to accept his losses, or he needed to move from primarily an investor in Pixar to truly setting the vision and strategic direction of the company and mandating the execution of that vision. Jobs was riding on one Pixar victory: the team had used its technology to create an animated short called "Tiny Toy," which won an Oscar for the best animated short film in 1988. With that data point, Jobs began to contemplate transforming Pixar to making full-length animated films instead of selling the technology that made them.

In 1989, Jobs began mandating change at Pixar. He was unwilling to give up on the company after all he had spent, but Jobs demanded sacrifices in order to commit to another round of funding and the pursuit of a new strategy—his strategy. In 1989, he shut down Pixar's hardware operations. While Pixar was unprofitable, the hardware operations contributed a significant amount of Pixar's meager revenue. In early 1991, he cut the Pixar staff by more than half and took their promised stock options from them.

Pulling the options did not sit well with some of the Pixar employees. Pam Kerwin, a Pixar VP during those tumultuous years, said that the staff lived in fear of Jobs, according to the book *My Unlikely Journey with Steve Jobs* by Lawrence Levy. "We've long felt unvalued, unappreciated," Kerwin said at the time. "He's broken promises. And people are angry about that. . . . He promised [stock options] to us, and they've never materialized. . . . Many here have been waiting for years to own a little piece of Pixar."

Kerwin also made it clear that she did not agree with Jobs's mandate driven style of leadership, continuing, "Steve doesn't get Pixar. We're artsy and creative. We're like a family. We hug. And we're not a top-down organization; everyone here has a voice. Steve is the guy who owns us—but he's never been one of us."

With a downsized but refocused Pixar, Jobs took his vision to Disney, and in May of 1991 Pixar and Disney announce a partnership to produce a computer-animated feature film. Pixar began production of the animated movie *Toy Story*. The agreement was that Pixar would receive 12.5 percent of box office sales and Disney would own all the characters and maintain complete creative control of the project.

Steve would not forget some of his failures at Apple, which he was convinced were the result of compromise. It was obvious that his mantra was now *never ever, ever settle.* While the mantra of many technology leaders is to get something 80 percent there, push it out, and fix the bugs later, Jobs needed everything to be absolutely perfect. Larry Ellison, who is known for being difficult to work with in his own right, tells the story of how when Jobs was at Pixar there were numerous versions of *Toy Story* before Jobs would even come close to letting it be released. Jobs wanted everything perfect in terms of both the technology and the story. He almost tortured the rest of the team until the project got to where he thought it needed to be. In other words, he refused to settle even when others tried to convince him it was good enough.

In 1995, the film premiered, and its success or failure would determine the future for Pixar. On the opening weekend, *Toy Story* grossed $29 million, becoming an immediate success. One week later, Pixar went public, opening at $47 a share and making Jobs a billionaire. *Toy Story*, the first full-length animated feature film made by computers, went on to gross $373.6 million, and Pixar followed its win with the films *A Bug's Life* and *Toy Story 2*, finishing a three-picture deal with Disney. Pixar continued to deliver, going on an incredible commercial and critical run, producing *Finding Nemo*, *Wall-E*, *Up*, and *The Incredibles*. Jobs would eventually sell Pixar to Disney for $7.4 billion.

Once again, Jobs, echewing consensus-building in favor of Mandate Driven Leadership, propelled his vision to reality.

Jobs Returns to Apple and Finds Redemption

Steve wasn't sure that anyone could save Apple, but he wanted a shot at it. After Jobs's departure in 1985, Apple had ridden the founder's Macintosh computer to immense success and profitability, but more than a decade had passed. Absent Steve Jobs, Apple had no new successes. Apple was rotting, was close to bankruptcy, and on the horizon was a dismantling of its assets to the highest bidders. It had lost $1 billion in 1996 on $7 billion in revenue. In the last quarter of 1996, sales had plummeted 32 percent, and its stock was bottoming out.

A *Fortune* article from March 1997 roasted everyone involved in the disastrous results. "Apple Computer, Silicon Valley's paragon of dysfunctional management and fumbled techno-dreams, is back in crisis mode, scrambling lugubriously in slow motion to deal with imploding sales, a floundering technology strategy, and a hemorrhaging brand name," the first paragraph of the article read. "About all that Apple's 13,000 shell-shocked employees, its 30,000 hapless shareholders, and the 20 million queasy Macintosh faithful can do is look on in dismay, just as the company's chronically passive board seems to be doing once again."[15]

The return of Jobs to Apple was a whirlwind. On February 2, 1996, Gil Amelio became CEO of Apple. A year later, Apple purchased the NeXT operating system, which had been in development for a decade, from Jobs for $430 million. Jobs was also appointed as an adviser to the company. Within the year, Jobs orchestrated with the board the removal of Amelio, the man who had brought him back into the Apple fold.

Jobs became the interim CEO on September 17, 1997, a title he held for three years before becoming the official CEO. Within a few weeks of becoming interim CEO, he forced the resignation of most of the board that had given him the title, including Mark Markkula, the man responsible for incorporating Apple and funding the Apple II. Jobs then repositioned and streamlined Apple, cutting 70 percent of its products, which resulted in the layoff of more than 3,000 employees.

With his Mandate Driven Leadership skills honed further by the success of Pixar, Jobs was back for an encore performance unimaginable for anyone but Steve Jobs.

Now in his forties, Steve Jobs's management style, while possibly somewhat softer on the edges, was no less mandate driven and demanding. Shortly after returning to Apple, Jobs found out that chip maker VLSI Technology was having trouble delivering enough chips on time. Jobs's approach was to storm into a meeting with representatives from the company and start shouting that they were "fucking dickless assholes." Obviously, this was not the kind of candid expression people had come to expect from the CEO of a major computer manufacturer at the turn of the twenty-first century. As much as everyone was shocked, however, VLSI did end up getting the chips to Apple on time, and its executives made jackets that boasted on the back, "Team FDA." They viewed it as a badge of honor for surviving one of Jobs's infamous tirades. My guess is that Steve got a kick out of it too.

iMac

On August 15, 1998, under Steve Jobs's leadership, Apple released the first iMac. The low-cost, all-in-one desktop with an egg-shaped, futuristic design came in 13 different shades of translucent color. During the event that launched the product, a lighthearted Jobs took the stage and remarked, "The back of our computer looks better than the front of the other guy's. It looks like it is from another planet. A good planet. A planet with better designers."

Using all his Mandate Driven Leadership lessons, Jobs ensured that the iMac was not designed by marketing nor by consensus. Rather, it was designed by an industrial design team led by Apple's VP of industrial design Jony Ive, whom Jobs personally gave air cover throughout the corporation to obstinately stick to their vision and not be coerced by consensus or group-think. As an example, Jobs related the story that the plastic for the desired colors of the first iMacs simply did not exist. Rather than compromise on the color of the iMacs, an Apple research team spent six months determining how to produce the exact colors envisioned by the design team.

The iMac became Apple's fastest-selling Mac to date, and it made Apple profitable again, tripling sales from the previous year as 519,000 units were shipped out before the end of 1998. The iMac turned 20 years old in 2018, and through seven updated versions over the years, it is still the third largest revenue line for Apple.

The iPod

The prototype to the first iPod was cautiously presented to Steve Jobs by engineers, according to Amit Chaudhary, an Apple employee. "Jobs played with the device, scrutinized it, weighed it in his hands, and promptly rejected it," Chaudhary told *The Atlantic* through a Quora forum. "It was too big."

The engineers argued that their creation was a complete innovative rein-vention of the MP3 players before it, but it was impossible to reduce its size. Steve Jobs sat quietly for a moment and took a gander at an aquarium in the office. "Finally, he stood, walked over to the aquarium, and dropped the iPod into the tank," Chaudhary said. "After it touched bottom, bubbles floated to the top."

"Those are bubbles," Jobs quipped. "That means there's space in there. Make it smaller."

Apple had already proven to be one of the world's great disruptors while following the mandates of Jobs. Technology companies, including Mic-rosoft, had been chasing Apple ever since it introduced the graphical user interface of the Macintosh in 1984. In order to stay relevant, companies had to model their creations *after* the inventions of visionary Steve Jobs, because they rarely got ahead of his ideas. The iPod could be no different as far as Jobs was concerned. There were already clunky MP3 players on the market, and Jobs was not looking for a clone of those products. He wanted to tilt music's audience in his favor, or like a crime boss, he would send the product to the fishes. He got what he wanted.

Apple released the iPod to the masses on October 23, 2001, and it became the rage of music aficionados who needed their tunes with them at all times. The final product was small, elegantly designed, and synched with Macs in order to easily access music libraries and purchase music through a new online store Apple called iTunes. Eventually, it synced with PCs as well. The device looked like pure art on a rack compared to the other music players beside it.

"If there was ever a product that catalyzed what's Apple's reason for being, it's this," Jobs said in Steven Levy's book *The Perfect Thing*. "Because it combines Apple's incredible technology base with Apple's legendary ease of use with Apple's awesome design, it's like, this is what we do. So if anybody was ever wondering why is Apple on the earth, I would hold this up as a good example."[16]

iPhone

Jobs's venture into the phone market began because he was incensed that a Microsoft employee was blatantly bragging about its venture to create a small handheld computer tablet. On top of that, Microsoft was planning to create a tablet that had a tool that Jobs obviously took exception to using.

"This guy badgered me about how Microsoft was going to completely change the world with this tablet PC software and eliminate all notebook computers, and Apple ought to license this Microsoft software," Jobs told Isaacson. "But he was doing the device all wrong. It had a stylus. As soon as you have a stylus, you're dead. This dinner was like the tenth time he talked to me about it, and I was so sick of it that I came home and said, 'Fuck this, let's show him what a tablet can really be.' "[17]

The next day, Jobs asked a team to make a multitouch tablet without a stylus or a keyboard and, as an extra bonus, make it into a cellular phone as well. It took six months to create, and in June of 2007, Jobs released the iPhone, a handheld computer that people could also use to make phone calls. The larger iPad tablet came later, using similar technology.

The device reimagined the idea of a phone and disrupted the mobile market, which had no appreciation for touch screens at the time, relying on pull-out keyboards and number-to-letter conversions when using text applications. Simultaneously, it disrupted the laptop market because with the iPhone's large screen, a mass assortment of applications, and ample storage, it resembled a super-compact personal computer and reduced the need for one in certain situations.

Initially, the plastic display screen on the iPhone prototypes scratched easily, and Jobs wanted a better solution. Jobs began researching and came across "Gorilla glass," a nearly scratch-resistant form of glass created by Corning in the 1960s. Jobs called Corning's CEO Wendell Weeks and ordered a large shipment of the material to be delivered within six months. There was a problem with that order, though. Years before, Corning had stopped making the glass and had completely transitioned its factory to manufacturing another type of glass. It could not, under any circumstances, deliver a large volume of the material to Jobs. How does a conversation go with a technology god with reality distortion technology?

"You can deliver, don't be afraid," Jobs explained to Weeks, according to Steve Jobs. Weeks explained to Jobs that it was an impossible engineering feat, and could not be done.

"Yes, you can do it. Get your mind around it. You can do it."

Through Jobs's reality distortion field, Weeks complied. He called up his plant and told them to convert to Gorilla glass immediately. Corning delivered the product in six months.

Warner Music Chairman Edgar Bronfman Jr. told the *Mercury News*, "You need to look no further than Apple's iPhone to see how fast brilliantly written software presented on a beautifully designed device with a spectacular user interface will throw all the accepted notions about pricing, billing platforms, and brand loyalty right out the window." This is one aspect of the iPhone that is underappreciated. The mobile phone industry began with a business model where the telecommunications companies paid for the vast majority of the hardware. That was the price of doing business and owning the customer and the revenue stream. Steve Jobs threw that model out the window. The customer was Apple's, not the telecoms'. And customers would pay Apple for a digital experience that they quickly could not live without.

If Apple had been led by a management team rooted in consensus management, the iPhone would not have been launched. Engineers said it could not be produced to the size Jobs required. Designers said it would be too brittle to be practical. Industry and market analysts stated that consumers would not pay for a cell phone when they could get one free or heavily discounted with their cell phone subscription. Shareholders did not want Apple to lose focus on the personal computer market. The music industry said it was not going to support further music streaming or downloading on devices. The technology industry was estimating it would take decades before a reasonable number of applications would be available to download to the phone for use—"There is an app for that" was not in our nomenclature.

Jobs ignored each and every one of the naysayers and pressed on, mandating his vision to reality. Today, Apple has sold more than one billion iPhones, and while it has never been an inexpensive device, people find ways to acquire one. And many historians would agree that the iPhone was integral in propelling the digital economy that is disrupting business today.

iPad

The iPad took the ideas of the iPhone a step further, creating a device that fell somewhere between a smartphone and a laptop. The iPad was easier to carry and was more intimate than a laptop but exceeded the capabilities of an iPhone. The iPad had a larger screen and could be many things: a computer, an e-book, a video player and a video maker. Original music could be made with it. It was also a video game console.

The iPad appeared on the cover of the January 30, 2010, edition of *The Economist*, with an illustration of Jobs, dressed as Jesus, holding it—a technological messiah with a light blue robe and a halo of light behind his head. The iPad completed Steve Jobs's wave of disruption: iPod, iPhone, and iPad all powered by "Apps," a term firmly rooted in our lexicon. However, the iPad would be Jobs's last great creation, and nothing could prevent his early departure from our world.

The Death of a Legend

In August 2011, Jobs left his position as Apple CEO. A fight with cancer, which resulted in three leaves of absence and a liver transplant, made it impossible for him physically, mentally, and emotionally to continue daily business activities at Apple.

The walls of Apple stores all around the world were covered with hand-written letters and cards as the technological icon slipped away. Many people wanted a piece of him during his last days, but he controlled his final act, according to his friend Dean Cornish: "for Steve, it was all about living life on his own terms and not wasting a moment with things he didn't think were important," Cornish said to the *New York Times*. "He was aware that his time on earth was limited. He wanted control of what he did with the choices that were left."

Steve Jobs died on October 5, 2011.

The Legacy and Lessons of Jobs

The citizens in Apple's 1984 "Big Brother" Macintosh advertisement march like zombies through futuristic tunnels, while an oppressive military force is seen chasing an athletic woman who is running with a large sledgehammer. The brainwashed citizens reach a theater-like room where they are still engaged in a trance and operating through the verbal commands of their controller, who is on a large screen before them. The curator of their thoughts holds their attention through purification directives that include the dissolving of all notions that are contradictory to the dystopian world's pure ideology. The rebel woman—who is consumed by color and energy though all around her are varying shades of gray—enters the room as a swarm of heavily geared troops gain ground upon her. She throws the hammer at the screen, shattering it, releasing a bright light upon a captive audience.

The advertisement appeared in the third quarter of Super Bowl XVIII. It won dozens of advertising honors. The ideas in the commercial, and in nearly every Apple advertisement that involved Jobs's direction, reflected a counterculture theme. Jobs wore the badge of the outsider. He seemed to revel in the fact that he was different from the corporate stiffs who tried to control him and his tactics in the business world. Jobs was selling his philosophical and lifestyle notions more than he was selling a product.

"Here's to the crazy ones," read the advertising copy for a 1997 commercial that marked the return of Steve Jobs to Apple.

Jobs was able to operate in the way he did because he acquired people around him who felt the same way he did—were counter to culture like he was—at least enough of them to keep the regulars and conformers at bay, for the most part. Jobs was aware of his limitations, according to Ron Johnson, who led Apple's retail group from its beginnings.

"I think Steve learned over time that he had to surround himself with people who could help create the culture he desired because he didn't necessarily have the day-to-day skills to do it himself," Johnson said in *Think Simple*.[18]

A lesson we can learn from Steve Jobs is to *improve the world, not just your product*. While the rest of the high-tech world was focused on fixing bugs and incremental improvements to their individual products and the other peripherals, Apple was developing devices like the iPod, iPhone, iPad, and iTV (later called just Apple TV). When they were combined into the full Apple ecosystem with iTunes, the Apple App Store, and the wide array of content, they helped realize Jobs's vision of a *digital lifestyle hub* to make our everyday lives better. Sure he drove everyone around him nuts to get it there, but there is no question the value it has added and the business disruption it has caused.

Jobs's legacy is a conundrum because he is both a cautionary tale and an inspirational story. "He oozes smug superiority, lacing his public comments with ridicule of Apple's rivals, which he casts as mediocre, evil, and—worst of all—lacking taste," Peter Elkind wrote in 2008. "No CEO is more willful, or more brazen, at making his own rules, in ways both good and bad. And no CEO is more personally identified with—and controlling of—the day-to-day affairs of his business."[19]

Yes, Steve Jobs will go down in history as one of the most challenging leaders to work with of all time. Shortly after his death, *The Atlantic*'s Tom McNichol referred to Steve Jobs as "a world-class asshole."[20] Biographer Walter Isaacson repeatedly talks about how there was *Good Steve*, and there was *Bad Steve*. While *Good Steve* could inspire those around him to achieve groundbreaking innovations that the world didn't realize it needed, *Bad Steve* could just as easily tear people down and make them hate life and run them off.[21]

At the end of the day, Steve Jobs is and will always be known as perhaps the greatest innovator of all time. He is also, beyond debate, the prototype of a Mandate Driven Leader, which begs the question: could he have accomplished the same adopting a different leadership model? While there are some management gurus who will undoubtedly disagree, the answer is an absolute *no*.

Jobs's adoption of a Mandate Driven Leadership model was integral to his success. At first, he may have adopted the style purely by accident or circumstance. However, as he matured it became very deliberate as Jobs recognized that Mandate Driven Leadership was essential to being "crazy enough to think they can change the world." Ryan Himmel wrote in *Entrepreneur*, "He had an extraordinary ability to push his company and employees to the limits without going over the edge."[22] Susan Kalla, an investment manager, wrote in *Forbes*, "his high aspirations spilled over onto Apple employees who believed they too could accomplish anything."[23]

The same traits that made Steve Jobs a "world-class asshole," were the traits that enabled him to achieve great things. The same passion that made him lose his temper was the obsession that drove him to relentlessly drive forward his vision. The same lack of self-awareness that made him think the rules didn't apply to him was what allowed him to find ways to fill needs we didn't know we had. Those same traits that made him a tyrant to work for also made him a Mandate Driven Leader.

Steve Jobs was crazy enough that he did change the world.

CHAPTER 3

THE HISTORY AND PITFALLS OF CONSENSUS LEADERSHIP

A genuine leader is not a searcher for consensus but a molder of consensus.

—MARTIN LUTHER KING JR.

There is an old story in management consulting about an entrepreneur who starts a business and over many decades builds it up from a one-man show to a thriving corporation that provides employment to thousands and goods and services to millions of customers. Along the way the man marries, has a family, and sends his children off to college and business school, because that's what good fathers do. As part of his legacy, he brings his children and their well-educated friends into his business, and over time they become the executives. While the entrepreneur is a hard-nosed, practical leader with decades of real experience about what it takes to grow a business, his children's and their cohorts' heads are full of ideas about things like consensus management and employee empowerment. They want to build a company culture that embraces their employees and enables them to do their best. The entrepreneur is having none of it. Hard work, discipline, and financial rewards are all that he needs. Try as they might, his children and their compatriots cannot sway him.

After quite some time the entrepreneur takes a vacation, his first in many years, to a CEO retreat where he plays golf with other captains of industry and hears speeches from the best business thinkers of the day. After a full two weeks, he comes back tanned, rested, and reinvigorated. He calls a meeting of all his senior staff where he shares with them that he has had an epiphany. He has finally seen the light. They should change their culture; they should have a more empowered workforce. He wants his people to feel engaged. He wants to establish a culture driven by consensus management. Everyone in the room breathes a sigh of relief and embraces the excitement of a new day within the organization. That is of course until the entrepreneur announces that he wants it all done by Thursday.

This is one typical story of many alluding to the virtues of consensus management and the evils of directive leadership. Stories like these and other anecdotes are often used in the academic and private sector in teaching that effective leadership begins with collaboration and consensus management. Is this underlying premise true? Or are there obvious pitfalls to a consensus management culture in an age of digital disruption? To understand the pitfalls of consensus management, we first must understand its definition and history.

Consensus decision making is a process wherein the decision is at least supported, even if not enthusiastically, by all the group members. In fact, the word consensus originates from the Latin *cōnsentiō*, which essentially means "to feel together," which is what is meant when the group members lend support to a common decision in a bid to stand by a common sentiment or principle for the greater good.

Consensus decision making and the principles that comprise consensus management can be traced back centuries. Many Native American cultures were based on nonhierarchical structures and were managed through consensus for hundreds of years. Five Native American societies, the Cayuga, Mohawk, Oneida, Onondaga, and Seneca, established the Haudenosaunee Confederation. This confederation, which is still active today, is based on the principles of consensus. Consensus building was at the foundation and used extensively by various utopian communities like the Christian Herrnhüter settlements of the 1700s and the Boimondeau communes in France in the mid-1900s.

In Europe, many governing bodies and associations, like the town councils and the guilds, have operated on consensus management principles for hundreds of years. Since the 1970s, Christiana, a district in Copenhagen, Denmark, has been totally self-governed through consensus. The Dutch polder model is often cited as an apt example of consensus decision making, where organizations work in a synergistic manner building consensus among employers, employees, and governments. The polder model, often described as "cooperation despite differences," received much acclaim when it was used by the Dutch for consensus-based economic and social policy making in the 1980s and 1990s.

In more recent times, social and political activists find the principles of consensus management essential to their work. According to the organization Seeds for Change, many current social and political movements believe that the methods for achieving change must match their vision and goals of a free, nonviolent, egalitarian society. The 1999 protest against the World Trade Organization (Battle of Seattle), the 2005 G8 Summit protests, and the Occupy movement of 2011–2012 utilized consensus leadership and management. In these cases, there were no designated leaders who established a vision and mandated action. Rather, the collective whole moved through recognized consensus to action.

Proponents of consensus management include Ethan Mitchell of Rutgers University, who has published at length the highly successful unanimous decision-making process employed for centuries by the Religious Society of Friends, commonly referred to as Quakers. During meetings, the Quakers use consensus-building techniques to assimilate the beliefs and opinions of each Friend in order to arrive at the best decision for the Society. According to Mitchell, the Quakers' practice of consensus decision making has its own vocabulary, ideology, and tradition and is an integral aspect of their religious experience.

Consensus management principles first made their way into the business world via the cooperative movement. The cooperative movement began in England and France in the nineteenth century. The industrial revolution was transforming society. The increasing mechanization of the workplace was threatening the livelihood of large portions of the worker base. This gave rise to many labor and social movements including the cooperative movement. The cooperative movement allowed workers to unite around a common economic goal, with leadership as well as the economic output of the cooperative being equally shared.

The first consumer cooperative can be traced to Fenwick in Scotland. Formed in 1769, the Fenwick Weavers' Society handled bulk purchasing of food, books, and other materials to benefit all members equally. Within the cooperative movement, decisions are made only by consensus of the cooperative members. By the early 1800s, hundreds of cooperatives were in operation throughout Europe. However, most of these failed by the mid-1800s due to management challenges. Though a few such as the Galashiels and Hawick

Co-operative Societies are still in existence today. We can still see the legacy of this early cooperative movement in the housing co-ops found throughout the world today.

So, while history has numerous examples of the use of consensus management, there is no well-defined moment in time where it can be pointed out that consensus management became in vogue in business. Early on, toward the middle of the twentieth century, social scientists began to understand that people behave very differently in groups than when they are alone, and this understanding started having implications on management theories. For example, Kurt Lewin's experiments revealed that people are likely to adopt the views of their groups and move toward the achievement of a common goal even when they may have held very diverse perspectives as individuals. This opened the possibility of using groups to arrive at consensus-based decisions that could lead to better societal or organizational outcome. Other scholars like Victor Vroom and Phillip Yetton postulated the numerous benefits of participative decision making, which included having a better chance at exploring more options and the better likelihood of decisions being accepted and implemented in the longer term.

In the 1950s and 1960s, scholars like Kees Boeke were advocating that a majority-driven approach to decision making is fundamentally unjust and detrimental to the interests of the minority, as well as limiting as there is less likelihood that the group will consider diverse opinions and suggestions. He advocated for three fundamental rules to decision making. "The first is that the interests of all members must be considered, the individual bowing to the interests of the whole. Secondly, solutions must be sought which everyone can accept: otherwise, no action can be taken. Thirdly all members must be ready to act according to these decisions when unanimously made."[1]

There is some indication that the Japanese economic miracle from post–World War II to the end of the Cold War (roughly 1991) accelerated consensus management principles becoming mainstream. During this time, the Japanese economy had phenomenal success. With that success, there was no shortage in the study of Japanese management techniques and theories. According to Peter Drucker, the Japanese have a strong perspective on management and have resorted to involving all employees from all levels on all issues to arrive at a consensus. This gave the alternatives to all decisions a chance to be debated and cross-checked by a large number of people before getting rejected. This consensus style of leadership and management was initially overlooked or rather shunned by Western organizations, owing largely to the thought that consensus building would take forever by giving rise to indecision or would lead to ineffective decisions that were accepted only because they pleased everyone. But, only initially.

The consensus style of management gained prominence owing largely to the promise that consensus-based decisions would lead to a more equitable and better decision—since decisions that hurt or negatively affected some members would not be passed as in the case of decision-making by majority vote. The idea of consensus building became popular with the trend to involve or engage all stakeholders in the decision-making process, which in turn evolved with the acknowledgment that people who gave their voluntary consent were more likely to stand by the decision and be accountable as well as take responsibility in the implementation process.

Thus, by the mid- to late twentieth century, consensus decision making was *norm de rigueur* within business schools and corporate management.

While consensus management may contribute to the positive feelings of the whole, however, it is also counterproductive and detrimental to the decision-making process if misapplied, which it often is. Consensus is often misconstrued to mean or portray unanimity in the context of decision making. Group members who want to pursue a particular course of action may want to translate consensus to mean unanimous agreement in order to quell any legitimate opponents of their decision. *Unanimous* means that all the members of the group agree to the principal involved in the decision-making process and also in the practical manifestations of that decision; while *consensus* is ideally a scenario where the team members agree to a decision but with their own unique understandings and expectations of the outcomes as well as their plausible reservations on the decision that they may have set aside in the spirit of agreeing to the concept only.

The fallacious interpretation of consensus as unanimity is forced upon other members who may have valid questions or doubts but can be cowed into consent by the group's desire to reach a unanimous and strong decision. On the other hand, group members may resolve not to follow any action unless consensus is manifested in unanimous agreement, and unless each and every member of the group has acquiesced. Another pitfall exists when there are dissenters but they are ignored to ensure that a unanimous agreement is projected, and thus the opinion of the minority is not even heard or discussed.

While the need or pressure to ensure that all members of the group are on the same page is high and often deliberately applied by strong or vocal group members, the subtle aspects of this pressure are too equally potent. It is often an inherent trait of the group members to lean toward the opinion that is being expressed by the majority. Several social or psychological factors may lead the members to avoid confrontations or to suppress their original opinions and agree to the consensus. These factors may include fear of appearing different from peers or discomfort at being the one who is seen as delaying the group's proceedings or creating a nuisance by presenting non-mainstream and different perspectives.

In reality, many of today's organizations reward likeability. The trait might be encased in the terms *collaboration, consensus building,* and *team-oriented,* but at the end of the day many organizations reward individuals whose thought processes and actions are not at odds with the mainstream. While Mandate Driven Leaders like Steve Jobs are usually not concerned with appeasing the majority, it is a limiting factor in many organizations.

Other factors that contribute to what is called groupthink are the propensity of some individuals to conform to others and the tendency of some people to get their own way. Both types of individuals may be contributing to the effect of groupthink, where almost all the members of the group end up agreeing to the predominant or the vocal theme.

Groupthink is likely to occur when there is a strong central and directive leader and when the group members feel cohesion. Also, when the group is devoid of actual experts on the problem, or of people whose opinions are relevant and credible to the problem at hand, then it is likely that most members of the groups will conform to the theme proposed by one or two strong members. However, the idea that groupthink is always negative has been debated by scholars as non–evidence based and predating the behavioral science era. This has led to new insights about the reasons why groups may fail. This includes the supposition that groups under the influence of groupthink may omit using the diverse expertise of all the team members and undermine the basic benefit of using teams, which is to be able to harness the distinct and diverse capabilities, knowledge bases, or skills of different team members in order to look at problems in a more holistic manner.

Also, in order to show consensus, groups may drive all the members away from the basic or the original thought toward one that is acceptable to all. This leads to the dilution of ideas, which may have had their own merit and utility if they had been pursued, but were instead discarded or toned down to appease the majority and build a consensus in decision making. Jobs would cite the failed Apple III project as an example of the pitfalls of consensus.

The Apple III was a design by committee often being led by Apple's marketing department as opposed to the engineering group. The project lacked a strong, visionary leader. Continual compromise on the design and production components by the group ultimately led to performance issues. Most of the initial units had to be recalled, and the Apple III was quickly discontinued. The cause of this early failure was one that Jobs would not forget.

In addition, group consensus may also result in what is called social loafing, where at least some of the members are not invested in doing any thinking on their own or contributing to the group in any way, and hence they just accept whatever the prevailing view is, thus leading to so-called consensus.

It can, therefore, be seen that while group decision making, even by consensus, could be a good approach, provided all the members of the group are able and willing to participate without hesitation in the debate, and that all the ideas and suggestions are tested and discussed on their merits, this is rarely what happens in practice. More often than not, consensus building leads to abandonment of difficult ideas that may be better suited to the problem at hand, or it may lead to inaction even when there is logical clarity on what needs to be done and how.

In the context of Japan, consensus decision making is effective because the consensus is built not for the end decision, but rather for questions like whether a decision is needed and what is it that needs to be decided. This allowed the Japanese to arrive at the exact question that needed to be decided, which helped make finding the most effective answers logically clear and easy. This is not necessarily the same thing as the eventual decision being made by consensus.

There are many examples of the perils of consensus management and groupthink in political and military realms. An example of groupthink was seen in the failure of the US military enterprise to anticipate the Japanese attack at Pearl Harbor, in spite of numerous warnings and signals available to them. The military leaders continued to presume that Japan would not take such a bold action, that they had adequate military power in the region to act as deterrent, that the United States had enough power to preempt and negate the attack even if it was launched, and that the enemy lacked sufficient military tactical or strategic capabilities to do any damage to the US interests. Such beliefs were closely held by the military leaders, and any attempt to question them was subdued to create a consensus in viewing the situation.

Groupthink also seems to have held sway in other political and military actions taken by the United States, like the Vietnam War and the invasion of Iraq. After the dreadful events of September 11, 2001, the US administration was under stress to deliver results, and the enormous pressure to take action led to a change in belief about Saddam Hussein's regime, which was reinforced by the patriotism prevalent at the time. The US leadership led a campaign to build consensus around the idea that Iraq had weapons of mass destruction (WMDs) and the need to invade Iraq, and the decision to do so was the result of this groupthink. It has now been widely established that Iraq in fact did not possess any WMDs and the invasion of Iraq has sparked instability throughout the region.

There are numerous examples of companies that have built themselves to formidable positions but failed ultimately because their culture encouraged consensus building, which led to groupthink that put them on a path to poor decision making. There are basically two types of errors that can be detrimental to any organization—errors of omission (when the company fails to invest in a new idea or technology and loses the opportunity) and errors of commission (when the company invests in a new idea or technology, but it is not successful).

The consensus-building approach is more appropriately followed in organizations that fear errors of commission—where the decision making may result in disastrous repercussions. However, consensus may also be an approach that is followed inadvertently because of the company's culture or its aspirations. One example of how consensus management can backfire is that of British Airlines when it initially opted for globalization in the 1990s. The company was confident of its ability to be resilient even in difficult times and had been generating continuous profits. This profit confidence gave top management the impetus to push for globalization, and the consensus building within the company resulted in subduing of doubts and rational questioning that could have prevented it from making rash decisions. The poor strategy adopted resulted in major setbacks for British Airways in the 1990s.

In the same manner, the management of the British retailer Marks & Spencer was rooted in a history of consensus management. This too led management to indulge in the frenzy of globalization-directed growth. The presumed invulnerability of the profitable company was used to quell anyone who questioned the strategy. The result of an unquestioned growth strategy was disastrous. "If Marks & Spencer are not on the cusp of a seismic change in business strategy, we think they should be," has stated Phil Dorrell, a partner at consultancy group Retail Remedy. "Marks & Spencer have been trying to dig their general merchandise business out of trouble for several years, but for now it seems that the time has come to stop digging."[2]

Another company that suffered from groupthink was Swissair, where the company's leadership cohesion and belief in their righteousness as well as invulnerability, led to the collapse of the company. One of the main reasons for the groupthink was found to be the fact that the board members were too similar in their sociocultural background and held similar values and norms with little variation in their expertise or experience. So, while they were able to build consensus on almost everything, their decisions were not sturdy, relevant, or even accurate, leading to disaster.

Enron's less than ethical accounting practices were condoned by management as the corporate culture encouraged employees to push for keeping profits and stock prices high. There was a culture of consensus building and groupthink around overlooking risky investment and accounting practices and activities that ultimately led to the downfall of the company.

Volkswagen suffered public relations problems as well as a financial disaster as it was caught manipulating the results of emissions testing for its automobiles. The car manufacturer installed "defeat devices" in its diesel vehicles that altered emissions levels so they would test at lower levels. While it is mind-boggling how and why the organization could have taken this path, it is easier to understand it within the framework of groupthink. Volkswagen suffered from intense competition, and its employees were under pressure to meet targets. It had an internal culture that did not take well to failure, and hence the employees felt under obligation to deliver, even at the cost of cutting corners and taking unethical paths to achieve an objective. A postanalysis of the entire episode at Volkswagen revealed that the devices were introduced by the company through a process of rationalization where it was okay to do so in order to remain competitive and doing so was accepted and supported by consensus as the organizational culture encouraged the employees to make decisions to beat the competition.

Some would argue that Mandate Driven Leadership would have a higher potential for this type of ethical lapse within an organization. For example, we know that Mandate Driven Leaders like Steve Jobs and Jeff Bezos are demanding. Many would say they establish unrealistic expectations but are still unrelenting in demanding the outcome. Surely the pressure to achieve the unrealistic expectations of these leaders may spur ethical problems?

Research indicates otherwise. In consensus cultures like Enron and Volkswagen, ethical concerns were hidden or ignored by groups. Individual action or leadership was discouraged. Groupthink presided, and actions or thought processes that were not supportive of the group were discouraged. In comparison, Mandate Driven Leaders eschew the status quo. They want disruptive innovation and, therefore, encourage a culture where individuals would not shield the group from an ethical lapse.

A consensus culture or consensus-based leadership have resulted in the failure of many acquisitions and mergers. A failure to utilize synergies and to agree on management and leadership styles often points back to a challenge with consensus management and groupthink as a core problem. An example can be cited with the AOL–Time Warner merger, where the boards of both the companies had arrived at a consensus approving the merger. The driving factor for the consensus sentiment was the history of working with each other successfully, which prevented the board members from voicing any doubts regarding the potential problems that might be faced in future collaboration or working more closely as merged companies.

Hewlett Packard is a classic example of where dramatic industry changes coupled with a culture of consensus can lead to disastrous results. Bill Hewlett and Dave Packard established a set of business principles—encapsulated in the "HP Way." These principles helped establish a heritage of consensus management within the company that has often been cited as the ideal state. In the early years, Hewlett Packard's engineering acumen allowed the company to grow and thrive. However, the well-entrenched consensus management culture proved to be disastrous for the company during times of industry disruption. The lack of the directive leadership necessary during these times resulted in a string of failed strategies and acquisitions including Compaq, EDS, and Autonomy. What was at one time the largest technology company in the world was ultimately dismantled.

Doubtless, there are more examples where a culture of consensus management has done more harm than good. At the heart of it all is the fact that, for all the talk of wanting to be agile, nimble, and innovative, most companies that practice consensus management are stiff and unresponsive. Indeed, it is arguable that except during times of extreme stability, a consensus management leadership style is not the prominent trait you want to see in the executive suite.

In *Unsafe Thinking*, Jonah Sachs discusses how organizations managed by consensus can lose sight of how to compete successfully compared to those organizations who have individual champions of a vision. The US drugstore chain CVS and Helena Foulkes, the executive vice president of CVS Health and president of CVS Pharmacy, are profiled as the example of a Mandate Driven Leader who shunned consensus at much risk. In 2014, CVS announced it would stop selling tobacco, a product that generated $2 billion a year in revenue for the company. While receiving much internal and external pushback on this decision, Foulkes championed the vision and insisted that "the business was moving more into health care and that the potential gains there would soon make the items that drug stores traditionally sold—such as cleaning supplies, candy, and tobacco—a sideshow."

A risky bet driven by a visionary leader who eschewed the status quo and industry and corporate consensus. And, what a successful decision it proved to be.

In the end, consensus leadership is an approach to management where the process is deemed more important than the outcome—where it is deemed more important to involve and engage everyone and to create an atmosphere of participation and agreement, rather than a vision of change. History is littered with examples of failed projects, failed companies, and failed visions due to the reliance on consensus. And, most of these failures were in normal times. Today, times are not normal. We are in the midst of a major inflection point where digital technology is disrupting everything. Now is the time for a new leadership paradigm built around the Mandate Driven Leader.

CHAPTER 4

JEFF BEZOS OF AMAZON: REGRET MINIMIZATION

What we need to do is always lean into the future; when the world changes around you and when it changes against you— what used to be a tail wind is now a headwind—you have to lean into that and figure out what to do because complaining isn't a strategy.

—JEFF BEZOS, Founder, Chairman and CEO, Amazon

I t was the ultimate risk.

Amazon.com founder Jeff Bezos learned of the Internet in early 1994 when the information superhighway started to buzz after a few years of development. The grand possibilities of the unchartered technological hinterland bewitched Bezos, and a few months later, he quit his stable, high-paying Wall Street VP job with the crazy notion that he would sell books on the World Wide Web. He decided to get out of his Manhattan apartment immediately, and like many American pioneers before him, he migrated west to help develop a new frontier.

The evolution of Bezos's life was so abrupt that when the moving company arrived to ship Bezos's belongings, he was unsure of where he would start his enterprise, so he told them to head toward the Pacific coast, and he would call them later with a final destination. He decided upon Seattle, and Amazon.com was born.

Fathom the idea of Bezos as the lone employee of his company, which now has 613,300 people onboard as of January 2019. Imagine him, unemployed and in the middle of a road trip to Seattle, at the age of 30, his car being his first office space and current residence, his head full of entrepreneurial ideas, and numerous levels of uncertainty masquerading as bravado as he crossed the miles to Washington state. Consider, 22 years ago, Bezos had yet to register Amazon.com as a domain, and his wife of less than a year was now at shotgun on this adventure. Imagine Bezos as he rambled across interstate highways tangled up in a complex web of notions that would eventually unscramble and alter the course of retail history, making Bezos a $100 billion net worth Internet idol.

Jeff Bezos's actions that year and ever since are undoubtedly those of a Mandate Driven Leader.

The Regret Minimization Framework

In a speech at Lake Forest College in 1998, Bezos recalled the day he decided to leave his secure job at a financial services firm to head into the unknown.[1] He coined an idea that day when he mentioned his "regret minimization framework" (Figure 4.1), which was a mental contraption he used to determine the rewards of personal fulfillment and life goals regardless of the odds. At the time, he had to make a decision that he would not regret on the day of his passing. In other words, he used the potential of future regret and his deathbed as a motivating factor.

"I knew that when I was 80, there was no chance that I would regret having walked away from my 1994 Wall Street bonus in the middle of the year," he said in an interview for *Time*.[2]

The regret minimization framework made his decision an easy one, according to Bezos, saying, "I was not going to regret trying to participate in this thing called the Internet that I thought was going to be a really big

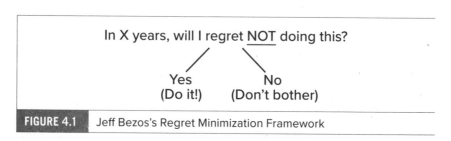

FIGURE 4.1   Jeff Bezos's Regret Minimization Framework

deal. I knew that if I failed I wouldn't regret that, but I knew the one thing I might regret is not ever having tried. I knew that that would haunt me every day."

This mentality continues to drive Bezos, a mogul who can seldom be swayed from his own ideas of how things should work at the company he founded and still operates as the chief executive. All major decisions come from the top and work their way down as he continues to innovate and disrupt the retail market and its associated technology. He is brash, stubborn, and, his colleagues say, always right and always on target, and it is why he has made billions for both himself and Amazon shareholders.

From the Lazy G Ranch to Princeton University to Wall Street

Jeff Bezos was not a prodigy computer programmer as a youth. While Bill Gates was writing code and creating a business as a teenager, Bezos was on his grandfather's farm working on tractors. Surrounded by rural agricultural folks, Bezos learned the spirit of initiative and resourcefulness to get things done efficiently.

"That kind of self-reliance is something you can learn," Bezos said in *One Click: Jeff Bezos and the Rise of Amazon.com* by Richard L. Brandt, "and my grandfather was a huge role model for me: If something is broken, let's fix it."[3]

Bezos did the work of a ranch hand every summer in Cotulla until he was 16, creating within him a strong work ethic. He cleaned stalls, branded and castrated cattle, worked on the plumbing, and fixed farm equipment like windmills. His grandfather's expansive knowledge of science also influenced the developing mind of the boy, who admired his grandfather immensely.

At the age of 10, Bezos found out for the first time that his father, Miguel Bezos, had adopted him when he was three years old after his mother had divorced his biological father. Bezos's biological father, Ted Jorgensen, met Bezos's mother, Jacklyn Gise, when the two attended a high school in Albuquerque. On January 12, 1964, their son Jeff was born. Ted attended the University of New Mexico where he earned a degree in math and computer science. He got a job at Exxon as a petroleum engineer and moved the family to Houston.

When Bezos found out that Miguel wasn't his father, he initially cried, but quickly moved on from the news. Today, Bezos says that he only thinks about his biological father when a doctor asks about his family's medical history.

Author Brad Stone writes in *The Everything Store: Jeff Bezos and the Age of Amazon*, "It is, of course, unknowable whether the unusual circumstances of his birth helped to create the fecund entrepreneurial mix of intelligence, ambition, and a relentless need to prove himself."[4]

Many people who are personally familiar with Apple's Steve Jobs and Oracle's Larry Ellison, both given up for adoption by their biological parents, say they were motivated to succeed by an inner force created from their feelings of abandonment.

"In Bezos's case, what is undeniably true is that from his earliest years, his parents and teachers recognized that this child was different—unnaturally gifted, but also unusually driven," Stone writes.

Ironically, while in elementary school, Bezos's was put into a gifted student program, and he was featured in a book titled *Turning on Bright Minds: A Parent Looks at Gifted Education in Texas*.[5] In the book, the author describes a 12-year-old Bezos as friendly and serious, but "not particularly gifted in leadership." However, there were glimpses even as a child of Bezos's future "never accept no" personality. As a 10-year-old Bezos was concerned that his grandmother's cigarette smoking habit was causing damage to her life, and he wanted her to stop smoking. However, when he mentioned the subject, his grandmother did not agree to quit. To persuade her, Bezos began doing mathematic calculations to determine how many years the cigarette smoking habit had taken from his grandmother's expected lifespan. He came up with a definite figure: cigarette smoking had removed nine years from his grandmother's life. Hearing this frightening fact caused his grandmother to weep openly—and she gave up smoking.

As a child, Bezos was not completely absorbed in any one thing. He was a well-rounded kid who loved helping out on the ranch, was a bookworm and took his academics seriously, tried his hand at football, started a small summer academic camp for a handful of kids one year, was inventive, and had an interest in store-bought science kits.

"I think single-handedly we kept many Radio Shacks in business," his mother told *Wired*.

In addition, Bezos was not a college dropout like many technology start-up geniuses, including Steve Jobs, Bill Gates, and Mark Zuckerberg.

No, Bezos earned high grades in high school, won a slew of academic awards in science and math, was the valedictorian of his class, and got early admission into Princeton, while working at McDonald's.

After high school, Bezos shipped out to New Jersey to attend Princeton. Few people have vivid memories of him in college. It is said that he liked to play beer pong, that he was in an eating group called the Quadrangle Club, and that he was not a hit with the ladies.

He told *Wired* that he was "goofy" and has never been a guy women met and thought, "Oh my God, this is what I have been looking for!"[6]

When he began his studies at Princeton University, he wanted to become a theoretical physicist like Albert Einstein. However, Bezos made a pragmatic decision to switch majors after he examined his classmates in the physics lab and formed an understanding that he would never be the best in that room, even though he was a top 25 student in the Princeton honors physic program. Being at the very top was important to him, and he felt he fell short in physics, so he switched his major to computer science.

"[I]t was clear to me that there were three people in the class who were much, much better at it than I was, and it was much, much easier for them," he told *Wired*. "It was really sort of a startling insight, that there were these people whose brains were wired differently."

In 1987, he graduated from Princeton, Phi Beta Kappa, with a bachelor of science degree in electrical engineering and computer science. Next, to his picture in the Princeton yearbook, he chose to put a quote from the dystopian author Ray Bradbury: "The Universe says No to us. We in answer fire a broadside of flesh at it and cry Yes!"

With an Ivy League degree in hand, Bezos turned down job offers from Andersen Consulting, Intel, and Bell Labs to become the eleventh employee of a start-up called FITEL, a telecommunications company that was in the early stages of building a worldwide telecom network for trading firms. He worked there for two years and eventually grew impatient with its slow growth, so he turned to stability instead and took a job with Bankers Trust as a product manager with the task of developing its computer system. Within two years, and at the age of 26, he became a VP. He was still unsatisfied, though, and he jumped ship, moving over to a New York City hedge fund, D. E. Shaw, where he became a senior VP after four years.

It was at D. E. Shaw that Bezos met his future wife, MacKenzie Tuttle. "My office was next door to his, and all day long I listened to that fabulous laugh," she told *Vogue*. "How could you not fall in love with that laugh?"[7]

Not everyone was as appreciative of his laugh—more on that later—but MacKenzie was a fan of the booming bray, and she talked him into a lunch date. They got married six months later.

Nothing More Than a Vision

While doing research for D. E. Shaw, an exploration of a global computer network called the Internet, Bezos came across a statistic that said this World Wide Web was growing at a rate of 2,300 percent per year. Bezos instinctively knew he had to be a part of this. After analyzing potential opportunities for a business on the electronic grid, which included only a sparse collection of information at the time, he decided he should sell books. Yes, the physicist turned electrical engineer and computer scientist decided his fate was intertwined with selling books.

To obtain more insights, he attended the 1994 American Booksellers Convention in Los Angeles. He established that key booksellers already had electronic catalogs of their inventories, but they were only used for wholesale pricing. He concluded that Internet connectivity that could place such inventories in one place online was the missing link to disrupting an entire industry.

During a speech at a baccalaureate ceremony for the Princeton University class of 2010, Bezos said, "I'd never seen or heard of anything that grew that fast, and the idea of building an online bookstore with millions of titles—something that simply couldn't exist in the physical world—was very exciting to me."

He brought the idea directly to D. E. Shaw. "I went to my boss and told him I wanted to start a company selling books on the Internet. He took me on a long walk in Central Park, listened carefully to me, and finally said, 'That sounds like a really good idea, but it would be an even better idea for someone who didn't already have a good job.'" Bezos continued, "Seen in that light, it really was a difficult choice, but ultimately, I decided I had to give it a shot."[8]

With hardly any hesitation, Bezos and his wife rolled out of Manhattan with only a vision. On the way west, he spoke to a friend in Seattle who agreed to let them store their belongings at his house. Then, Bezos notified the movers that Seattle would be his new home. His thinking was that in Seattle, he would have unfettered access to Ingram Book Group, one of the largest wholesalers of books, and access to the pool of talented computer experts in Seattle.

While MacKenzie drove, Bezos typed out his business plan, and after a few nights at roadside motels and an evening camping on the edge of the Grand Canyon, the online innovator arrived in Seattle to start Amazon.com.

The Foundation of Amazon.com

The beginnings of Amazon, the creation of the first Amazon.com website and the distribution and logistics planning, occurred within the folds of Bezos's three-bedroom house in Bellevue, Washington, a suburb of Seattle. After the site was launched in July 1995, Bezos moved his company into a 1,000-square-foot office space in a brick industrial complex (Figure 4.2), which also housed an out-of-business pawn shop and a needle exchange program. The frugal businessman only had a 400-square-foot warehouse in the basement of the complex, where a couple hundred books could be stored when they arrived from distributors before being turned around and sent to waiting customers.

FIGURE 4.2 The Original Amazon Warehouse

Bezos's little company with a skid row address was only selling five or six books a day to start; consider that today, Amazon now has days in which it sells 6,000 orders per minute. From the get-go, Bezos was offering discounts of 10 to 30 percent off what brick-and-mortar bookstores were charging, and book lovers immediately took notice of the great deals. However, it wasn't until he received a call from Jerry Yang, cofounder of Yahoo, that things really got cooking. Yahoo wanted to put Amazon on its "What's Cool" page.

"We thought about it some, and we realized it might be like taking a sip from a fire hose, but we decided to go ahead and go for it," Bezos said.[9]

Back in the late 1990s, Yahoo was *the* search engine, and Yahoo's approval of Amazon put Bezos on the map. Orders immediately soared, and Bezos couldn't keep up with the boom. Late into the evening, until 2 and 3 a.m., his employees worked without workstations, on hands and knees on a concrete floor, attempting to pack, address, and ship $12,000 in book orders in the first week after the Yahoo announcement, and $15,000 in orders the second week. He told one of his employees he was going to have to get his staff kneepads, and at a speech at Lake Forest College on February 26, 1998, Bezos recalled that the employee "looked at me like I was a Martian" before saying, "buy some tables."[10]

This moment marked the beginning of Bezos's legendary penchant for frugality. He quickly developed a reputation that the needs of his employees would always be secondary to those of the customer. From that point, Bezos's employees felt the demand to keep pace with both Amazon.com orders and Bezos himself. Today, his staff still feels Bezos's pressure to meet Amazon patrons' fever for fast customer service response and delivery of their products.

Bezos used that drive to achieve his vision with his distributors as well. At the time Amazon was founded, book distributors required retailers to place orders of at least 10 books each. They could be different books, but the minimum order that would be fulfilled was for 10. This requirement constituted a significant hurdle for Amazon because his new company did not have the money to purchase 10 books per order, nor did it have the need for those 10 books. Not willing to cede his business vision in the face of such requirements, Bezos hatched a strategy for getting around this obstacle. Bezos would place an order for a copy of the book Amazon needed together with nine copies of some obscure book that was out of stock at all times. Through this strategy, Bezos enabled Amazon to continue its operations despite the limiting requirements of book distributors. His Mandate Driven Leadership style, the unrelenting forward motion to achieve a vision regardless of obstacles, was taking hold.

Bezos beat every bookstore to the Internet in 1995. Many brick-and-mortar chains crashed as Amazon took their customers. Even the biggest survivor of the traditional book retailers, Barnes & Noble, scrambled to keep pace with Amazon, and it didn't launch its retail website BN.com until May 1997, the month that Bezos took his virtual bookstore public. His competitors have been in the fumes ever since.

Amazon's Disruptive Innovation

In May 1997, Amazon made a public offering with a simple Bezos-esque definition of its product: "Amazon.com is the leading online retailer of books." Included were its statistics, which were just as simple: "Average daily visits (not 'hits') have grown from approximately 2,200 in December 1995 to approximately 80,000 in March 1997." The offering provided data regarding the future prospects of book sales, and the $26 billion book market that he quoted from 1996 is less than Bezos's net worth today. The company, which employed 256 people at the time, was losing money: $5.78 million in 1996 with gross revenues of $15.75 million. Amazon's revenue growth of 2,982 percent from the year before superseded the prediction that Bezos had read that the Internet was growing at 2,300 percent a year. At this time, there was no discussion of Amazon moving into markets outside of book sales. The initial public offering opened at $18 a share and closed the day at $23.50, raising $54 million to make Amazon's value $438 million.

In 1998, Amazon expanded to CDs and DVDs, and in 1999 it started selling toys. In 2000, it changed its logo to include an arrow running from A to Z, signaling its desire to sell all products A–Z. In March 1999, *Wired* wrote, "Bezos's vision has always been about taking advantage of a new platform and new tools to change shopping itself. Long before he launched the company, he had dreams of making Amazon.com broader than books and music."[11] For the holiday season of 1998, analysts had projected revenue for Amazon of $190 million. Actual revenue exceeded $250 million, sending Amazon's stock as high as $350 by early January. Amazon was now a force to be reckoned with in the retail world.

Bezos has always represented himself as a savior of the retail world. He claimed that he wasn't trying to trick people into buying any of his products and called for merchants of the era to build communities, not destroy them, and to be honest with consumers.

"What consumerism really is, at its worst, is getting people to buy things that don't actually improve their lives," he said. "The one thing that offends me the most is when I walk by a bank and see ads trying to convince people to take out second mortgages on their home so they can go on vacation. That's approaching evil."[12]

Bezos was even willing to disrupt his own business for the sake of building a better marketplace and advancing Amazon's customer service experience through honesty and trust and shifting consumer power from merchants to consumers. He allowed people to post negative reviews on his website, and he sold secondhand books, both of which he was advised not to do by his executives and shareholders because they felt it would decrease the bottom line. However, Bezos stuck to his vision that a marketplace where the customer was truly in charge would propel Amazon forward.

While Bezos held to his vision, there were many naysayers. On many occasions, business analysts, including Forrester Research president George Colony, saw the end for Amazon, calling the company "Amazon.toast" in a 1999 report.[13] After the Internet bubble and market crash in 2000, many gave up on the company. An article from *Barron's* had the headline "Amazon.bomb" after the company lost 20 percent of its value in a single day.[14] A 27-page Lehman Brothers analysis of Amazon said the company probably would not survive, reporting that Amazon had a "weak balance sheet, poor working capital management, and massive negative operating cash flow—the financial characteristics that have driven innumerable retailers to disaster through history."[15]

On one particular day, Bezos personally lost more than a billion dollars on the value of his Amazon stock, and business reporters stalked him for comment. He remained hard-nosed and practical, but at the time, financial experts didn't find him very sensible.

Bezos was never worried about Amazon's short-term stock price nor his net worth. "I know a lot about e-commerce," Bezos stated to the *Guardian*, "but it's because I think about it all the time. I'm constantly thinking about Amazon.com, e-commerce and the internet. It's in my every waking moment and most of my sleeping ones. The internet truly is a big deal, so it hasn't been over-hyped in that sense. It will probably be a bigger deal than anyone realizes. Long term, there is an irrational under-exuberance."[16]

Bezos, who only a year before was *Time* magazine's person of the year while running a company that had yet to turn a profit,[17] would prove all the naysayers wrong. Amazon would make a profit for the first time in the fourth quarter of 2001, driven by holiday sales. It would continue to rise, and in 2017 Amazon reported $3 billion in profit on $177.9 billion in revenue.[18] In 2018, Amazon was generating more than $2 billion of profit each quarter.[19]

As Amazon ascended to become the largest retailer in the world, its innovations and disruptions to the sector became routine. Amazon revolutionized the e-commerce shopping sphere when it introduced its One-click purchasing feature in September 1997. Here, Amazon freed customers from the lengthy checkout processes that are typical of most online merchants.

Amazon rolled out Amazon Prime, yet another disruptive service offering, in 2005. With this service, users pay a flat yearly fee in exchange for privileges such as same-day shipping, instant videos, music, photos, and unlimited storage space in the Amazon Cloud. Amazon now has more than 100 million subscribers to its Prime service.

It's easy enough to say that Amazon disrupted not only the traditional brick-and-mortar bookstore business but the entire retail industry and beyond. The company pioneered online consumerism, grew it, and has become so powerful and dominating of the online retail market that many argue it is single-handedly responsible for the shuttering of hundreds if not thousands of traditional brick-and-mortar retailers including industry behemoths Circuit City, Borders, and Toys"R"Us.

Others will argue that Amazon's emergence has been integral in driving the digital economy forward, creating hundreds of thousands of new jobs and economic opportunity. Regardless, Bezos was not settled with disrupting just the retail marketplace.

The Cloud

At the turn of the millennium, Amazon's system infrastructure was a tangled mess because of its fast growth and layers of software that were desperately attempting to work together. The connected web of software was both confusing and slow, and it was critical that the engineers streamline it for easier management and faster results as the company continued to grow.

"It turned out to be way harder and more time-consuming than any of us imagined," Andy Jassy, head of Amazon Web Services, told the *Washington Post*.[20]

Given time, the engineering group built a straightforward and autonomous computing system that became the pride of the organization. Bezos wanted to show off the system and sell the technology if possible, so Amazon Web Services (AWS) was launched. The new arm of Amazon brought cloud infrastructure to the mainstream. The cloud was a revolutionary change in how information could be stored, shared, and used. Instead of using a local hard drive to store data, information was stored on multiple servers and accessed over the Internet from any device at any time. Other companies were developing the technology, but they were attempting to evolve it for traditional businesses of size to make big money with less work. Amazon had different ideas. "We wanted to enable any individual, in his or her dorm room, to have access to the same price and cost structure and scalability and infrastructure as the largest companies in the world," Jassy said.

Amazon pushed the accelerator and moved quickly into the market.

"Large tech companies usually wait to launch until they've built all the bells and whistles their development team can imagine," he continued. "We thought it was very important to be first to market."[21]

Four months after Amazon launched the service in July 2006, it was holding on tightly to 800 million client files in its cloud, beating its competitors to the punch, creating a buzz about its product, and working through numerous kinks on the go. The next year, start-up Dropbox began using Amazon Web Service, and its biggest client today is Netflix. In a huge sign of confidence to the market, Amazon began providing cloud services to the CIA. Today, Amazon owns more than a third of the market for cloud infrastructure services and exceeds $17 billion a year in revenue from its Web Services division.

Against all advice, Bezos and Amazon initially targeted the low-end market that the industry ignored—literally, any developer using a computer—and now Amazon is the undisputed industry leader in cloud hosting.

Watch a Movie or Have Alexa Make My Coffee at 9 a.m.

Bezos is not finished disrupting, and he understands that the Internet of Things is still in its infancy. Understanding that traditional television will eventually be bypassed by streaming content on the Internet, Bezos created a streaming TV and movie service, and while he was at it, he created original content to stream on the service, keeping pace with Netflix, which is both his competitor and his client. Bezos created Alexa, a voice-controlled assistant that will order you takeout food or set a timer for you in the kitchen. It will give you the weather and traffic, and buy you a Kindle e-book then read it to you. He continues to advance the Kindle e-reader, and he is not afraid to bring something brand-new or improve someone else's concept at a low price.

Entire books are being written about the disruptions that Jeff Bezos has spurred, and the ones that have been mentioned are only the more prominent. What is evident is that Bezos is a visionary who understands what it takes to bring those visions to reality. He consciously and unconsciously is the epitome of a Mandate Driven Leader. His day-to-day work is powered by a vision of the future, not a view of how to make the status quo more efficient. We see that vision at work in each of his innovations. He then takes that vision and through mandate makes it a reality. With gusto, and at times a lack of patience, he demands that everyone in his ecosystem turn his visions into reality, and he provides them the tools to accomplish the task. His work ethic is beyond reproach, and naysayers are cast aside in favor of unrelenting drive. And at the foundation of every vision is the customer.

Customer Service and the Empty Chair

In the world of Bezos, the customer comes first. In fact, the customer participates in nearly every meeting with the online kingpin; an empty chair in the room symbolizes the customer's position. While Bezos indulges his customer's wishes, he does not coddle his employees like many of today's technology companies. The stories are endless about the demand he places on his staff members, especially those in his warehouses, where turnover is scary. In 2013, Amazon had the least loyal employees with a median tenure of one year, according to PayScale.[22]

However, in a 2015 University of Michigan survey of 9,358 customers chosen at random, Amazon was ranked the number one Internet retailer, and the same results are seen in nearly all online shopping experience surveys in every year for the past decade.

Bezos says that Amazon works every decision around the customer to stay competitive, and not the other way around.

"When they're [Amazon competitors] in the shower in the morning, they're thinking about how they're going to get ahead of one of their top competitors," Bezos told *Fortune*. "Here in the shower, we're thinking about how we are going to invent something on behalf of a customer."[23] Perhaps no quote better epitomizes the Mandate Driven Leader.

In a 2012 article in *Forbes*, the writer makes this fact clear, writing:

> More than a century ago another legendary retailer, Chicago's Marshall Field, championed the fatalist's slogan: "The customer is always right." Bezos, perhaps more than anyone, has taken that mantra into the digital era, incrementally cracking one of the business's great mysteries: figuring what customers want before the cash register rings and then making those insights pay off. In an era when high-flying tech companies outdo each other with worker perks, no-frills Bezos is proving the potency of another model: coddling his 164 million customers, not his 56,000 employees.[24]

Nadia Shouraboura, who was an Amazon VP in charge of technology for Amazon's global supply chain and fulfillment operation, said that Bezos often ignored discussions taking place at his own meetings because he was reading customer e-mails.

Bezos understands that by having a direct dialogue with the customer, he will have a deeper understanding of the customer experience. Forwarding e-mails of customer complaints is just one method Bezos utilizes to ensure customer responsiveness. "My initial reaction was, you want me to be working on a Friday night on an order that was messed up by half a day?" Shouraboura said. "Then it sank in. If one customer wrote to Jeff, there are others who didn't. And Jeff wants to understand the screw-up to make sure it gets fixed."[25]

Yes, there really is a Jeff@Amazon.com e-mail, Bezos does read e-mails that come to his box, and employees must figure out a solution to every customer problem, especially those that come from him. Once a resolution is considered by the tagged employee, a series of managers review the response and send a final proposal to Bezos.

One particular escalation in 2010 involved lubricants in the category of sexual wellness. A customer who had browsed the section without making a purchase began receiving e-mails that pitched other items within the category. The shopper was not happy to be receiving e-mails on such a personal item, and the patron e-mailed Bezos to tell him about the experience. The e-mail marketing department received the forwarded message and the question mark.

A nervous crew patched together a response, which focused on the successes of that particular brand of marketing—e-mail follow-ups to virtual window shoppers—which generated hundreds of millions of dollars in revenue for Amazon.

Bezos cared little, storming into a conference room in Amazon's Seattle headquarters to confront the VP of marketing, Steven Shure, as others sat in attendance.

"So, Steve Shure is sending out e-mails about lubricants," an upset Bezos declared.

He stood, staring straight into Shure, and continued, "I want to shut down the channel. We can build a $100 billion company without sending out a single fucking e-mail!"[26]

A debate began, and Bezos, who is overt at his tactic of starting confrontational squabbles in order to get further faster, would not tolerate customer mistrust for any amount of revenue, while Shure argued that embarrassment over this sort of item was childish, considering you can buy lubricants over the counter at any pharmacy. Bezos demanded that the marketing department ban any item of a sensitive nature from e-mail follow-ups.

Bezos is direct with his communication. While others may find his directness harsh, for Bezos it is to ensure there is no misunderstanding of the vision. Understanding and propelling the vision forward is the only outcome acceptable to the Mandate Driven Leader.

The Bezos Theory of Communicating

Bezos's approach to PR is as simple as its core message: Amazon has everything you need at a lower price, presented in a friendly manner. Bezos takes a red pen to the rest. He is not interested in fluff or overexplaining in any press release, product description, speech, or shareholder letter, so he edits out everything that isn't put into simple terms. John Doerr, who was on the Amazon board of directors for a decade, calls it the "Bezos Theory of Communication."[27]

Remember MacKenzie, Bezos's wife, remarking about his incredible laugh? Well, that laugh can be used as a rifle. Bezos will laugh at you and lob insults if you don't deliver his requests and back his vision with an absolute loyalty that is proven by working more than anyone else and following his orders. His animated cackle lets you know that you are a joke and so is your work if you do not comply with his direction or meet his standards. It's like a grenade.

"You can't misunderstand it," said Rick Dalzell, former Amazon CIO. "It's disarming and punishing. He's punishing you."[28]

Brad Stone writes, "His drive and boldness trumps other leadership ideals, such as consensus building and promoting civility. While he can be charming and capable of great humor in public, in private he explodes into what some of his underlings call nutters. A colleague failing to meet Bezos's exacting standards will set off a nutter. If an employee does not have the right answers or tries to bluff, or takes credit for someone else's work, or exhibits a whiff of internal politics, uncertainty, or frailty in the heat of battle—a blood vessel in Bezos's forehead bulges and his filter falls away. He's capable of hyperbole and harshness in these moments and over the years has delivered some devastating rebukes."[29]

Within the Amazon ecosystem, Bezos's nutters are one of the mechanisms he uses to keep Amazon focused on the vision. An empty chair in every meeting to represent the customer is another. When you listen to Bezos you understand that there can be a lot of wasted bandwidth in an organization. Therefore, there are specific leadership attributes, styles, and management systems that are necessary to keep individuals focused on what matters most. One of these is "The Narrative."

"The Narrative" and Creating the Virtual Book

E-mail anecdotes, or an anecdote in general, has no place in the Tuesday gatherings when departments have their meetings. Tuesdays are when data is analyzed, and it is the numbers that do the talking, and through their analysis, those things that are broken are fixed. To make the point clear, Bezos has his senior executives read *The Black Swan: The Impact of the Highly Probable* by Nassim Nicholas Taleb, which is an essay on the human tendency to be simplistic in their explanations of events. The book drills into them the idea that every declaration must be supported on a higher level with numbers.

Stone writes, "Humans are biologically inclined to turn complex realities into soothing but oversimplified stories. Taleb argued that the limitations of the human brain resulted in our species' tendency to squeeze unrelated facts and events into cause-and-effect equations and then convert them into easily understandable narratives. These stories, Taleb wrote, shield humanity from the true randomness of the world, the chaos of human experience, and, to some extent, the unnerving element of luck that plays into all success and failures."[30]

In addition, Bezos does not allow employees to use PowerPoint presentations during meetings. Instead, he wants his staff to use "narratives," which he feels are more impactful because they are not snippets of information but deep thoughts. In a 2004 memo, Bezos gives the directive to stop the use of slide presentations and begin writing narratives:

> Well structured, narrative text is what we're after rather than just text. If someone builds a list of bullet points, that would be just as bad as a PowerPoint. The reason writing a good memo is harder than "writing" a 20 page PowerPoint is because the narrative structure of a good memo forces better thought and better understanding of what's more important than what, and how things are related. PowerPoint-style presentations somehow give permission to gloss over ideas, flatten out any sense of relative importance, and ignore the interconnectedness of ideas.[31]

The narratives allow all personality types, even introverts, the luxury of expressing their ideas by writing them out and not performing them, which eliminates bias. In other words, some people sell ideas of no substance because of their charisma and ability to give lively, engaging speeches. This cannot be done in a narrative. Ultimately, the narrative challenges more rigorous thinking.

As meetings begin, no one commands the room. Instead, the narratives are passed out, and everyone reads them quietly. The memos are six pages long in full sentences with topics and action verbs. Essentially, they are to be written like a dissertation defense, using the following structure:

1. The context or question.
2. Approaches to answer the question—by whom, by which method, and their conclusions.
3. How is your attempt at answering the question different from or the same as previous approaches?
4. Now what? That is, what's in it for the customer, the company, and how does the answer to the question enable innovation on behalf of the customer?

"Full sentences are harder to write," Bezos told *Fortune*. "They have verbs. The paragraphs have topic sentences. There is no way to write a six-page, narratively structured memo and not have clear thinking."[32]

The "written" part of the narrative is crucial because nothing is lost in the delivery of the message, and the message is backed by raw data. "For the new employee, it's a strange initial experience," he continued. "They're just not accustomed to sitting silently in a room and doing study hall with a bunch of executives."

The narrative has distinct value to prevent groupthink and avoid the pitfalls of consensus management. Oral presentations and PowerPoint slides when used for decision making inevitably bring into the decision making the personality, charisma, and qualitative properties of the presenter at the sacrifice of the quantitative data and facts. For the Mandate Driven Leader, the theater is to be left outside of decision making.

Gladiator Culture: Taking a Hammer to Social Cohesion and Consensus Building

Bezos gets no joy in seeking consensus. In fact, he hates it and pushes his employees to clash. On Amazon's job site, the company's leadership principles are posted for all to see (Figure 4.3), and the one stands out is near the bottom of the 14 rules. The title of Rule Number 13 reads: "Have Backbone; Disagree and Commit." In other words, Bezos, who is involved in all statements to the public, is telling his employees as a directive to challenge, contradict, and oppose.

The rule states, "Leaders are obligated to respectfully challenge decisions when they disagree, even when doing so is uncomfortable and exhausting. Leaders have convictions and are tenacious. They do not compromise for the sake of social cohesion. Once a decision is determined, they commit wholly."[33]

Bezos follows his rule to the extreme, but at times he may neglect the "respectfully" part, according to his colleagues. Former employees say the message is clear, a "gladiator culture" is the preferred method of doing business, but many cannot handle the climate and have had to leave the combative chaos never to return.

Bezos himself will often practice the rule to disagree. And he has an uncanny ability at analyzing data and process that makes it difficult for him

1. Customer Obsession	8. Think Big
2. Ownership	9. Bias for Action
3. Invent and Simplify	10. Frugality
4. Are Right, A Lot	11. Earn Trust
5. Learn and Be Curious	12. Dive Deep
6. Hire and Develop the Best	13. Have Backbone; Disagree and Commit
7. Insist on the Highest Standards	14. Deliver Results

FIGURE 4.3   Amazon's Leadership Principles

to be the recipient of disagreement. For example, a team of five engineers spent nine months working on a project to make fulfillment centers more efficient. Former supply chain VP Bruce Jones presented the findings to Bezos. The documents and preparation were erased in a moment when Bezos declared that the team had failed because they were all wrong.

Bezos stood up, began scribbling on the whiteboard, and dismantled all of their claims with his own observations of how things should run.

"He had no background in control theory, no background in operating systems," Jones says. "He only had minimum experience in the distribution centers and never spent weeks and months out on the line. . . . It would be easier to stomach if we could prove he was wrong, but we couldn't."[34]

In another situation, Bezos commissioned Jones to change the way that Amazon accounted for its inventory in order to distinguish it from its partners' merchandise. The process was difficult and complicated, and after two days of dealing with malfunctioning software that made Amazon's revenues invisible to the company's umbrella systems, Bezos blasted Jones during a "nutter" with a series of insults.

"He called me a 'complete fucking idiot' and said he had no idea why he hired idiots like me at the company," he continued, "and said, 'I need you to clean up your organization.' It was brutal. I almost quit."[35]

Faisal Masud, who worked in Amazon's retail business sector for five years, received a letter threatening legal action from Amazon after he left Amazon to work for eBay. Amazon believed his new position breached his noncompete clause. However, Masud was not upset by it and said he enjoyed the culture of conflict at Amazon.

"Everybody knows how hard it is and chooses to be there," said Masud. "You are learning constantly, and the pace of innovation is thrilling. I filed patents; I innovated. There is a fierce competitiveness in everything you do."[36]

As with many Mandate Driven Leaders, Bezos believes that complacency and the status quo is the ultimate enemy. A culture of innovation, of disruption, needs a level of stress. A certain amount of conflict. Great things can happen when individuals are outside of their comfort zone. And that competitiveness and no-lose attitude are not reserved just for internal management.

Competitive Intelligence Gathering

"Competitive Intelligence," a clandestine research organization within Amazon that resembles the FBI, began tracking an organization called Quidsi in 2010. Part of the department's job was to buy merchandise from other online stores and measure their service against Amazon's. Their gathered intelligence found that Quidsi, a retailer of baby supplies from diapers to strollers, was providing top-notch service on a level equal to Amazon. In an article in *Bloomberg Businessweek*, the founders of Quidsi admitted to idolizing Amazon and modeling their company after it. They even referred to Bezos as "sensei," making it clear that they believed him to be a master at retail.

Amazon's VP of business development, Jeff Blackburn, sent an e-mail to the cofounders of Quidsi, Vinit Bharara and Marc Lore, making it clear that Amazon was about to battle the baby boutique in their category, so they might want to consider a buyout. Bharara and Lore were not interested in selling, preferring instead to remain independent and build their own brand.

Bezos was not happy, so he flexed his retail muscles and dropped Amazon's prices 30 percent in the Quidsi niche of baby products in an attempt to rattle the upstart competitors into partnering with Amazon. Executives at Quidsi caught wind of the scheme and decided upon an experiment to see how Amazon's prices would change if they changed their pricing. In the process, Quidsi found out that Amazon was using a system bot to monitor the company, and every time Quidsi changed its prices, Amazon would match and discount them. Quidsi's revenue started to slow, and venture capitalists began to turn away from providing additional funds to the company. They were not answering the phone anymore.

Then, Bezos really got serious by creating "Amazon Mom," a monthly subscription service for parents with free two-day shipping. The service was so inexpensive to its subscribers that experts predicted that Amazon would take a $100 million loss in the diaper domain every three months.

It was about that time that Walmart stepped into the fray and began discussions with Quidsi in an attempt to buy it and compete with Amazon. The panicked cofounders were ready to settle for fear that Amazon would make them completely irrelevant as a retailer in short order. Bezos told Quidsi that he would give diapers away if the cofounders continued to go down the road with Walmart, and on November 8, 2010, Quidsi agreed to a $545 million acquisition proposal by Amazon.[37]

Bezos has a reputation for buying retailers that compete with Amazon in the area of customer service. Quidsi is one of several acquisitions, and each one has a similar type of culture, which Bezos explained himself in a video to the employees of Zappos, a shoe company that Amazon acquired for $850 million in 2009.

"Zappos has a customer obsession which is so easy for me to admire. It is the starting point for Zappos. It is the place where Zappos begins and ends," he said in the video. "And that is a very key factor for me. I get all weak-kneed when I see a customer-obsessed company, and Zappos certainly is that. I've seen a lot of companies, and I have never seen a company with a culture like Zappos. And I think that kind of unique culture is a very significant asset."[38]

Zappos, Quidsi, and many others have found themselves caught in the neutralizing teeth of Amazon. All of them have found out quickly that it is better to ride shotgun with Bezos than to be driven off a cliff through price manipulation and intimidation. Mandate Driven Leaders such as Bezos are focused on the outcome. And just like an effective military leader, the measurement of the outcome is to win. That often includes eliminating your competition.

Mandate Driven Leadership Becomes Central to Amazon

The culture that Bezos has built at Amazon is one where the customer is always at the center of discussions, where groupthink and consensus are discarded in favor of vision, innovation, unrelenting movement forward, competition, and facts. Bezos has demonstrated this Mandate Driven Leadership style from the time he was planning to launch Amazon.

Bezos wanted to launch an online bookstore that had every kind of book in its inventory. Nevertheless, a number of publishing experts advised Bezos to launch an online bookstore that included only a few genres and bestselling titles. In his characteristic unyielding style, Bezos rejected the advice of these publishing experts and instead implemented his personal idea of what Amazon should be. "Every well-intentioned, high-judgment person we asked told us not to do it. We got some good advice, we ignored it," Bezos has stated.[39] Here, Bezos owns up to the fact that he did not cede his ideas to the ideas of his advisors.

Stories abound where Bezos's legendary demands illustrate his Mandate Driven Leadership style. Clearly, the Kindle is one product that would be much different now if it were not for Bezos's demands.

Early in the development process of the Kindle, after analyzing numerous data points, Bezos came to the conclusion that consumers wanted an e-reader that had the capacity to download any book in a maximum of one minute. While setting this target, Bezos did not mind potentially impeding technical issues such as transmission speeds or compression ratios for book files. Rather, Bezos instructed his engineers to achieve this target and to resolve any arising technical issues in whatever way they deemed fit. Bezos presented Amazon's software engineers with a tough challenge and failed to consider the possibility for failure. In his characteristic Mandate Driven Leadership style, Bezos focused on the goal of pushing Amazon forward.

As the development of the Kindle moved forward, solving the technical problems became costly. Bezos had one interaction with an Amazon finance executive who was worried that Amazon had spent too much money over several years in an attempt to create a Kindle e-reader that satisfied Bezos's specifications. This finance executive asked Bezos how much money he was ready to spend on the Kindle development process. This otherwise polite query apparently infuriated Bezos, who retorted angrily by wondering what amount of money Amazon had on hand at that particular moment. In this situation, Bezos was so focused on creating an "ideal" Kindle that he did not pay equal attention to the cost of development of the project. Bezos did not mind hurting the emotions of this finance executive to get across the point that vision is paramount.

One of Bezos's favorite quotes is "We are stubborn on vision. We are flexible on details." His point, like many Mandate Driven Leaders, is that once you have a vision you must immediately start forward progression to achieving that vision. If you wait for everything to be perfect, your vision may indeed become someone's else's reality. Bezos's demands of the engineering team on the Kindle parallel Steve Jobs's demands of the engineering team on the iPhone—don't worry that the technology is not all there to do what we want—we will solve those problems along the way. But go ahead and start development now.

Once development of the Kindle was complete, the Amazon team that was involved in creating this e-reader believed that this gadget should be named after a character named Fiona in Neal Stephenson's novel *The Diamond Age*. Even though the development team had logical reasons to support their choice of name, Bezos disregarded them and instead named the e-reader Kindle. Bezos maintained that Kindle was an appropriate name because it evokes the thought of lighting a fire.

When marketing began, Bezos roundly rejected a particular advertisement for the Kindle. Tina Patterson, who served as a senior brand manager for Amazon between 2007 and 2011, describes an enlightening experience she had with Bezos. According to Patterson, Bezos and the Amazon advertising team were reviewing a particular advertisement in which a Kindle user transforms into a courageous matador before being thrown in the air by a wild bull. While the rest of the Amazon advertising team giggled after watching this advertisement, Bezos was not amused. In response to the giggling responses of his team, Bezos adopted a stern outlook and gravely stated that there was nothing funny about an Amazon customer being assaulted by a bull. Bezos bluntly criticized the work that had been done by his advertising team. For Bezos, the team had violated the customer-centric vision. Why should he pay heed to the idea that such a response could hurt the egos of members of the team?[40]

Bezos's mandates related to customer service, and anything related to customer satisfaction, have obtained almost legendary status. He constantly reminded his executives that Amazon's only asset is the reputation of Amazon with the customer, and therefore, anything an Amazon employee had to do to not inflict harm to that reputation would have to be accepted. In 1998, when Amazon was inundated with an avalanche of orders, to ensure that the company's operations did not collapse, Bezos instructed that all of his employees had to take an extra graveyard shift in the fulfillment center. As a result, many employees would spend the night in their cars before reporting to work the following morning.

Moreover, early in the history of Amazon, Bezos required his employees to work 60 hours per week. To satisfy Bezos's demands, one employee who lived close to the office bicycled to work early in the morning and returned from work on his bike late at night. Over eight months of relentless work hours, he totally forgot to check on his car, which had been parked near his apartment. During all this time, the relevant authorities had been sending warnings to this employee about owing parking fees. When he finally had an opportunity to pay attention, he found several parking tickets in his mail, an alert that his car had been hauled off, several caveats from the towing firm about owing towing fees, and a memo indicating that his car had been auctioned.[41]

When Amazon implemented same-day delivery in select markets, it was a huge hit with customers. Bezos mandated that it be expanded to other markets. On this note, Simon Murdoch, a past executive of Amazon's UK operations, recalls that Bezos personally pressured him to begin providing same-day delivery services to customers. According to Murdoch, Bezos initially instructed him to broaden the delivery cutoff to orders placed before 6 p.m. Bezos subsequently pressurized Murdoch to further broaden the delivery cutoff to 7 p.m. Eventually, Murdoch had to give in to Bezos's unrelenting pressure. To satisfy Bezos's wishes, Murdoch had to radically change warehouse hours and require overtime for hundreds of line employees and managers with no notice.[42]

To ensure that every Amazon employee understands that the vision Bezos mandates for Amazon is not optional, Amazon has implemented what a former Amazon human resource director refers to as the policy of "purposeful Darwinism." According to this former executive, Amazon culls members of its staff who fail to internalize Amazon's stringent values. This is the process of "purposeful Darwinism"; staff members who fail to adopt the ideals of Bezos are sacked every year.[43] This way, Bezos illustrates that he is not ready to tolerate employees who do not support his vision about the values employees should have.

An Amazon employee who was interviewed by the *New York Times* further illustrates Bezos's Mandate Driven Leadership style, stating, "If you're a good Amazonian, you became an Amabot."[44] Here, the word *Amabot* refers to an Amazon robot. In other words, to be considered an ideal employee by Bezos and his junior managers, an employee has to internalize Bezos's 14 leadership principles to the level of becoming a symbolic "bot." From this employee's remark, it is evident that Bezos is so focused on having his employees follow his vision that he does not mind converting his employees into metaphorical robots.

This Mandate Driven Leadership style has followed Bezos into ventures apart from Amazon. In 2013, Bezos bought the Washington Post Company. The newspaper industry has been decimated by the Internet, with print newspaper advertising revenue falling from $60 billion in 2000 to less than $20 billion by 2015. Hundreds of newspapers have been shuttered. It is safe to say that every major financial advisor was against Bezos's purchase. However, he has a vision. Shailesh Prakash, the chief product and technology officer at the *Post*, has explained that Bezos pressured the technology team at the *Post* to create Arc, a compilation of publishing instruments. This was despite the fact that the *Post* could easily obtain identical off-the-shelf publishing tools. Prakash noted that Bezos is "pushy . . . [and] very involved" in the affairs of the product and technology team at the *Post*. To defend his adamant stance on this matter, Bezos explained that, at its inception, Amazon could have utilized IBM software. Amazon nevertheless took a different path; it created its software that eventually led to the establishment of AWS that has since become hugely profitable.[45]

Today, Arc Publishing is available for purchase by publishers throughout the world.

Bezos demonstrates that after creating a particular vision, he henceforth primarily concentrates on actualizing the vision. During this process of actualizing the vision, Bezos does not mind what actions or steps he has to take. According to Bezos, such obstinate focus on vision enables Amazon to experiment until it finds what works. Bezos is sensible enough to exercise flexibility, but only when it does not sacrifice the vision. That is what a Mandate Driven Leader is all about.

The Businessman and the Legacy

The way Bezos does things is unorthodox and can be mean, and the slight five-foot-eight-inch man is scared of nothing and no one. Bezos bought the *Washington Post*, a newspaper that roasts President Trump on a daily basis, a paper that the president calls "fake news," but Bezos will casually sit with Trump during summits on technology, seemingly without prejudice, and supplies the CIA with Amazon Web Services. No insecurities exist.

In 2012, Bezos was *Fortune* magazine's Businessperson of the Year. He was called the "ultimate disrupter" in the announcement on December 3.[46] It could have easily read "ultimate Mandate Driven Leader." Other visionaries lauded him. Marc Andreessen, the Netscape cofounder, said that Bezos has "staying power and willingness to withstand beatings."[47]

Beatings aside, Bezos's leadership and business acumen has formed over the course of three decades. The form it took was that of a Mandate Driven Leader. In an Internet world of fierce competition, skeptics, and critics, he fights, and he brings that fire into the culture of his company as he projects the spirit of his vision down into his company and into the culture of everything that his employees do. Yes, at times Bezos's drive to achieve the vision results in some mean-spirited actions. True, if you don't play on his team, he may try to neutralize you. And it does take a certain personality to tolerate the pressure, pace, and maniacal customer centricity that Bezos demands.

At the end of the day, Bezos's leadership style for Amazon is summed up in a comment he made to *Forbes* magazine: "Our culture is friendly and intense, but if push comes to shove we'll settle for intense."[48]

CHAPTER 5

MANDATE DRIVEN LEADERSHIP DEFINED

The best executive is the one who has sense enough to pick good men to do what he wants done, and self-restraint enough to keep from meddling with them while they do it.
—THEODORE ROOSEVELT, President of the United States

When discussing leadership, one of the more amusing opinions that gets tossed around is a false belief that there are no new ideas. There seems to be a fallacy that either everything has already been done, or anything new is simply a rehash of what has been discussed in academic and management circles to date. I once heard a very well-known industrial psychologist call this the "old wine in new bottles" dilemma. I won't name this person as that statement was part of a larger and very colorful late-night rant in the bar at a Society for Industrial and Organizational Psychology annual conference, but I will say the person was fairly emphatic that this idea was correct. I will also say that the person was not as correct as the individual emphatically believed. In fact, we are in dire need of a new look at effective leadership models.

If you ever want to see a fascinating review of the flaws on the current views on effective leadership, go to YouTube and type in "On Leadership: A Discussion with Robert Hogan."[1] Dr. Robert Hogan, PhD, from the University of California–Berkeley, is a renowned authority on personality assessment, leadership, and organizational effectiveness. Watch this video and you will see this eminent psychologist rightfully vent about how the

77

study of leadership has failed because we have forgotten what it is all about. We have forgotten that leadership initially evolved because the group needed to identify someone who could *make decisions for the survival of the group.* It began at a time when finding the right leader was not a matter of being the next big thing in the market, but it was literally about life and death. The group with an effective leader survived and thrived. The groups without that leader did not. Dr. Hogan continues discussing how today many views on effective leadership are often views on how to rise to the top of the corporate ladder. We think of effective leaders as those who have been promoted over the years at a company. However, moving up the corporate ladder only proves that an individual was effective at the internal politics and inner workings of that company. It usually has nothing to do with whether the individual is truly an effective leader.

While the stakes today may not be about individual death, the stakes are about business death. We are in a major inflection point in business history. Digital technology is powering massive business disruption, and no industry or value chain is unaffected. Today's leaders must recognize that no company is sacrosanct from being disrupted right out of business. The result is a corporate landscape of billion-dollar companies that were merely a vision a few years ago—littered with many iconic companies now failed because of their ineffective leaders. Daily we are seeing companies entering bankruptcy and being liquidated because of a lack of vision, a lack of effective leadership. This list is long with many iconic names, including the once great retailer Brookstone, as well as the gun manufacturer Remington..

To compound the challenges of today's business disruption, effective leaders are scarce these days. Leaders are failing at an astounding rate—along with their organizations—as represented by a recent study by APQC of 547 businesses. The research by the benchmarking and best practices company found that 79 percent of organizations have ineffective leadership practices. The study also found that organizations do not spend enough time or money on leadership development, and they often rely on leadership selection and reward practices that encourage outdated leadership styles such as consensus management.[2] Current business challenges demand a specific type of leader, but many organizations resist change to the detriment of their survival.

Since many businesses place little or no priority on leadership development, it is up to the individual to evolve in a way that ensures success and a long career of accomplishing objectives, with or without an organization's support. This process of self-determined leadership development begins with an understanding of the styles of leadership and then deciding which works best for the leader's personality and the particular work environment and situation.

This word *situation* is key to the thesis of this book. The disruptive business environment of today requires a very specific type of leader—the Mandate Driven Leader. Upon reading the profiles of Steve Jobs and Jeff Bezos, it can be confidently stated that these two individuals are the epitome of the Mandate Driven Leader. But, what exactly does that mean? How is a Mandate Driven Leader defined, and more important, how can each of us develop into this type of leader? How does the Mandate Driven Leadership model differ from the transformational, transactional, servant, authentic, or any other leadership approaches that pop up from blogs to academic peer-reviewed journal articles?

Much like Douglas McGregor's Theory X and Theory Y,[3] Mandate Driven Leadership is about the assumptions leaders make, not just the actions they take. One can be a Mandate Driven Transactional Leader. One can also be a Mandate Driven Transformational Leader. In fact, if the leadership profiles in this book show us anything, it is that many Mandate Driven Leaders are transformational leaders. One can even be a Mandate Driven Servant Leader. In fact, even though our consensus-driven business environment has morphed servant leadership's accepted definition into some concept of the leader serving the team, the original context from Howard Greenleaf was about the leader serving society. Servant leaders drive a mandate about the societal benefit of their organizations. And anyone who worked with Green-leaf will tell you that he didn't have a lot of patience for people who didn't agree with that mandate.

So what are the characteristics that are core to a Mandate Driven Leader? Upon researching this book and interviewing some of the most successful businesspeople of our time, I have found that these leaders share characteristics that can be collapsed into three simple themes. In the most simplistic diagnostic, successful Mandate Driven Leaders have a vision, drive to an outcome, and are unrelenting until it is accomplished. These three themes are seen in the leaders profiled in this book as well as numerous other corporate leaders who have transformed companies or changed entire industries.

A Well-Communicated Vision of the Future

Sir Richard Branson, the founder of the Virgin Group, once said, "I believe in benevolent dictatorship provided I am the dictator."[4] An apt nickname for the Mandate Driven Leader would be benevolent dictator. Merriam-Webster defines benevolent as "marked by or disposed to doing good, organized for the purpose of doing good."[5] What is common to Mandate Driven Leaders is that they see a future that is better than the status quo. In fact, they hate the status quo. Steve Jobs said succinctly, "Innovation distinguishes between a leader and a follower."[6] This begs the question, can one be an effective leader maintaining a successful status quo? No, one cannot. In that case, the person is simply an effective manager, which is vastly different.

Mandate Driven Leaders recognize that the necessary outcome for today's leader is nothing short of survival. They fear the landscape littered with failed companies. They understand they have an ethical obligation to protect the livelihoods of their employees and the extended families those employee support. Jeff Bezos has stated, "In business, what's dangerous is not to evolve." At the core, the Mandate Driven Leader recognizes that survival starts with a vision for a better future.

The vision for a better future is obviously situational depending on industry, organization, company, or even service or product. Steve Jobs did not want to make a better computer. His vision was to create a better world through designing beautiful technology enablers that became part of our lives. "Apple is about people who think 'outside the box,' people who want to use computers to help them change the world, to help them create things that make a difference, and not just to get a job done."[7]

The vision of the future for a leader might be a new product. It might be a better business process. It might be a completely new business paradigm for an industry. Jeff Bezos, in a presentation in 1999 when Amazon was four years young, was asked about the vision for Amazon. He stated "It's customers helping customers make purchasing decisions. And that's what is community . . . businesses cannot create community. All businesses can do is facilitate community."[8] Bezos's vision was not to create the largest online bookseller or retailer. He was creating a community marketplace powered entirely by the community members themselves—their reviews, their rankings, their search results, and in many ways their product mix and their prices. Bezos still ingrains that vision into everything Amazon does. Without exception, a common theme among all Mandate Driven Leaders is that they have formulated a vision for the future state, and they are able to clearly communicate that vision into the rank-and-file management of the company.

These leaders all use variations of what academics would call the path-goal theory. First developed by Martin Evans in the 1970s, the path-goal theory simply means that individuals should have established goals and an expected path to achieve those goals. Within path-goal theory, leaders may use different leadership styles depending on the situation: participative, support, achievement-oriented, and directive. While directive management is not necessarily the only way to take the leadership vision of the future and weave it into the fabric of the organization, it has proven to be the most successful. And, as discussed previously, today's business disruption demands it. The survival imperative is what leadership was initially about, and it is part of the reason why command-and-control and directive management are considered more classical approaches to leading groups. It is also why military organizations still use directive management. Today's Mandate Driven Leaders understand this, and more often than not, they use directive management to ensure that the leadership vision of the future is understood, accepted, and implemented within the organization.

The importance of vision to the Mandate Driven Leader cannot be overstated. Rather than the Mandate Driven Leader giving power to the vision, it could be stated that it is the vision of a better tomorrow that powers the Mandate Driven Leader.

Drive to the Outcome Instead of the Process

Once the vision of the end state is established, a Mandate Driven Leader drives to the outcome. Death by process is actively avoided. A Mandate Driven Leader assumes that the *required outcomes* of the team, the organization, and sometimes society take priority over getting everyone in the team to agree on the strategy at hand. Does this mean that Mandate Driven Leaders don't listen to their team? Absolutely not. They make sure they are surrounded by qualified people with valuable insights and listen carefully to consider the options.

Make no mistake that Mandate Driven Leaders' first task in driving to the outcome is to assure that they have the right people on the team. Jim Collins in the seminal book *Good to Great* penned the memorable metaphor that an effective leader is a bus driver. The first objective of the leader is to get the right people on the bus and the wrong people off the bus. Mandate Driven Leaders expect and demand that individuals in the organization follow them and take their vision to reality, and they refuse to accept naysayers. Mandate Driven Leaders are OK with individuals questioning and debating the many details that are required to implement the vision to reality. In fact, they demand it. However, this is different from questioning or obstructing the vision. Mandate Driven Leaders continually assure themselves that the individuals in the organization have bought into the vision—or they ask them to exit the bus.

There is a segment of our society that may see this view of people management as an outdated and potentially unethical approach. But some simple math shows that this approach is even more relevant in the current fast-paced environment driven by digital disruption. If anything it is more ethical than spending inordinate amounts of time to get the key managers of a Mandate Driven Leader on the bus.

Let's say we have a company of 20,000 employees. Some of the people will be single, and others may have large families, but a good assumption would be that for every employee, there are say 2.5 additional people who are dependent on that income. This means that the leader of this organization is responsible for the well-being of approximately 70,000 people. And this is conservative as it does not account for partners, suppliers, investors, etc.

Let's say the leader of this organization has a vision for transformation that could improve the company and grow it by ten times over the next several decades, but this leader maintains the status quo. Or, the leader delays the decision and is eventually beaten to the market. For this leader, the challenge was that this new idea might seem too risky or the leader could not develop consensus in the organization on the value. Which approach is more ethical, wasting valuable time trying to achieve consensus for everyone to buy into the new idea? Or is it more ethical to be a Mandate Driven Leader and push toward a vision that will keep a company relevant and protect and benefit 70,000 people supported by the organization even if that results in the termination of employment of some employees not on board?

Jack Welch, yet another consummate Mandate Driven Leader, was the CEO of General Electric from 1981 to 2001. He quickly developed the nickname of "Neutron Jack." This nickname was earned through various strategies he implemented including exiting any business where GE could not be the market share leader and firing the bottom 10 percent of all employees each and every review period. In a short period of time, Welch terminated more than 100,000 employees and exited businesses with revenue in the billions. The result was that he turned what at the time was a company in crisis into a global power and increased the company's market value by more than $300 billion while achieving record revenue and profits.

Mandate Driven Leaders do not mind questions. If people have concerns, they hear and consider them, but at the end of the day, the Mandate Driven Leader takes responsibility for pushing the team constantly toward the vision. Remember the story about Bezos storming into a marketing meeting and demanding it stop sending customer solicitation e-mails in the sexual wellness category? Some would say that Bezos was not listening to his qualified people. A more accurate analysis is that Bezos was putting his people back on the path of the vision. They had strayed from the vision since the community was complaining about the e-mails. In other words, Bezos was simply preventing his team from straying from a customer-centric vision to a marketing-led vision.

Mandate Driven Leaders recognize that process can be a killer to outcomes. Hence, the phrase "death by process" that is often tossed about. One aspect of eschewing process over the outcome is to embrace disruption. Mandate Driven Leaders embrace disruption both in the industry and within their own companies. They must break down preconceived notions and any culture where consensus is valued more than survival. Jonah Sachs in *Unsafe Thinking* discusses the importance of communicating vision often by "applying two seemingly contradictory forces—disruption and security."[9] Worrying less about the process and more about outcomes requires teams to think differently. It requires them to embrace disruption. Mandate Driven Leaders want teams to stop thinking historically or linearly and access what some call information from the edges. Relying on the same historical data, gathered in the same way, and applying linear thinking often results in shared information bias. Much like consensus management, shared information bias often waters down or places at risk a path to the outcome of the vision.

Steve Jobs once said, "It's really hard to design products by focus groups. A lot of times, people don't know what they want until you show it to them."[10] A common characteristic of Mandate Driven Leaders is to be skeptical of status quo processes. The Apple III was designed through very common and established product and engineering design processes including deep involvement from a marketing group that "dictated a day-by-day definition of what the product had to be."[11] It was Apple's, and Steve Jobs's, most prolific disaster.

Remember New Coke? Most people may not know that Blockbuster had an opportunity to purchase Netflix for $50 million. Blockbuster is now dead. Netflix now has a market capitalization of $147 billion. The list is endless of poor business decisions that were powered by seemingly good decision- making or business processes. Mandate Driven Leaders are skeptical of status quo processes and often throw them out the window when they impede the vision.

To illustrate this point, Steve Jobs was a world-class rule breaker, both in business and in his personal life. He lacked understanding of why anyone would just accept the status quo as either right or best. This was a guy who was so convinced that the rules didn't apply to him that he traded in for a new car every six months to avoid ever getting a license plate because he was somehow morally opposed to them. While this kind of defiance of the status quo is usually frowned upon in normal people, it is often admired in people we consider visionaries. This can help explain why Jobs is often seen as some kind of counterculture guru as much as a technology visionary. This kind of status makes us more willing to accept extreme behavior.

Undoubtedly, creating and embracing disruption results in an atmosphere that can be emotionally demanding of the leadership team. This is where security plays a part. Mandate Driven Leaders must have a leadership team that embraces the same three traits of Mandate Driven Leadership: vision, outcomes, and unrelenting determination. And when these folks are identified, they become part of the inner circle secure in their path forward. This may seem ironic, but Mandate Driven Leaders are much more loyal to their management team than are consensus- styled leaders. When Mandate Driven Leaders identify individuals who share their vision and traits, this team tends to stick together, many times even moving together as a team over multiple corporate opportunities in a career. These "trusted lieutenants" are integral to the Mandate Driven Leader's success and equally rewarded.

Throughout the profiles of Mandate Driven Leaders you will find examples of them driving to the outcome of the vision without much concern about following established processes. The outcome is survival, and Mandate Driven Leaders often break what many believe to be the established rules of business processes to get there. The ride may be bumpy, but if you are on the bus the destination is phenomenal.

Unrelenting Focus and Determination
to Achieve the End State

Stated clearly, Mandate Driven Leaders do not take no for an answer. They do not accept excuses. They hold individuals accountable. And they do not stop driving relentlessly forward until the end state is achieved. It is not unusual for some people to confuse Mandate Driven Leaders and their unrelenting focus and determination with leaders who are narcissistic, poor team builders, and just plain mean-spirited. They may look at examples like Steve Jobs and Jeff Bezos pushing their teams to cutting-edge concepts and never being satisfied with the results and assert that they were tyrannical despots. This view is wrong.

Jobs was obsessed with the outcome because he truly believed that his vision, what he was relentlessly pushing forward, was for the good of the company, its employees, and society overall. In fact, you could characterize Steve Jobs as a Mandate Driven Servant Leader. Yes, he was reportedly a pain to work for at times, but he was that way because he was driving a mandate to change the way we use technology to create better lives.

Business leaders who are tyrants and dictators are not directive leaders for the common good; they are in it for their own selfish gain. Such leaders may claim they are champions of the people, and some even start out that way, but they quickly devolve into enriching themselves. One of the clearest examples of this comes from the Enron scandal. Ken Lay and Jeff Skilling were reportedly very difficult and demanding, but their mandate had nothing to do with helping anyone other than themselves. And as we all know, they ended up being prosecuted for it.

This, of course, is another difference between a Mandate Driven Leader versus dictators and tyrants: dictators and tyrants tend to have very limited life spans. Over time people get sick of their foolishness, and they are removed from their positions of authority. Mandate Driven Leaders, on the other hand, add value to those around them and the world in general. This makes people want to be around them and work with them, regardless of whether they are easy to work with or challenging. There are plenty of not-so-flattering stories of Steve Jobs and Jeff Bezos. Prior to his death, however, Steve Jobs had one of the highest employee satisfaction scores in the Fortune 500.[12] A recent outside study of employee satisfaction for Amazon found "Of the 18 workplace-related dimensions Kununu surveyed, Amazon's employee satisfaction rate exceeds the national average in 12 categories, most notably in gender equality, diversity, career development, compensation and company culture."[13] Of course, being easy to work with is preferred, but Mandate Driven Leaders would say that with the current velocity of business disruption, don't let employee satisfaction get in the way of pushing the vision forward. Eventually, employee satisfaction will catch up as the vision is realized.

The common characteristic of the Mandate Driven Leader's unrelenting focus and determination to achieve the vision is clearly perseverance. Steve Jobs has stated, "I'm convinced that about half of what separates successful entrepreneurs from the non-successful ones is pure perseverance."[14] In an aptly titled *Washington Post* article "The Willingness to Pursue a Long-Term Vision Was Critical to the Rise and Persistence of Amazon.com," Jeff Bezos's belief in perseverance in driving to the long-term vision is profiled. Both Jobs and Bezos as well as other Mandate Driven Leaders recognize that a fault of many ineffective leaders may not be the vision, but the lack of perseverance in driving toward making the vision a reality. My belief is that the best example of lack of perseverance to achieve a vision and perhaps one of the biggest corporate mistakes of all time was Viewtron. Viewtron was perhaps the first online service, as we know them today, offered to the mass market. Developed by Knight Ridder and AT&T from 1983 to 1986, Viewtron offered online news from the various newspapers owned by Knight-Ridder, e-commerce from JCPenney and other merchants, airline schedules from the Official Airline Guide, real estate information from Century 21, online auctions, financial services from American Express, some online banking services from 20 different banks, and standard features such as chat and e-mail.

Knight Ridder had invested $50 million into the venture, and AT&T another $100 million. While the service had not made a profit, it was forecasted to turn a profit by 1988. Despite the many positive reviews by analysts and consumers, Knight Ridder pushed for the service to be discontinued, and Viewtron closed on March 31, 1986. Analysis indicates that the primary impetus to closing the service was not financial—it was the concern that the Viewtron's success would erode Knight Ridder's core newspaper business.

Viewtron closed in early 1986, and the services Viewtron offered were replaced by some of the most venerable innovators of our time: AOL founded in 1985, Amazon 1994, eBay 1995, and Zillow 2004. These companies took services similar to those offered by Viewtron and through their effective leaders' perseverance propelled them to reality, resulting in combined market values exceeding $1 *trillion*. Knight Ridder does not exist anymore. After years of revenue, profit, and subscriber erosion, the company was broken up and sold off in 2006. I myself was a midlevel manager at Knight Ridder from 1994 to 1998. From firsthand experience, I know that the company was perfectly positioned to not only survive but thrive in the digital world except that it lacked a true Mandate Driven Leader with perseverance.

Unrelenting focus, determination, and perseverance of course does not mean no limitations. Reckless perseverance is naturally a course to disaster. Mandate Driven Leaders understand the right kind of perseverance

What Is It That Mandate Driven Leaders Do That Is Different from Others?

What does need to be clearly understood is that the three behavioral themes that all Mandate Driven Leaders clearly exhibit—a well-communicated vision of the future, drive to the outcome instead of the process, and unrelenting focus and determination to achieve the end state—are a summation of a myriad number of individual characteristics and behaviors used each and every day by these effective leaders. Aside from the three main themes, Mandate Driven Leaders can be recognized by how they are both similar to and different from other types of leaders.

For example, many leaders will say they have a clear vision. However, how much of that vision has been diluted by consensus building or groupthink? Mandate Driven Leaders not only have a vision but it has not been diluted and, frankly, they couldn't care less who agrees or does not agree with it. Many leaders including Mandate Driven Leaders will take risks. The difference is that you will never hear a Mandate Driven Leader say, "that can't be done" or "the technology is not there yet." Mandate Driven Leaders do not accept these types of obstacles, and these phrases will often invoke "nutters." Mandate Driven Leaders also exhibit other very specific characteristics, including the ones shown in Figure 5.1.

Some individuals, even academics, will say that it is hard to define effective leadership, but you will know it when you see it. A Mandate Driven Leader would disagree. Effective leaders are ones who ensure their organization is first surviving, then thriving. These leaders can be seen embracing the key behavioral attributes of a well-communicated vision of the future, a drive to the outcome instead of the process, and unrelenting focus and

LIKE OTHER LEADERS	DIFFERENT FROM OTHER LEADERS
Have a clear vision of the outcomes they want/need	Suprised when others don't see the value in the vision
	Don't really care if they do or not
	Ruthless about getting there
Willing to take risks	Won't accept failure in themselves or others
Try to inspire those around them	Not afraid to scare the crap out of those who won't get on board
Prefer happy and engaged team members	
Delegate the process	Micromanage the results
Have some unique technical expertise	Not afraid to disrupt the status quo
Seek approval	Assume they are in charge
	Customer/stakeholder first, employees second
Not selfish	Won't allow others to be selfish

FIGURE 5.1 Similarities and Differences Between Mandate Driven Leaders and Other Leaders

determination. These behavioral attributes are then augmented by a myriad of characteristics exhibited daily that can be mapped back to these themes. Yes, the correct leadership style to be effective is *sometimes* situational. However, a Mandate Driven Leadership style is what is demanded today and what is usually always demanded at the very highest level of an organization.

CHAPTER 6

MIKE LAWRIE OF DXC: TRANSFORMING THE GIANT

Not every person or CEO or senior leadership member is able to practice different leadership styles. Most CEOs—in fact, most people in general—have a dominant leadership style. Over time, the good ones learn how to exercise different leadership styles depending on the situation.

—MIKE LAWRIE, Chairman, President,
and CEO, DXC Technology

Here are some facts about Mike Lawrie. He was one of IBM's most successful senior executives during the 1990s and early 2000s. In the early 2000s, he was one of the first executives to recognize *digital transformation*, and in fact, he may have started the discussion. By 2004, he was the CEO of Siebel Systems and was accurate in his forewarning that Salesforce .com would become an early disrupter of both customer relationship management technology and the software industry in general. Today, Mike Lawrie has built one of the most successful IT services companies, DXC Technology, with a market capitalization of $17.6 billion as of April 2019 from the remnants of two legacy firms that were both on the verge of extinction. However, unlike many of the leaders profiled in this book, the reader may not readily recognize his name.

Mike Lawrie spends large chunks of his time with clients, analysts, partners, and employees; however, spending time with the press is not his priority nor his style. He is a roll-up-the sleeves, let's-get-it-done leader who prefers that his company, not he, be placed in the spotlight. For the stockholders and investors of the firms he has led, that is just fine. While CEO at Misys and subsequently CSC, which became DXC Technology from the merger with the Enterprise Services division of Hewlett Packard Enterprise, he has delivered shareholder returns well in excess of 100 percent in short periods of time, firmly establishing himself as the turnaround expert within the IT services industry and the digital economy.

Along the way to the top of the IT services field, Lawrie earned a degree in history from Ohio State University and an MBA from Drexel. He is partial to his 1967 Mustang convertible and enjoys golf, hiking, and powerboating. He is a father to a son and daughter and, along with his wife, Kim, runs a "consensus" household. A place where Mandate Driven Leadership simply has no place. Outside of his family and work, Mike is a rabid Philadelphia Eagles fan. In fact, there are a lot of similarities between his beloved Eagles and his business successes.

The Philadelphia Eagles went from a 7–9 season in 2016 to winning Super Bowl LII in 2017 against the New England Patriots. Lawrie was at that game and not surprisingly ecstatic with the result. In his interview for this book, Lawrie said there are similarities in the use of leadership styles when turning around a professional football team and a Fortune 500 company. "It's very important to match what the company needs with the leadership style," Lawrie asserted. "A great analogy is a football team. Now, if you've got a team that is absolutely in need of completely rebooting, you do not want some consensus leader in there that is into 'Kumbaya.' That's not what you need. You need someone that can provide some tough love. Then, once you have some successes along the way, you begin to introduce other dimensions of that leadership style. It's about the leadership style needing to be right for the situation." He noted that Coach Doug Pederson had to make some tough decisions, and they paid off for the Philadelphia Eagles. "He made the decision that I am going to call the offensive plays. Yes, I have an offensive coordinator, but no, I'm going to call the plays. Now, he listens to his players, he listens to his coaches, he spends the time reviewing the tape, but he makes those decisions, and he took on the responsibility and the accountability for those decisions."[1] The same can be said for Mike Lawrie and the companies that he has turned around.

Lawrie cannot stress enough the importance of using the right leadership style for the right situation. He readily acknowledges that a directive leadership style, a Mandate Driven Leadership style, is often what is needed during times of major disruption or when turning around a company. He emphasizes that the corporate vision and objectives must be clear, concise, and mandated from the company's leadership. Vacillation or excuses in implementing and achieving that vision cannot be tolerated. Lawrie makes clear that directive leadership should not be confused with tyrannical, egocentric, or uninformed leadership. While cutting his teeth at IBM, Lawrie had some great mentors who taught him early both the value and absolute necessity of information and data gathering prior to directives and the importance of team building once a vision and objectives are mandated.

Lawrie Helps Usher in the Digital Transformation Era

During his 27 years at IBM, which began in 1977, Lawrie's ride up the chain of command was steady, eventually becoming the senior vice president and group executive with responsibility for sales and distribution of IBM's products and services worldwide. In addition, he was general manager for IBM's $25 billion EMEA (Europe, Middle East, and Africa) business with a staff of more than 90,000 employees and operations in 124 countries.

At the time, the international segment for IBM was not doing very well, and here Lawrie first showed his knack for quick turnarounds. "We were able to bring in a new team, innovate, and get much closer to our customers and market, turning the business around," Lawrie said.

Part of the strategy was taking everything IBM understood well in hardware and software development and manufacturing and adding *business value*. In other words, instead of only helping a company install a physical technology infrastructure, IBM began helping companies look at their overall business processes. Then, he and his team would reengineer the processes by selecting the best technology applications to help automate or digitize them.

In many ways, Lawrie—atop the shoulders of IBM's iconic brand—enabled and ushered in the dawn of the "digital transformation" era, which involves the utilization of digital technology to reengineer a company's business processes as well as to fundamentally change and improve its key business and marketing strategies. While the topic of digital transformation is the norm today, 16 years ago Mike Lawrie was at the forefront of the discussion.

In an August 2002 interview on NDTV, Mike related that "we think we've really seen the beginnings of a new cycle in the information technology industry where companies are beginning to *digitize* not only the transactions in their enterprise but *digitize the processes* that link many vital business activities together." He goes on to state that "the ability to integrate an enterprise, the ability to share information seamlessly allows a company not only to be more efficient and productive internally but also allows that company to link with its customers, its business partners, its suppliers, and its shareholders in a much more efficient and productive way."[2]

During this interview, Lawrie used terms that were new in 2002 such as "e-business on-demand" and an "e-utility model." Lawrie further stated that "we are increasingly moving towards what we call business value, where we help companies look at their business processes, in many instances reengineer those business processes, then select some of the best applications to help automate or *digitize* those business processes."

Looking back, Lawrie's revelation was spot-on. Today, everyone is discussing digital transformation in the same context that Lawrie first did in 2002. While the term *digital* is now the new normal, discussion on the leadership style that is necessary to achieve digital transformation is not as prevalent.

During his three decades at IBM, Lawrie worked with Lou Gerstner, who was the chairman of the board and CEO of IBM from 1993 to 2002. During Gerstner's time at IBM, he transformed IBM from a slow fading company back to its iconic status as an IT pacesetter. Lawrie watched him closely and worked alongside him, and he says Gerstner was key in developing many of his current leadership and management principles.

"I learned the power of communication, the power of keeping things simple, and the power of the normal tension between patience and wanting to get things done," Lawrie stated to the *Washington Post*. "I also learned about the significance of a disciplined management system and the need for an overriding focus on clients, markets, competitors, and tangible business results."[3]

About the time that Gerstner retired, Lawrie was ready for a change. After 27 years at Big Blue, Lawrie realized that he could either get comfortable at IBM or try to stretch himself. Ultimately, he decided to seek out new challenges. "I wanted to take everything I learned and apply it to a real-life situation where I had the ultimate responsibility for the results."

A Learning Experience at Siebel Systems

Having already developed a reputation as one of the best executives in the IT industry, in 2004 Lawrie moved from IBM to become CEO at Siebel Systems. The business software company specializing in CRM was once one of the fastest-growing IT companies. However, Siebel Systems fell on difficult times as the economy faltered and companies curtailed technology spending. Having recently suffered heavy financial losses, Siebel's shareholders revolted against its founder Tom Siebel and demanded new leadership. Siebel, though, maintained his spot as chairman.

"We engaged in the usual deliberative processes," Siebel said in a teleconference call at the time to introduce Lawrie. "We retained one of the top executive search firms to recommend to me and the board of directors the candidates we might approach. We are very, very pleased that our first choice (Mike Lawrie) ultimately accepted and assumes the role. This is a big day for the company."[4]

Tom Siebel was famous in Silicon Valley for his fiery temper and huge ego, and according to multiple sources, this got in the way of Lawrie's progress. Lawrie and his team had identified a major shift in the market toward software as a service (SaaS), but the founder was not willing to move forward into a new paradigm. "He thought our future competition was SAP, and I thought the future competition was Salesforce.com," Lawrie told *The Telegraph*. "And I wanted to move the majority of our development dollars into competing with Salesforce.com, and Tom did not think that was the right strategy."[5] Lawrie believed that Salesforce.com, while small at the time, was correct in its belief and strategy that a new model of software delivery, SaaS, would be one cornerstone in the fundamental disruption of the software industry.

As CEO, Lawrie advocated to the board a fundamental shift from the traditional software paradigm of client-server software license and maintenance fee to this new cloud-based SaaS model. Ultimately, though, Tom Siebel convinced the board to ignore Lawrie's recommended strategy and continue with the traditional product line. With his hands tied, Lawrie's first year at Siebel Systems was difficult. The company failed to meet Wall Street expectations because of continued industry disinterest in the company's traditional product offerings. From there, things went downhill fast. "Founders are really difficult people to get along with," Lawrie said. "They are just not used to being told they are wrong."

Here we see two leaders, Siebel and Lawrie, with differing visions. A Mandate Driven Leader recognizes that everyone must have the same vision from the board to the floor, so to speak. Everyone must be on the bus. The board and Lawrie mutually agreed to a resignation. "The founder and I didn't see eye to eye, and so I left from that situation, but I was proud of the fact that we identified the market shift," Lawrie said.[6]

When Lawrie left, Siebel and Salesforce.com were running neck and neck, as both companies had 200,000 seats of software and services installed. From that point forward, there was no race. Tom Siebel took over from Lawrie as CEO and continued to eschew SaaS and embrace its traditional model. In September 2005, amid continued stagnation, Siebel was acquired by Oracle for $5.8 billion. Under Oracle, the Siebel platform continued to lose clients and market share and is now generally not considered a major player in the CRM space. Salesforce.com, embracing SaaS, continued to experience phenomenal growth and quickly became and continued to be the market share leader in CRM. As of fiscal year 2018, Salesforce.com had $10.5 billion in revenue, and as of April 2019 the company had a market capitalization of more than $124 billion and is still growing.

I'm sure many Siebel employees and shareholders of that era actively wonder what the future would have held if Tom Siebel and the board would have allowed Mike Lawrie to implement his strategy. According to Lawrie, "I learned a lot of lessons. That was my first time as a chief executive of a public company, so I didn't do everything right, but it was a very meaningful and positive experience."[7]

Surely, this experience helped define for Lawrie when the use of a directive, Mandate Driven Leadership style was critical.

Lawrie Establishes His Turnaround Credentials

Lawrie moved on to ValueAct Capital Partners, a San Francisco–based investment company, and for the first time in a while, he was not in an executive role. Now, Lawrie was the investor sitting across the table advising the CEO how to improve the value of the company.

"It was an enormously powerful lesson for me," Lawrie said. "Whatever business moves you're going to make, both short term and long term, you must understand how that plays out in terms of the valuation and value you create for your shareholders. Sometimes you need to get smaller to get more profitable. I learned how to stick with my convictions as I began to turn a company around. It's very easy to get sidelined into activities that don't significantly bring value."[8]

While in the United Kingdom working as a partner for ValueAct and organizing major investments, he identified Misys—a British software company with a focus on retail and banking—as a great investment. As a result, ValueAct purchased 25 percent of Misys and then pushed for Lawrie to be appointed as the CEO in October 2006 after cofounder Kevin Lomax was ousted after a failed management buyout.

During his time at Misys, the company expanded from its roots, developing banking software for Bahrain's banking conglomerate Al Baraka, as well as other work in Dubai and Oman. Recognizing the growth in Asia banking, Lawrie began work in China creating an advanced platform for 30,000 Chinese banks that had previously used an outdated system of spreadsheets to organize their finances.

Under Lawrie's leadership, Misys merged with Allscripts, maintaining a majority stake and creating the largest provider of information technology to US physicians, helping one-third of all American physicians digitize their prescriptions and medical records and organize payments from health insurance companies. The results are clear. While revenue began to grow modestly, up 5 percent during his time at Misys, profits grew an astounding 90 percent. This was accomplished by doing the things that Lawrie does the best today: establishing vision and strategy and mandating that vision and strategy to implementation while bringing costs and assets in line. Poor-performing or nonstrategic business units of the company were sold. Costs were meticulously controlled; videoconferencing replaced non-customer-related travel, four separate office locations were moved to a single building, and unnecessary vacant positions were not filled.

In six years at Misys, Lawrie is credited with a successful turnaround of the company. Lawrie's leadership drove significant growth in shareholder value by positioning Misys as a leader in the financial services and healthcare application software industry. Implementing a process of continual innovation, Lawrie advocated the development of the world's first fully open source health information exchange solution. Success was not only seen in shareholder value, but these changes also resulted in an impressive gain in client satisfaction.

Feeling that he had accomplished what he had set out to do at Misys, in 2012 Lawrie was ready for a new challenge and set off to lead a troubled CSC.

Taking the Helm of a Sinking Ship

When Mike Lawrie took over the top spot at Computer Sciences Corp. (CSC) in March 2012, many were stunned. The company was in a dire situation—one that many thought was irreversible. The IT services company stock was in a state of perpetual freefall from $49.91 a share at the beginning of 2011 to $23.40 by the first of 2012. Moreover, after decades of success through innovation since its beginnings in 1959, CSC was heading toward a huge net loss of more than $4 billion in 2012. In fact, CSC's anticipated net loss in 2012 would exceed the total revenue of the average Fortune 1000 company.

CSC clearly needed a new direction to turn things around, and in stepped Lawrie, the bold 27-year veteran of IBM, advocate of digital transformation, and successful corporate turnaround CEO at Misys. The board at CSC liked the sound of a "turnaround" and Lawrie's reputation for market foresight and vision. The board issued a challenge to their new CEO when he arrived at CSC's Falls Church, Virginia, headquarters: increase the company's stock price by 80 percent in five years. Most executives would shudder at the directive, but with a laser-like focus on both customers and investors, Lawrie went to work, displaying intolerance to inefficiency and mediocrity while showing an erudite ability to predict and adapt to market conditions and changing technology.

The challenges that Lawrie inherited were immense. Clients were not happy. In 2011, CSC was in turmoil, facing $2 billion in losses and write-downs because of a distressed contract with Britain's National Health Service. So troubled was the agreement with NHS that the Security and Exchange Commission was threatening CSC with penalties because of accounting lapses and the company's failure to disclose the issues with the NHS deal. There was also a troubled deal with America's IRS to modernize its computer systems, which resulted in the agency mistakenly sending out $300 million in refunds for fraudulent tax returns. Furthermore, CSC held a contract with the US Air Force to overhaul its logistics management system, but the billion-dollar project was fraught with irreconcilable problems between CSC and the air force.

From a sales and operational perspective, CSC's technology and cost structure were not competitive. "We were close to slipping under the waves," Lawrie told the *Washington Post*. "When I took my first look at the company before taking the job, honestly, I couldn't figure it out."[9] As Lawrie dug into the facts, he found a highly decentralized company in both CSC's corporate structure and management systems. The business units were free to adopt their own practices, so they did their own procurement, structured their own contracts, chose their own technology, and even developed their own incentive programs. Nothing unified the business units, and there was no overall vision.

"Every business could do what it wanted to do," Lawrie said. "So, taken separately it looked successful, but as a whole, we were going bankrupt. Individual motivations and decisions that weren't linked to overall strategy were driving the company into the ground."[10]

Lawrie began the turnaround. One thing that Lawrie freely discusses and emphasizes is that it is not all about Lawrie. Successful leaders must surround themselves with other successful leaders who share the same vision and passion for what needs to be accomplished. One of Lawrie's early hires at CSC was Jim Smith, who became CSC's executive vice president of customer advocacy and joint ventures. Smith recalls telling Lawrie before he was hired, "CSC is a freaking disaster. The last place I want to go to work is CSC. Everything is broken."[11] Lawrie agreed and told Smith that was exactly why he needed him because he saw things for what they were.

"He described a vision for how we could create a new world for IT services which was really going to be about speed and change," Smith said of Lawrie. "He said with the right people and the right leadership we can create the future. He was relentless. Relentless about the vision and about what it would take to create something with meaning." For Smith, the debate in his mind quickly switched from "there is no way I want to work at CSC" to "how could I pass on an opportunity to work with Lawrie to help transform CSC into something special?"

To cost-effectively support CSC's customer's transformation programs, first Lawrie had to drive out the inefficiencies endemic at CSC. CSC had to bring expenses back in line with revenue while simultaneously ensuring the expense reductions were supportive of CSC's vision and strategy. Naturally, some decisions were easier than others. Lawrie and his team consolidated computer centers and moved them to lower-overhead locations or closed them completely. Lawrie also immediately addressed the CSC workforce including overall expense, organizational design, management layers, and performance plans. The overall CSC workforce was thinned by 20 percent. Lawrie cut the number of vice presidents by 80 percent, from 350 to 75. However, this was not entirely about expense control. The workforce transformation was about both expense control and building a management team, structure, and systems that supported the strategy. Lawrie firmly advocates that building the right team in the right management structure using the right management systems can occur in parallel with expense reduction.

To achieve a true transformational change of magnitude, you have to have the right culture and the right team in place alongside you, while still making the hard expense cuts that are necessary to survive. "You've got to have people who are fully in, who believe both intellectually and emotionally in your strategy," he states. "Frankly, when I started, the CSC team didn't have emotional or intellectual buy-in. So we made some changes to bring people in who were onboard with the direction."[12]

Lawrie, Smith, and the core leadership eliminated 6 layers of management, going from 14 layers to 8. While many people to this day assume that the reduction of management layers is to save cost, Lawrie reduces layers because it forces a more productive, focused management. It forces people to work on what is important. Smith states succinctly, "The more infrastructure and management layers involved the more people produce work for the sake of work." Work that is not critical or central to the strategy of the company. A flat management structure is a core principle to the management systems that Lawrie institutes to this day. Lawrie admits that the company "lost some people that we would not have liked to lose," but addressing the prevailing culture was imperative to growth and investor confidence.

In parallel to these work streams, Lawrie knew that he had to realign CSC's assets and portfolio to be in line to support the vision and strategy. "Looking at the bigger picture, we needed to have the right assets to execute our strategy correctly," said Lawrie. "That's not exactly a surprise, right? You need to have the proper businesses in your portfolio. So, we had to unload assets that weren't relevant to where we wanted to go." CSC began divesting businesses that did not fit into CSC's strategy or operating model. These divestitures included its Australian IT staffing unit, its credit services business, and an Italian IT services company.

One particularly hard decision for Lawrie in the turnaround at CSC—maybe the hardest of all—was to divest the government business. Since its establishment in 1959, government work had been central to CSC's mission. "What was unique about that decision compared to other hard decisions is that it's irrevocable," said Smith. "Most of the decisions we had to make were reversible if they didn't work out. And we didn't take years to decide; we decided in 30 days."

In the end, CSC divested seven businesses that were noncore units, whether they were profitable or not. But it was not just about divesting nonstrategic or underperforming assets. CSC also acquired eight companies that were necessary to help CSC achieve its long-term goals and to shore up gaps in cybersecurity and cloud computing.

When you discuss directive or Mandate Driven Leadership, perhaps no example better exemplifies Lawrie's leadership team during the CSC turnaround than their directive to divest clients. Yes, by mandate of the leadership team, CSC had to divest itself of unprofitable clients. Some contracts were restructured and renegotiated. Other client contracts were simply allowed to expire without any effort to renew. Some client contracts were proactively canceled by CSC. These are tough, directive decisions. However, it has to be emphasized that Lawrie would never advocate they be done in a vacuum. These decisions are made after thorough analysis of the data and facts and deep and transparent discussion with all internal and client stakeholders. But once the decisions are made, those decisions are mandated forward taking out all emotions or non-fact-based second-guessing. Simply speaking, Lawrie would state that decisions to divest clients were imperative to CSC's turnaround but also key to the client's success.

What was once a sprawling and uncontrollable collection of independent pieces became a considerably smaller and cohesive brand in just three years under Lawrie's leadership. Investor confidence followed. After instituting massive changes in 2012, Lawrie's changes truly took hold in 2013, and the results became evident. Stock prices climbed, and CSC saw a jump in net profit to nearly $1 billion—a net change of $5 billion in less than two years!

What many prognosticators had considered impossible when Lawrie took the helm of CSC was completed three years ahead of the stated goal. Lawrie had achieved the board's objective of an 80 percent stock price increase with an actual share price increase from $30.86 to $60.29, more than a 90 percent increase.[13]

Lawrie was rewarded handsomely for his hard and smart work, and I'm sure many close friends and families would be recommending that he rest on his laurels. However, life without challenge is not for Mike Lawrie. In fact, the industry rumor mill in early 2014 was that Lawrie was a leading contender to replace Steve Ballmer as CEO of Microsoft. Reuters reported at the time that "at least three of the top 20 investors" in the company "want a turnaround expert to succeed Steve Ballmer as chief executive." These investors recommended Mike Lawrie or Ford Motor Company CEO Alan Mulally.

While Satya Nadella was eventually named to replace Ballmer, Lawrie would not stand still. He was looking at something even bigger than CSC.

CSC Acquires a Much Larger Sinking Ship

In a 2016 announcement that caught many in the IT services industry by surprise, it was announced that Hewlett Packard Enterprise (HPE) would spin off its $18 billion in revenue Enterprise Services (HPES) business unit. In a complex financial spin-merge transaction, HPES would merge with CSC creating a new, independent NYSE traded digital IT services firm called DXC Technology. It was widely acknowledged at the time that HPES was struggling. At the time of the announcement in May 2016, revenue was in a free fall, and the fate of the business was up in the air, while CSC with $8 billion in revenue had just emerged from a successful turnaround with a tremendous increase in shareholder value. So, why would Lawrie acquire a failing company twice the size of CSC?

With this spin-merge, Lawrie was setting himself and his leadership team up for a challenge greater than the CSC turnaround. And, he was willing to place the now successful and profitable CSC at risk. To understand the rationale and risk, the initial leadership structure of this new entity must be understood. The spin-merge was positioned upon announcement as a merger of equals though HPES was twice the size of CSC. Financially, upon completion, the spin-merge would result in HPE stockholders owning 50.1 percent and CSC stockholders owning 49.9 percent of the new entity. The board of directors would be composed of five appointed by HPE including HPE CEO Meg Whitman and five appointed by CSC including Mike Lawrie, who had been named from the day of the initial announcement as the chairman of the board, CEO, and president of the new entity, DXC.

What was evident from the time of the spin-merge announcement and throughout the premerger activities was that this was Mike Lawrie's vision and strategy. As both chairman and CEO, Mike Lawrie was in charge. In other words, it was his to implement and succeed, or his to fail.

The decision to spin off CSC's government business paled in comparison to Lawrie's decision to mastermind to completion the formation of DXC. Lawrie and the CSC leadership had a vision and strategy rooted in digital transformation services that required scale to implement. They were looking to address the business disruption occurring in almost every industry by transforming the very core of what IT services firms provided their clients. But first, they had to convince the CSC board and investors.

Lawrie reiterates that the decision to purchase HPES was not easily made. "Making the decision to buy [HPES] was not a simple decision to make because of the risks associated with large-scale integrations and mergers. They often destroy value; they don't create value. This one has happened to create a lot of value, but most do not create value."[14] This decision was not simply about using scale to achieve financial efficiencies. The decision was about a vision to create a new IT services company where digital disruption would be embraced.

Once the spin-merge was announced, the name of this new entity had to be determined. Undoubtedly, emotions for keeping the Hewlett Packard or the CSC name were high. With data and facts reviewed, however, Lawrie ultimately mandated a rebranding effort. At the end of the day, Lawrie's vision and strategy were not to grow something existing bigger. He and his leadership team were creating something new in the IT services arena.

"We did this rebranding for several different reasons," Lawrie told Jason Hancock for his book *The Change Agent: How Mike Lawrie Transforms Cultures and Companies*. "One, both HP and CSC brands felt sort of tired, and this brings new energy. But more importantly, we're signaling that this is about the future. This is about being a leader in the industry. This is entirely new. And this is one of the biggest cultural shifts that we have to make in the company, to think as a leader in this industry. That's a subtle but important shift, and our model supports that way of thinking and leading as we go forward."[15]

The spin-merge was completed on April 1, 2017, and DXC emerged. The task of combining these two organizations into one while simultaneously transforming the company was daunting. This was the second largest merger in the technology services industry ever, second only to the $67 billion Dell-EMC deal. Transformations or turnarounds like these in the era of digital disruption would necessitate a directive, Mandate Driven Leadership approach from the executive suite.

Five Leadership Principles Leading to a Successful Transformation

Lawrie has very specific leadership principles that serve as the foundation for a successful transformation initiative (Figure 6.1). To be successful, the entire leadership team must acknowledge and be in synch with these principles. And once these principles are understood by the leadership team, a directive leadership style ensures that the principles are embedded into the

1. The right vision and strategy communicated,

2. Assets must be aligned through divestiture, acquisition or build,

3. Financial model understood and attractive to investors,

4. Right leadership in place, and

5. Leadership culture based on metrics and incentives that embraces accountability.

FIGURE 6.1 Lawrie's Five Principles for a Successful Transformation

overall fabric of the company. Thus, a successful transformation is rooted in both these principles and the leadership styles that ensure their adoption.

VISION AND STRATEGY

First, a successful transformation requires a very clear vision and strategy, without any ambiguity. What Lawrie makes clear is that the vision and strategy mandated is never devised in a vacuum. Lawrie relies on a network of people and institutions to help him understand an issue and formulate a solution. He has a reputation of being a master at recognizing and synthesizing patterns within the feedback he receives.

"I listen very carefully to a very broad network of people, whether it be bankers or customers or business partners, or McKinsey & Company, or Boston Consulting, or people within the company, or peer managers," he states. "From there, I glean patterns. Then, I take those patterns, and I try to synthesize them into very simple concepts that can be absorbed and actioned. I've always done that throughout my career. Always."[16]

Moreover, according to Gary Stockman, DXC's senior vice president, chief marketing and communication officer, Lawrie is very realistic about what it takes for the company to be competitive in the spaces in which it needs to play. Therefore, once Lawrie achieves clarity regarding vision and strategy, mandates become a necessity.

"One of the difficult things to do is to convince people who have been used to doing things a certain way, and are very comfortable with that, that the world has changed around them," Stockman said, "And that what made them successful before will not make them successful now. In fact, part of it is just convincing them that they're not actually succeeding, because it can be difficult to get people to see reality."[17]

To DXC, the strategy and vision were about creating a new IT services firm rooted in digital transformation. An IT services firm that helped clients thrive on change. A firm that assists clients with harnessing digital technology as an enabler to innovation. The firm envisioned by Lawrie and the leadership team was more than an IT services firm, it was a firm where technology is used as a core enabler to optimizing business processes and drive strategy and business value.

A firm where digital disruption was to be embraced, not feared.

ASSET ALIGNMENT

Lawrie's second principle to a successful transformation is to have the assets in place to support the vision and strategy. DXC acquired the assets by taking on partnerships and joint ventures, buying companies, and shedding assets not linked to the vision and strategy. For example, in June 2018, DXC divested its US public sector business through a spin-merge with Vencore Holding Corp. and KeyPoint Government Solutions to form Perspecta, a publicly traded IT services provider to the federal government. According to Lawrie, "Separating our global commercial and USPS business, and combining it with Vencore and KeyPoint, will accelerate transformation with two strategically focused companies, each uniquely positioned to lead its market by prioritizing the needs of its clients."[18]

As with the decision of Lawrie to shed the US public sector business at CSC, spinning off the US public sector business from DXC was a difficult decision. This was a business with substantial revenue and good margins. However, it took the focus away from DXC's core vision and strategy to focus on commercial companies and their digital transformation, and Lawrie was going to stay true to his transformation principles.

FINANCIAL MODEL

Third, it is critical for a company's leadership to build the right financial model that can be communicated and shared with investors, so that everyone shares in the vision and strategy. Both at CSC and DXC, Lawrie gave stockholders and investors clear multiyear guidance on the turnaround road map and the key performance indicators.

Lawrie and the leadership team devised and implemented a communication plan for investors and shareholders that was clear as to both objectives and time frame. The three-year plan from the completion of the spin-merge in April 2017 consisted of key objectives that investors, shareholders, and employees both understood and could track.

"It's not just getting employees and customers to invest in the vision and strategy," Lawrie states. "It's also about getting your investors to invest. DXC was able to do that, and it more than doubled the value of DXC from a market capitalization standpoint in a year."[19]

RIGHT LEADERSHIP

Fourth, the right management leadership, from top to bottom, must be in place because it takes the right team and blends of people to execute the vision and strategy. Lawrie fully recognizes that people decisions are among the toughest. Bright, capable managers may simply be in the wrong job for the current situation. New thinking may be needed. The imperative is to make those decisions quickly. "Those are tough, tough decisions. Leadership changes that needed to be made. We just made a whole series of those in the last two or three months. We've reshaped the entire senior leadership team of the company in the last three months." This is also an area where direct leadership is of absolute necessity. In fact, leaders that rely too heavily on delegation should be questioned. "So, what I find is that when you are really an active, engaged leader, and you're not delegating, by the way, a mandated leadership is not about delegating to someone else, it's about understanding what needs to be done, and having the courage of that knowledge and those convictions to make the decision, make the changes as necessary, and drive execution and implementation."[20]

With big transformations or turnarounds like DXC, companies may have many good leaders but not necessarily the right leaders for the situation. "People were very accustomed to explaining why there were problems, and explaining why there were shortcomings," Lawrie said. "But they never really took on the responsibility and accountability to actually drive a different outcome. A directive mandated leadership team takes on the accountability and takes on the responsibility to drive to a different outcome than would be achieved by just ordinary standard operating procedures."[21]

Having the right leadership also means having the right leadership structure. For Lawrie, that is a structure that is not hierarchical. In fact, he hates hierarchies. Therefore, just because somebody reports to him does not mean that person always has the best ideas or even has a clue as to what is going on as problems are narrowed down. "If you really just summarize Mike's approach to a flat structure, it is that he believes management is a verb, not a noun," Jim Smith relates. "You have to be active; you have to be engaged, you have to be doing things. In order to do that, you have to be close to the business—and to be close to the business, you can't have layers and layers separating people from the business. To execute management as a verb, you need a flat management structure. To require leaders to contribute and not simply review, that requires a flat management structure."[22]

CULTURE OF ACCOUNTABILITY

Finally, leadership needs to have the right culture that is built on incentive and accountability. It's about metrics and measurement systems and how the company holds individuals accountable. Along with a revamped management structure, Lawrie at both CSC and DXC implements guidelines for performance reviews based on a strict bell curve that management uses to issue raises, bonuses, and promotions. Furthermore, only employees who supported markets deemed critical for corporate growth and who ranked in the top 15 percent of the curve—meaning they exceeded expectations— would be considered for merit raises.

Donna Lesch, CSC's former executive vice president and chief human resources officer, has stated that the company's success depended on CSC's ability to build a high-performance, results-driven workforce. "We have a framework in place that holds each employee accountable for delivering results, provides guidance for managers to differentiate individual performance, and appropriately compensates our strongest performers for their strong leadership and outstanding contribution to CSC's growth."[23]

While often useful for encouraging managers to set goals for themselves and their teams and drive higher performance, bell curve assessments have also been shown to reduce morale and drive out employees if implemented poorly. In Lawrie's case, at CSC the new standards used a quota system that required managers to grade 40 percent of the workforce as not meeting expectations or only partially meeting them. "I expect a wave of resignations," a former CSC manager told the *Washington Business Journal* at the time, under anonymity. "Some of my people that are unbelievably dedicated to their work are no longer dedicated to CSC. The morale is so low."[24] Lawrie and other Mandate Driven Leaders would probably have a differing view.

Simply stated in the case of CSC, a company that lost $4 billion dollars in 2012 probably needed a housecleaning, and a Mandate Driven Leader would recognize this. Ensuring accountability does require hard decisions related to personnel. For Lawrie, these hard decisions are required to protect the well-being of the overall employee base.

The results of Lawrie's transformation principles applied to DXC Technology are clear and impressive. By merging CSC and the Enterprise Services business of Hewlett Packard Enterprise, Lawrie and his management team created the world's largest end-to-end IT services company with $21 billion in annual revenue and 6,000 clients in more than 70 countries. Immediately prior to the merger announcement on May 24, 2016, CSC's stock price was $35.65. At the end of its second fiscal year in March 2019, DXC's stock price was $64.31. In addition, DXC spun off its US public sector business into a new, publicly traded company, Perspecta, on June 1, 2018. DXC shareholders received one share of Perspecta for every two shares of DXC owned. Including that value, shareholders have earned an impressive 113 percent return in less than three years.

While the returns are impressive, the analyst view of DXC perhaps better solidifies Lawrie's turnaround credentials. Industry analysts such as Gartner and IDC rank DXC Technology as number one or two in the industry in almost all of the company's core offerings.

Creating the leading IT services company speaks for itself, but some say that if Lawrie were not a recognized turnaround expert and successful Fortune 500 CEO, he would probably simply be a teacher. DXC's CMO Gary Stockman when interviewed said, "My view is if he wasn't doing this, he should be teaching at Harvard Business School, or Wharton, or someplace similar. Because, for our clients and senior leaders, he is a great source of knowledge and insight."[25] Yes, Lawrie is a hard-driving, intense business person. Losing is not in his vocabulary, and if you want to work for him, then there is no option but to succeed. That being established, those interviewed all view Lawrie as an invaluable teacher and mentor.

Lawrie's Views on Leadership and Management Systems

While Lawrie believes mandates drive change and accountability, he also believes this is not incompatible with an inclusive leadership style. Directive leadership is not about making decisions in a vacuum. Input is critical in the beginning before final decisions are made and actions put into place. "I always get people involved in the early part of the decision-making process," Lawrie said. "I want people to participate. It's a very, open, transparent, inclusive leadership style."[26]

Leadership is as much about the process and the steps a leader takes and the results necessary in each step. "It's not just one thing that you do," he continued. "It's a series of steps, as a leader, that you take your team through." Inclusion and being open and transparent in the beginning requires certain styles and steps, as does the actual decision-making or execution process. The first step is to get people to understand there's a problem, or understand what the issues are, and make sure those issues are articulated and understood. "Frankly, you want a lot of people involved in that process," he said. "But then, over time, that needs to be narrowed down. This is what an effective leader does. They need to be narrowed down to issues that are actionable because leaders tend to like to talk a lot, but they don't tend to root it back in facts and data that support a certain set of outcomes and decisions.

"I tend to spend a lot of time out in the field, out in the regions talking with reps," he says. "Talking with people in our delivery organization or our build organization. I listen very carefully to their insights. Again, this is another major source of input into recognizing and discerning patterns. Because it's only with that knowledge, and with that conviction, that you can take on a more mandated leadership style. One of the requirements of a mandated leadership style is that you actually have to know what you're talking about, because if you don't know what you're talking about, anyone can talk you out of it."

Once the data is understood, all of the facts have been laid out, and everyone has had a chance to voice their opinions, Lawrie then makes a decision. "I think you draw a distinction between a consensual leadership style and a more mandated leadership style in the actual decision-making process itself. In a consensual process, it's usually much longer, it really requires a lot of deliberation, buy-in, cajoling, trade-offs, compromise. I use the word compromise because that often leads to regressing to the lowest common denominator, which often provides a mediocre response to what is a critical environmental situation." At the start of the process, you want the data gathering. You need the facts. But in the end, the decision must be the leader's rooted in the vision and not watered-down by consensus. "That's where the leader has to have the courage of their own convictions to make those tough calls and then drive action and execution," he states "That's what I think you're getting at with a more mandated leadership style, as opposed to a consensual leadership style."[27]

Stockman has said that a company can have a strong leader with a clear vision, but it will not impact the end result unless the leader can also bring other people onboard, and Lawrie has a system for doing that. "He's got a regular cadence," Stockman continued. "His direction is that you're expected to speak and to offer opinions, and they'd better be fact-based. Then a decision is made and we move forward. This notion of mandate driven leadership is not only whether you can express the mandate, but whether you can carry it out. What is your system for doing that? Ultimately, the system for executing the mandate is an equally important factor."[28]

Vacillation only occurs with Lawrie if there is a new set of facts. If there's a new set of facts, then he places them on the table. "There's nothing wrong with admitting you've made the incorrect decision and going back and changing that decision if there is a new set of facts," Lawrie said. "But, I do not believe in making or changing decisions based on personalities or opinions."[29]

The ability to make tough decisions is what stands out most about Mike Lawrie. Through his years, Lawrie has never been afraid to make the difficult decisions that must occur to turn around a company toward a path of success. In fact, he has made a whole host of really tough choices over a long period of time. With CSC, Lawrie sold the most profitable business to raise the cash to be able to refinance the company's debt and top off pension plans. Both at CSC and later at DXC, he also made the decision to remove large swaths of management hierarchy including a large percentage of senior management, and in effect, he let that institutional knowledge walk right out the door because it was the right thing to do in the long run. Furthermore, he divested businesses, acquired businesses, and allowed others to come to their natural conclusion. But, he knows that if difficult decisions are not reached, and no changes are made, nothing gets accomplished.

"Never in my wildest imaginations did I think that I could say that in five years, we would be where we are today," Jim Smith related. "Don't get me wrong, I was committed to doing something successful, but the degree to which we have made the very difficult, difficult, difficult choices and stuck with them to get here, has been nothing short of a testament to exactly that. You've got to really instill the belief in everyone to get to the vision."[30]

As to being a Mandate Driven Leader, Lawrie is different from the other visionaries in this book. While the others built companies from the ground up, Lawrie takes crumbling businesses and fixes them with streamlined tactics that would make an aerospace engineer proud. Like a high-level mechanic fixing a broken machine, he assesses the situation, maps it to a vision, finds out what still works and what needs repair, and then tactically puts the pieces back together again, eliminating all that is defective and fractured and finding better parts more suited for the task. In the end, the final product is well-oiled, polished, and more efficient than it was before and pointed to a clear vision for the future.

"I think a mandated-oriented leadership style gives people a chance to either get on the bus or get off the bus," Lawrie states. "Some people get off the bus voluntarily, others, you need to open the emergency door and throw them out. You have to have the right people around you because, in a mandated leadership style, you need to have people that share that vision. In a consensus model, not everyone agrees, which can lead to a lot of passive-aggressive behavior, and on a turnaround or at a start-up situation that can be endemic to success."[31] Like many high-caliber change agents, Lawrie is not a friend to every employee down the line, especially those affected negatively by necessary changes. That being said, stockholders love him, and so do many employees as well.

When you speak to Lawrie about a topic he is passionate about, whether the Philadelphia Eagles, digital transformation, or management accountability, the passion of a teacher does quickly surface.

However, don't expect Lawrie to move to the academic realm anytime soon, as he is glad to be at the top of the highly competitive and cutthroat IT services world. It is a nice view, and it took a while to get there, though all who know him doubt he will be taking time to smell the roses anytime soon.

CHAPTER 7

WHAT WE KNOW ABOUT LEADERSHIP

Thus we may know that there are five essentials for victory:
(1) He will win who knows when to fight and when not to fight.
(2) He will win who knows how to handle both superior and
inferior forces. (3) He will win whose army is animated by the
same spirit throughout all its ranks. (4) He will win who, prepared
himself, waits to take the enemy unprepared. (5) He will win who
has military capacity and is not interfered with by the sovereign.

—SUN TZU

Before we start delving into what it takes to be a Mandate Driven Leader, we have to set the context of what we know about leadership and the way people think about it to date. Concepts of what it means to be a good leader such as servant leadership and participative leadership have only existed for a few decades. Concepts of effective leadership in an industrial and organizational setting only began evolving at the dawn of the industrial age. Prior to that, the only models of leadership that were consistently applied were concepts around military leadership. A Mandate Driven Leadership approach is a very specific type of leadership style. However, a Mandate Driven Leadership style does not reside in a vacuum. What is apparent in the profile of these leaders is that they incorporate many other leadership principles, characteristics, and traits professed over the years.

Military leadership undoubtedly is the epitome of Mandate Driven Leadership. For the better part of human history, leadership was associated with military rule. For military leaders, the chain of command was more distinct—one person was in charge, and that person's orders were followed. Leadership effectiveness was easy to determine—the outcome of the battle. In today's disruptive digital economy, Mandate Driven Leaders recognize both the value and necessity of the chain of command as well as the imperative of the outcome.

The eminent industrial and organizational psychologist Robert Hogan is known for regularly discussing how leadership, like much of human innovation, evolved from warfare, and when we look at the evolution of leadership, we must first look at it through the military lens. One of the earliest known treatments on leadership was Sun Tzu's *The Art of War*.[1] Depending on which source you believe, this document was written as early as the sixth century BCE. In the late twentieth century it became wildly popular among MBA students in reference to strategic planning, but anyone who has actually read any of the various translations will tell you that it is much less about strategy and much more about how a leader wins the battle.

Sun Tzu's fifth essential for victory is "He will win who has military capacity and is not interfered with by the sovereign." Military leadership exists in a command and control structure. While the title of various ranks may change, at the end of the day there is a strict hierarchy in which the leader gives orders to soldiers, and the soldiers are expected to follow those orders. This is most important when the military is engaged in battle against an opposing force. This expectation or demand that the organization follow them and their vision to reality is a common characteristic of Mandate Driven Leaders like Steve Jobs.

Steve Jobs had some failures and huge successes in business. Throughout it all, Jobs was extremely passionate and fearless when it came to commanding Apple and his other ventures. Himmel related in *Entrepreneur*, "Many actions in his career were controversial and at certain points risked the future of the company."[2] For Jobs to take those actions, he understood the pitfalls of consensus and compromise. However, when he commanded his vision to reality with military precision, great things could be accomplished.

When looking at leadership through the military lens, it is pretty easy to define effectiveness—victory. And victory, according to Sun Tzu, is the primary responsibility of any leader. "The art of war is of vital importance to the State. It is a matter of life and death, a road either to safety or to ruin. Hence it is a subject of inquiry which can on no account be neglected."[3] In the past, understanding impactful leadership was quite simple; *who won*. Why should it be different today when discussing corporate leadership?

The theory of effective leadership being tied to the notion of military principles is evident when we recognize that most of the great leaders in early history, from Alexander the Great to Dwight D. Eisenhower, had ties to military training. As the industrial revolution took hold, the idea of effective leadership evolved from pure military principles to being about influencing the performance of nonmilitary teams, groups, and organizations. This became increasingly evident with Frederick Taylor's work at the Midvale Steel Plant in 1878. Taylor was one of the first people to try to analyze and understand how various jobs were performed so as to increase the effectiveness and efficiency of the people in those jobs. Admittedly this approach was more about management than leadership, but it did begin the process of thinking about how we get people and organizations to focus on what matters most.

Management Versus Leadership

This, of course, brings up the entertaining question of what is the difference between management and leadership. This is a much-nuanced debate, due in no small part to the nonstandardization of titles across various organizations. A general manager in one organization may have the same responsibilities and commensurate compensation as a vice president in another organization. Conversely, you may have a go-to-market leader who outranks an account manager in one organization, but that same go-to-market title might be in an individual contributor, implementation role in another organization.

I once had the pleasure of meeting and chatting with Seth Godin, who at the time was head of direct marketing at Yahoo during its heyday. He left me his card with his title: *Marketing Yahoo*. To this day, it is still my favorite individual title.

We must think about leadership in terms of what individuals do rather than what it says on a person's business card. In simplest terms, *leaders inspire and produce a dynamic change* in those around them, while *managers seek to maintain efficiency, order, and stability in implementation*. Leaders inspire for change, while managers maintain control, focus on task-level problem solving, and inspire for efficiency. You can be a leader without being a manager, and you can be a manager without being a leader. But if you're doing it right, you are probably both.

The difference between leadership and management is significant, especially when it comes to discussion about consensus. At the management layer of responsibility, at the layer seeking efficiency, order, and stability, groupthink and consensus management might be a proper tool to surface all concepts, ideas, and processes and achieve broad level support in the implementation of a specific task or process. However, that is vastly different from the dynamic change a Mandate Driven Leader seeks to propel. But today's organizations tend to reward individuals who excel at collaboration and consensus building by promoting them into leadership positions where many fail miserably. Why? Because organizations have confused effective management with effective leadership.

Ethical Leadership

Ethical leadership and being a good corporate citizen is an integral supporting trait of the Mandate Driven Leader. Superficially, one might think that Mandate Driven Leaders because of their unrelenting drive might be prone to ethical lapses. Not true. Mandate Driven Leaders can still lead ethically—one cornerstone of being a good corporate citizen. There has been a lot of talk over the past couple of decades of ethical leadership. A lot of that talk has been sparked by unethical behavior on the part of business leaders.

From the fall of Enron in the early 2000s to the subprime mortgage scandal of 2007, there never seems to be any shortage of examples of organizations where a leader's bad behavior and selfish intent creates problems. No matter how many new laws get passed, or how much oversight is provided, those who want to benefit themselves at the expense of others always find a way. For better or worse, those in positions of corporate power have the capability of doing more harm than the average worker.

Somehow individuals may think that Mandate Driven Leaders veer toward unethical behavior while consensus-driven leaders by the nature of groupthink veer toward ethical behavior. The data suggests otherwise. Warren Buffett once said, "In looking for people to hire, you look for three qualities: integrity, intelligence, and energy. And if they don't have the first, the other two will kill you."[4] This applies to both mandate and consensus-driven leadership styles. In fact, the number of corporations on the garbage dump of history due to unethical behavior that was driven by a *group* of unethical managers is large. More than 20 individuals at Enron either pled or were found guilty of crimes in Enron's downfall; in WorldCom more than 10. We should never confuse mandating a vision with mandating unethical behavior.

The challenge in trying to apply an ethical lens to our discussion of leadership is that unlike laws that are clearly defined, ethics tend to evolve and change as the moral and fairness canons of society progress. There is often a significant delay between when something begins to be considered unethical and it becomes illegal. Sometimes it takes a significant negative event for those ethical standards to become legally codified. Therefore if we want to encourage more ethical leadership behavior, we can't just depend on leaders sticking to legal standards at the time. Leaders, including Mandate Driven Leaders, will usually have distinct opinions on four things:

► What does ethical leadership mean?
► What is ethical behavior, and how do we engrain it in our culture?
► How do we encourage our managers to be ethical?
► What governance is established to ensure ethical behavior?

Deciding what really constitutes ethical leadership can be tricky. It seems to be like great art in that it is hard to define but we know it when we see it. Or to be more precise, we know unethical leadership when we see it. For example, Joel Amernic and Russell Craig in the *Journal of Business Ethics* talk about the News Corporation phone hacking scandal in the United Kingdom and how it was largely a result of News Corporation CEO Rupert Murdock driving a culture where anything goes, even unethical behavior. In other words, he was leading a culture where outcomes were more important than ethics.[5] While this approach may produce outcomes in the short term, without fail it will come back to haunt the leader and the organization. A leader who is promoting outcomes at any cost is not the Mandate Driven Leader we are advocating or one that succeeds. Outcomes regardless of ethics are vastly different from a leader mandating a vision of the future where the company is propelled to the forefront of its industry.

This of course gets to the question of what ethics actually means when we are talking about leadership and organizations. The question of ethical behavior is one that scholars have wrestled from the beginning of time. Traditionally ethics has been thought to mean fair and equitable treatment toward customers, business partners, and even competitors. More recently that term has evolved to include corporations being concerned with corporate social responsibility and their impact on society including the global environment. For Mandate Driven Leaders, their vision of change and innovation is as much about societal improvement as it is about corporate profit. Steve Jobs was adamant that the objective for Apple was to "change the world." Mark Zuckerberg stated, "My goal was never to just create a company. It was to build something that actually makes a really big change in the world." Within the DNA of a Mandate Driven Leader is the desire for disruption, the abolition of the status quo. The disruption is not to bring about chaos and anarchy; it is to enrich and benefit society. And, yes, to make a profit along the way is always nice.

The idea that one cannot be ethical without taking into account things like social benefit did not even exist a few decades ago. Clearly the idea of what is (or is not) ethical is largely a function of the zeitgeist and ecosystem in which the organization operates. To lead ethically, leaders must be tuned in to these evolving standards. But let's be clear, being a Mandate Driven Leader and an ethical leader are complementary, not at odds.

Servant Leadership

One of the more popular discussions about leadership models is what has become known as servant leadership, which is an approach by leaders who are driven by the belief that they are in their roles for the benefit and support of the people that they are charged to lead. This concept can be traced back to the writings of people like Robert Greenleaf in his 1977 book *Servant Leadership: A Journey into the Nature of Legitimate Power and Greatness.* These leaders place other people's needs, aspirations, and interests above their own. Calls for servant leaders came in response to the unethical and self-serving behavior seen in many corporations at the time. With many of the recent financial crises and corporate scandals over the past decade or so, the calls for servant-based approaches have only intensified.

The challenge with servant leadership is that it has become so popular that many people espousing its value are not completely clear on its definition. Case in point, I had a dissertation student recently who wanted to do her study on servant leadership. My first question to her was to define servant leadership. She hemmed and hawed a bit before coming back with the reply of "a servant leader is just a leader who's not a bad person."

The confusion about what servant leadership is can partly be traced to one of its core differences compared to other leadership approaches. Whereas most approaches to leadership focus on what the leader does, servant leadership is focused on why they do it. This is not a slight nuance. A servant leader is driven by a particular set of principles, values, and beliefs. Most important among those beliefs is that leaders are there for the benefit and support of those they are charged to lead. Their behaviors, their actions, and even how they interact with others are driven by this core principle.

The behaviors that result from these drivers are often considered to be more ethical and prosocial than the outcomes of other leadership approaches. While the ethicality and prosocialness is often debatable depending on the cultural context, from a leadership study standpoint our main concern is that servant leadership places more value on what makes leaders want to take on that role and how they make behavioral decisions while in that role as opposed to the actual outcomes of their leadership. In this theory the *why* is more important than the result.

So what is it that makes a servant leader different from other leaders? As stated earlier, it is not so much an issue of what the leader does but why that leader leads. Servant leaders are driven by a calling to take care of those they serve and lead. They accept their leadership roles for reasons greater than personal gain or self-satisfaction. Because of this focus, servant leaders often do not exhibit a command and control persona, but act as cheerleaders, listeners, and facilitators. They focus on how they can serve their followers, rather than how their followers can serve them.

There is a place for a servant leadership style, and it can coexist within a Mandate Driven Leadership model with an important clarification that is often overlooked in the discussion. The list of venerable companies that have failed due to the business disruption being experienced continues to grow. Servant leaders must recognize that if they are truly to benefit the individuals they lead, they must first ensure that the organization will survive and thrive. An early mentor reminded me of this fact whenever I had to terminate an underperforming worker or reorganize a low-performing business unit. Leaders can be empathetic to the individual they are impacting, but they need to be beholden to the entity and ecosystem—the thousands of individuals that remain in the organization, their families, suppliers, and the entire human impact of that value chain. Undoubtedly Steve Jobs knew this when he downsized both Pixel and Apple to restructure to his vision. In other words, servant leadership must be practiced at the collective, not the individual level and begins with ensuring that the organization will survive and thrive.

Ultimately, advocates of servant leadership theory believe in a Zenlike irony: leaders who focus on serving others rather than commanding others to follow are ultimately easier to follow. With this in mind, servant leadership theory is still not at odds with the Mandate Driven Leadership model. Hard decisions will still be made that may negatively affect individuals. The vision of change these leaders are mandating may be to ensure survival for both the company and the welfare of all its employees, partners, and shareholders. Or, it may be to disrupt or create an entirely new industry with societal benefits. What is common for both the servant leader and the Mandate Driven Leader is to think of the greater good of the entity they are leading.

The Organizational Champion

While there are a lot of ideas recycling around the subject of leadership, there are also quite a few new ideas that are helping drive new knowledge around what it is to lead and what type of leaders are needed. Today, we are seeing entire industries and sectors of the economy being disrupted by digital technology, and at no time is the identification of not just leaders but Mandate Driven Leaders of greater importance. One of the more interesting ideas I've found is the notion of an organizational champion.

This is a fairly new construct that has been floating around the past few years and seems to be gaining some steam in the popular press, even though the academic researchers have not caught up. It is tied to the idea of someone who leads not just internally but externally as well. These organizational champions are change agents not only for their companies, but for their industries. It starts to touch on the fact that today, the definitions of leader and change agent become intertwined. This notion has been supported by a number of leading thinkers including Mike Thompson in his 2009 book *Organizational Champions: How to Develop Passionate Change Agents at Every Level*.

So what is the difference between a leader and an organizational champion? A leader and a change agent? In a nutshell, organizational champions are leaders who commit themselves and their organization to win in the global marketplace through innovation, agility, and disruption. They are not afraid to make bold moves that not only benefit their organizations but also serve the greater good. They are not beholden to the traditional go-to-market strategies and tactics of a marketplace. They eliminate rungs in the value chain. They create new markets. They disintermediate. In other words, they are not just focused on motivating top performance now, but also on helping their organization evolve to meet future needs. Moreover, they are looking at not just the organization, but the broader world. This is quite an intriguing concept that fits well with the goals of a Mandate Driven Leader.

Motivation

In a 2013 issue of *Harvard Business Review* in the article "Connect, Then Lead," Cuddy, Kohut, and Neffinger had a great debate about whether it is better for a leader to be feared or loved, assuming that they can't be both. They suggest that it is more important to be loved and trusted because without trust there is the risk of trepidation, resentment, and envy from those that you are meant to lead. This concept is particularly interesting when it is considered in terms of Douglas McGregor's original work on Theory X and Theory Y.

Originally developed while McGregor was at the MIT Sloan School of Management in the early 1960s, a Theory X manager *assumes* that people are lazy and must, therefore, be motivated by economic incentives and kept under constant surveillance or they will start slacking off. A Theory Y manager *assumes* that people are basically self-motivated and therefore need to be challenged and channeled, not controlled.

Theory X managers would claim that a Theory Y manager's approach would not make any sense because employees aren't going to trust managers no matter what they do. They just want the path of least resistance to perform their task, receive their compensation, and go home. Traditional management techniques, including consensus management, might work under Theory X. If employees saw how providing input or using teamwork might make their jobs easier and increase their compensation, they would be all in.

Theory Y managers, on the other hand, would want to build that trust to extend the employees' natural motivation. They would want to instill a vision into each employee. They believe that employees have a natural motivation for success and with it an insatiable appetite to be directed to achieve a vision greater than the individual task. While McGregor's Theory Y addresses the individual as opposed to the collective, it begins to address the absolute need for vision that Mandate Driven Leaders use to propel organizations to success.

Whether they agree with McGregor's Theory X, Theory Y, or neither, Mandate Driven Leaders understand the importance of motivation. They also understand that motivation is often inextricably linked to having and being able to articulate a clear, impactful vision.

What Is Leadership Employee Development?

There is a growing view that one of the most important things leaders can do is develop the employees who work for them. There was a rather pithy article in *USA Today* in 2013, "On the Job: Best Bosses Help You Add Skills," that cited numerous research projects that suggest the best leaders are the ones who help their employees build their skills. The thesis was that those in leadership positions should focus on making the people around them better, rather than worrying so much about maintaining control or asserting authority. While these are interesting insights, they are not exactly news. Leadership gurus and researchers have been beating this drum for years. This knowledge base has been applied to everything from "muddy boots" well drillers to C-level executives. That being said, employee development is an obvious supporting characteristic of the Mandate Driven Leader.

The general consensus seems to be that the best leaders focus on developing and growing their people rather than just transactional outcomes. The idea is that organizations tend to evolve in the direction of where they focus their energies. As such if they focus their energies on developing quality people, that is how the organization will grow, and the rest of the transactional outcomes will eventually take care of themselves. This is great in theory, and it is supported by some longitudinal research, but those transactional outcomes are how most managers are evaluated and compensated. For better or worse, however, most employees have come to expect this kind of personal development, so modern managers are faced with the challenge of two often conflicting priorities: development of their workforce over transactional business outcomes.

One of the places where the challenge of balancing these multiple priorities becomes particularly apparent is when we start dealing with the multiple generations we now find in the workplace, especially when it comes to what many people like to call millennials.

Millennials (normally defined as those born between 1982 and the early 2000s) tend to take a very different view than baby boomers and Generation

X in terms of their attitudes toward work and their expectations about how they want to be treated at work.

There is the talk of their willingness and desire to work across teams, as well as their constant need for feedback and reinforcement. There is praise for their tech savvy, but also lamentations about their inability to focus on one thing at a time for very long. Depending on the author and the publication, Generation Y (an alternative name for this group) is either collectively a brilliant bunch or a bunch of spoiled brats. The one thing that all authors seem to agree on is that they are much more willing to speak up if they feel they are not being treated fairly. This means that they seem to place emphasis on personal development over transactional outcomes regardless of the priority the company places on each.

Sure there are some variances in what millennials want out of their work lives compared to earlier generations, but *how* we lead them to get there is not all that different. For example, if we go back to Warren Bennis's *On Becoming a Leader* (1989), we find that there are some basic ingredients to leadership that still resonate today. Those ingredients include guiding vision, passion, integrity, trust, curiosity, and daring. Those are ingredients that speak well to all employees no matter what their age. In *Zapp! The Lightening of Empowerment*, William Byham and Jeff Cox put forth the notion that empowering employees is the most important thing we can do as leaders. In the 1980s, authors such as David Campbell in his book *If I'm in Charge Here Why Is Everybody Laughing?* discuss that effective leaders take on roles like disseminator of valuable information and liaison between coordinating groups and colleagues. These are all the exact kinds of interactions that are valued by high-touch employees such as millennials.

Liked or Loved

Early in my career, I worked for an individual who exhibited many Mandate Driven Leadership traits. He was very outcome focused, was a West Point graduate, and was known for taking care of his "troops" as long as they were willing to work toward the organization's goals. One particular time he had a couple of young team leads who were pretty convinced they knew better than he what the group should do. In his efforts to "motivate" them to get with the program, he relayed one of the most interesting views on leadership that I've ever heard. While I don't remember his exact words, the gist was something to the effect of *I would prefer to have your respect and support, but if I can't get that I'll take fear and compliance.*

Mandate Driven Leaders expect and demand to be in command, but does this necessarily mean that they are disliked or feared? The answer is an unequivocal no. A Mandate Driven Leader model comes with some clear tenets as to vision, command, and the unrelenting pursuit of a vision. However, there are many facets of individual style that determine the likeability of a leader whether a Mandate Driven Leader or not. "I don't think I run roughshod over people, but if something sucks, I tell people to their face," Jobs once told Isaacson in an interview. "It's my job to be honest. I know what I'm talking about, and I usually turn out to be right. That's the culture I tried to create. We are brutally honest with each other. And we've had some rip-roaring arguments, where we are yelling at each other, and it's some of the best times I've ever had."[6]

There are many stories and anecdotes that portray Steve Jobs as someone hard to like. "Jobs could be so direct, it bordered on rude," Susan Kalla, an investment manager, wrote in *Forbes*.[7] But was he disliked? Unloved? These stories notwithstanding, Jobs still instilled in his teams a sense of pride, fellowship, and loyalty. In fact, Jobs regularly received employee approval ratings that topped 90 percent. In a 2011 Glassdoor survey, Steve Jobs received an employee approval rating of 95 percent. He came in second among CEOs after Google's Eric Schmidt, who received 96 percent approval. Amazon's Jeff Bezos, a fellow Mandate Driven Leader profile in this book, was at a respectable 83 percent. Meanwhile, Microsoft CEO Steve Ballmer, who generally is not considered a visionary, Mandate Driven Leader, was at 40 percent.

Generally, Apple employees under Jobs enjoyed their work and successes and appreciated and many loved Jobs's leadership, but there is no question he hurt feelings along the way. Pixar VP Pam Kerwin stated succinctly to *Newsweek* a few weeks prior to Jobs's death, "Nobody would ever call Steve an angel in the usual sense of the word. But somebody willing to go to bat for you—that's what he was for Pixar. A devilish angel."[8]

In the end, all leaders can either be liked or disliked. This is not dependent on whether they adopt a Mandate Driven Leadership model. Rather, it stems from a myriad of other traits, characteristics, and actions. What is evident in our profiles of Mandate Driven Leaders is that whether they are liked holds little import to them. Whether they are effective is what keeps them up at night.

Is Effective Leadership a Quantifiable Trait?

Whether you lean toward Theory X or Theory Y, how do you know if someone who *looks* like a leader is really an effective leader? The first thing we can do is, of course, consider how well the organization is performing quantitatively. If the organization's stock price and revenues are going up, then we can assume that an organization has good leaders, right? Well, maybe not. We only have to look at the behaviors of the people who led Enron and the scandal around Bernie Madoff to see that organizations that appear to be performing may not have the best leaders. Or, companies like Yahoo that were once the disrupters but in a fairly quick period of time became irrelevant. The question that comes of these examples is how we identify ineffective leaders before things get that bad.

Elizabeth Rupprecht, Jessica Waldrop, and Matthew Grawitch looked at this in 2013 when they developed a leadership scoring model, the General Inventory of Lasting Leadership (GILL) and the Multifactor Leadership Questionnaire (MLQ). It was their objective to identify measures to quantify and predict counterproductive work behaviors (CWB) and organizational citizenship behavior (OCB). The GILL is an instrument in which people rate their leaders' behaviors, and the MLQ is an instrument in which both the leader and the subordinates provide feedback. They are fairly robust instruments, and practitioners require some specialized training in psychometrics and behavior science to be able to use them properly. Regardless of those challenges, however, the principle is sound.

There are both quantitative and qualitative metrics that can be applied to leadership. However, when we put too much weight on the qualitative view of these traits, especially from the perspective of those being led, we may not be receiving the data that is most important for the collective whole. The qualitative data may not be most representative of the success of the organization, current and future. Undoubtedly, we will find that some leaders with high qualitative traits, while shiny on the outside, upon closer inspection do not have the effectiveness of the Mandate Driven Leaders.

Professionals in the business world and academia will continue to debate the merits of various leadership traits and characteristics. The only conclusion that is probably accepted is that no definitive model works in every situation. Effective leadership models recognize both style and situation. Individual characteristics of the leader coupled with situation specifics should determine which style to develop and model to use. Mike Lawrie's opinion is that

"Not every person, CEO, or senior leadership member is able to practice different leadership styles." He continues, "Most CEOs—in fact, most people in general—have a dominant leadership style. Over time, the good ones learn how to exercise different leadership styles depending on the situation."[9]

That being said, there has been much academic and private sector work on what it takes to be an effective leader. Somewhat like an à la carte menu, effective leaders utilize many supporting traits and characteristics including Mandate Driven Leadership. Some of the more important traits have been summarized in this chapter. What is vital to understand is that these traits and characteristics, while important, must be used to support an overall Mandate Driven Leadership model that is necessary for the disruptive business environment of today.

CHAPTER 8

MARK ZUCKERBERG OF FACEBOOK: CONNECTING THE WORLD

The biggest risk is not taking any risk. In a world that is changing really quickly, the only strategy that is guaranteed to fail is not taking risks.

—MARK ZUCKERBERG, Founder and CEO, Facebook

On a disruptive trek from Cambridge to Silicon Valley in 2005, a young Mark Zuckerberg, just 21 at the time, placed all bets on his own convictions rather than on the virtually guaranteed route to success: a Harvard degree. In a "devil be damned" roll of the dice, he dropped out of Harvard with a youthful belief that he could guarantee his own future. Zuck gambled that it was ultimately up to his intuitions and internal drive, not a Harvard education and not a hefty paycheck from one of the numerous mega-successful corporations snatching up Ivy League grads like candy from an expensive glass bowl.

A caveat in this sometimes romanticized "follow your dreams" story of Mark Zuckerberg dropping out of Harvard is that by the time he headed to Silicon Valley in 2005, he was taking with him an already successful one-year-old start-up version of Facebook with multimillion-dollar offers, including $75 million from Viacom. As a 19-year-old sophomore, Mark had created "theFacebook.com," a Harvard social networking website that spread like wildfire across campus. After its launch on February 4, 2004, more than 1,200 of his Harvard classmates reportedly joined theFacebook.com in its first 24 hours, followed by a majority of the undergraduate student body in just over a month. It then jumped the fire line and sparked anew at Columbia University, Yale, Stanford, and dozens of more elite institutions.

By the end of Zuckerberg's first year in Silicon Valley, Facebook exceeded 12 million active users. Today, there are more than 2 billion active users, and Mark Zuckerberg is firmly entrenched as a visionary and a Mandate Driven Leader.

Early Passion for Innovation

Mark Zuckerberg's passion for innovation was seen earlier than perhaps any of the other profiled Mandate Driven Leaders. In the early 1990s, home computer programming was in its infancy, but that did not stop Mark Zuckerberg. He mostly taught himself to program computers. By the age of 10, his self-cultivated programming skills had allowed him to build "ZuckNet," a program to link his father's home and work computers. By his teens, even with a pseudo-prankster streak that got him into trouble periodically, he had already created a number of programs on a whim and entered early talks with Microsoft about selling a music suggestion program called Synapse that he'd created as a high school senior at the exclusive Phillips Exeter Academy.

This solid upper-middle-class background and early recognition of his intellectual prowess landed this quasi-genius on the campus of Harvard, where he undoubtedly had access to resources and a fertile environment for experimentation. Mark launched two instantly popular college-oriented computer programs at Harvard. Coursematch allowed students to choose classes based on who else was taking them, and his Facemash attractiveness rating service was quickly banned by the Harvard administration.

Years later, author David Kirkpatrick explained in *The Facebook Effect* that Zuckerberg considered the initial programs he created in his Kirkland House dorm at Harvard as "these little projects" that were really more like hobbies. "I had like twelve projects that year. Of course, I wasn't fully committed to any of them," said Zuckerberg.[1] They were revealing nonetheless, as they showed a seed of thought and a pattern of "seeing how people were connected through mutual references."

Today, Mark Zuckerberg's last college project, Facebook, has a market valuation greater than $500 billion and more than 35,000 employees. Somewhere in the Facebook offices sitting at a nondescript open table, you will find the CEO, founder, and resident social networking visionary. They are all the same person, of course, and they are Zuckerberg. On most days, you will still find him in a gray T-shirt, zippered-up hooded jacket, jeans, and sneakers.

The Facebook offices are not offices, per se, because there are no actual "offices." In fact, there are no cubicles, either, or walls, except the ones that hold up the building and insulate its inhabitants. Even the main conference room is a box of glass in the middle of an expansive workspace. The name of the room is the Aquarium, and it provides a fine metaphor for the online world that its boss has created, a virtual space in which people offer up their lives for the world to see. Photos and random thoughts are found in the online fishbowl called a social network, which opens up everyone involved to positive reinforcement or negative criticism of their daily life in an addictive public forum.

This casual entrepreneur was *Time* magazine's person of the year in 2010, only seven years after he created "TheFacebook" in his Harvard dorm room at the age of 19. The simple website he created was billed as "an online directory" that connected people "through social networks at colleges." For a time it was meant for university students only, which makes sense since he was only a college sophomore at the time, and he was only attempting to impress people of his age.

His vision grew much bigger, though.

A Man and His Vision

Turning down the early lucrative buyout offers for Facebook and instead opting for relatively small investments to get his business off the ground, Mark headed to Silicon Valley, essentially creating his own mandate. With the bravery and some say arrogance of youth, and a conviction that he personally had the vision to see his pet project to fruition, he began the journey in which he would (not always gracefully) grow into his own larger-than-life shoes—while becoming a multibillionaire somewhere along the way.

"It takes courage to choose hope over fear. To say that we can build something and make it better than it has ever been before," Zuck told Matt Rosoff of *Business Insider*. "You have to be optimistic to think you can change the world. And people will always call you naive, but it's this hope, and this optimism, that is behind every important step forward."[2] That optimism within a few short years propelled Facebook to the forefront of the digital world.

As of December 2018, Facebook had 2.32 billion monthly active users, and the grand majority of those users check on to the site every day. Essentially, Zuckerberg figured out a recipe to link humanity to a single network. In doing so, he became the sixth richest person in the world with a net worth that fluctuates between $60 billion and $70 billion, depending on how well the stock market did that day. Yet, he still makes it to work on a daily basis even though he is a multibillionaire.

"The question I ask myself like almost every day is, 'Am I doing the most important thing I could be doing?' Unless I feel like I'm working on the most important problem that I can help with, then I'm not going to feel good about how I'm spending my time," he said.[3] For Zuckerberg, like most Mandate Driven Leaders, the vision of the future drives them more than they drive the vision.

As Zuckerberg grew his team of all-stars and racked up monster success, his style left little room for his investors to challenge his mandates. "Mark has retained nearly absolute control over his board of directors," said Joe Green, a former college roommate, and a friend who works with Zuckerberg on Facebook applications. "Facebook would be a zillion times OVER if not for Mark. Especially as you hire older people with direct financial needs, you get lots of pressure to get liquidity. But you need Zen-like confidence to turn down a billion-dollar acquisition offer."[4]

It is true, Zuckerberg pushed away numerous buyouts. He knew that someone would build the ultimate online social network, and he could not stand the idea that it would be anyone else but him. He needed that control. In 2005, a year after Facebook launched, MTV considered buying Facebook for $75 million, right before Yahoo! and Microsoft blew the offer to pieces with a billion-dollar deal.

"I'd never met anyone—forget his age, 22 then—I'd never met anyone who would walk away from a billion dollars," said Terry Semel, former CEO of Yahoo. "But he said, 'It's not about the price. This is my baby, and I want to keep running it; I want to keep growing it.' I couldn't believe it."

Chan, his wife, does remember some strife when he was offered a quick route to billionaire status, saying it was the most stressful time of Zuckerberg's life. "We try to stick pretty close to what our goals are and what we believe and what we enjoy doing in life—just simple things."

Along with the resolution not to sell, another key decision along the way to the top was that Zuckerberg held out for as long as he could on making a public offering. It was this independent spirit that allowed Zuck to maintain so much control when it actually occurred. Basically, if investors wanted an IPO, they would give him what he wanted, and it happened just that way.

After Facebook's IPO was settled in 2012, Zuckerberg managed to maintain 60 percent of the voting power of Facebook, which is more muscle than Bill Gates had at Microsoft (49 percent) and way more than the cofounders of Google have in their boardroom (16 percent each). This structure was not financial for Zuckerberg—it was about control. The ability to ensure he would always control the vison. Zuckerberg's share arrangement gives the rest of the investors in FB very little voice in the operation. Zuckerberg is the chairperson of his company's board and the CEO. He cannot be fired; he can only resign. He has ultimate control and extraordinary power over his vision, which has drawn scrutiny.

Charles Elson, a University of Delaware corporate governance professor, told the *New York Times*, "You're willing to take someone's money, but not willing to invite their participation. It makes meaningless the notion of investor democracy."[5] However, Paul Madera, an investor in the company and managing director at Meritech Capital Partners, says, "Mark's vision on the purity of the product really did benefit from his control and ownership. It wasn't subject to committee decisions. It was all Mark."[6]

Like most Mandate Driven Leaders, propelling their vision to the ultimate outcome is not something they will let go of easily.

Zuckerberg's Unrelenting Drive to Achieve the Vision

People have varying notions of Zuckerberg. Those close to him describe him as an intense and forceful speaker with the perfect annunciation of a grammarian. His rigid posture is that of a guard outside Buckingham Palace, which makes up for his five-feet-eight-inch frame, and when something or someone engages him, he may never blink his hazel eyes.

Often, in one-on-one conversations or on a stage, he is charming and energetic. However, when he is *not* enlightened by someone's ideas, he looks distant in such a way to be disorientating. Described as robotic, one of his friends says, "He's been over-programmed." He can be smug, brusque, flippant, and completely aloof when he is bored; he cannot fake excitement for anyone's benefit.

When *Fortune* named him Businessperson of the Year in 2016, the magazine said that it was due to his successful management approach, which rests on the following three pillars:

- ▶ His unique ability to look into the future
- ▶ His otherworldly consistency
- ▶ His business discipline, which he nurtures in an industry enamored with bright, shiny objects

"One of the things that defines Mark is that he takes a very, very long view of things, almost a geological view," longtime FB engineer Mike Vernal told *Fortune*. "Most people think day to day or week to week. Mark thinks century to century."[7]

Zuckerberg goes deeper than most successful founding CEOs on all issues and ideas concerning Facebook because he only looks for business concepts that make a difference, are disruptive, and add value. However, it is *always* Zuckerberg who defines the worth of an idea through his own values while considering no one else's. In other words, there is no doubt, Facebook is a mandate-driven operation, in which Zuckerberg asserts himself as supreme *leader*, who has no interest in following or doing anything on other people's terms.

Zuckerberg never backs down from his position, and in the entirety of his professional career, he has never blamed a soul for any of Facebook's shortcomings. Through his years, he has admitted to acts of poor judgment and irresponsibility. In a recent Facebook controversy involving the improper harvesting of the user data of 87 million Facebook members by a political consulting firm, Zuckerberg made it clear that it was entirely his fault and no one would be fired over the matter. For anything that Facebook does, good or bad, he takes all of the credit, and he takes all of the blame.

"What I think people should hold us accountable for is if we are learning from our mistakes," he told reporters in a conference call, "When you're building something like Facebook which is unprecedented in the world, there are things that you're going to mess up."[8]

The Facebook founder stays focused and does not mess around with other ventures that are not directly tied to Facebook. Since leaving Harvard, he has had two passions outside of his family life: Facebook, and being the only boss at Facebook. Along the way, he has pushed his staff to act swiftly and take risks, and he will pick up the pieces if something crumbles.

"Move fast and break things," he told *Business Insider.* "Unless you are breaking stuff, you are not moving fast enough."[9] He continues to take risks with philosophical approaches to business that are unique in Silicon Valley and the world, mostly because they are not commerce-driven.

"In a world that's changing really quickly, the only strategy that is guaranteed to fail is not taking risks," he said to a crowd, during an interview at Y Combinator's Startup School.[10]

Over the years, he has given up a substantial amount of revenue and personal wealth because he did not want to change the way Facebook looked or functioned. Zuckerberg does not live extravagantly, and he does not chase money. From early on, the most important thing to him was creating something "neat," and the commerce side and monetizing the website are not things that get him up in the morning. For business matters, Zuckerberg is fine with giving up some control to skilled employees who do the required commerce work, which he has always admitted is not his main interest, nor is he good at it.

When Zuck moved to the Valley for the first time, he rented a one-bedroom apartment that his friends described as a "crack den," before moving into a two-bedroom house and then a four-bedroom home that he said was "too big," right before Facebook went public, making him a billionaire.[11] Tyler Winklevoss once said Zuckerberg was "the poorest rich person" he had ever seen in his life.[12]

"Whenever anyone asked about his priorities, Zuckerberg was unequivocal—growth and continued improvement in the customer experience were more important than monetization," according to David Kirkpatrick. "Long-term financial success depended on continued growth."[13]

This has been his same mantra since the infamous Instant Messages of his college days. He is recorded as saying the following:

ZUCKERBERG: Eduardo is paying for my servers.
D'ANGELO: A sucker born every day.
ZUCKERBERG: Nah, he thinks it will make money.
D'ANGELO: What do you think?
ZUCKERBERG: Well I don't know business stuff.
ZUCKERBERG: I'm content to make something cool.

Prying him from this position has taken some work. He has always disapproved of anything that might clutter the site, including advertisements. He works on his own, most often without a net, constantly tweaking the site to the dismay of his users. In 2009, he updated Facebook on his own without consensus, and the change made private accounts open to public viewing, as a default.

When the Federal Trade Commission cited Facebook for deceptive business practices after the event caused user backlash, Zuckerberg simply apologized and remarked, "Better done than perfect."

His mind works in one way. When cornered about the decision that he made on his own for his millions of users without their permission, he proclaimed, "A lot of people who are worried about privacy and those kinds of issues will take any minor step and turn it into as big a deal as possible. We realize that people will probably criticize us for this for a long time, but we just believe that it is the right thing to do."

It seems very autocratic to have this opinion for a world of users. Many of Facebook's controversial moments deal with the philosophical battle over transparency, and Zuckerberg will always win those battles because if you want to be on his social network, you play by his rules. His rules, always.

Sean Parker, the infamous creator of Napster and investor and first president of Facebook, said, "There's a part of him that—it was present even when he was 20, 21—this kind of imperial tendency. He was really into Greek odysseys and all that stuff."[14]

While he might follow the rules of gods and demigods when issues grow big, he is not so self-centered that he won't ask for occasional advice; it's just that it is not his investors or employees that he seeks out. Instead, he has gone to Bill Gates, Steve Jobs, Google founders Larry Page and Sergey Brin, and other technology luminaries.

"There is no problem he doesn't think he can solve, but he constantly tries to find the smartest people he can to give him advice," an unidentified investor told the *New York Times*.[15]

More often, though, he rolls out plans, takes risks, and makes changes without advice. A former Facebook engineer likened Zuckerberg to Steve Jobs, who relentlessly went rogue when it came to a consensus and was involved in every new product and feature development at Apple.

In one particular case of supremacy, a team of employees worked long hours on a social calendar feature for the website, and the proud employees talked about it daily, for weeks. However, in an instant, they began working on something else. When they were asked about the calendar project, the group responded, "Zuck said, 'No.' He killed it. Not modified it. Killed it."

"It's clear that Facebook has, in fact, been at the center of electrifying change in the way that we communicate with the people around us and share information," CNET proclaimed. "And if Zuckerberg's relentlessly hands-on approach with Facebook—which seems to have grown even closer and more obvious over the years—is any sign, this could not have happened without the young, flip-flops clad CEO."[16]

For Zuckerberg, it is not personal. Some ideas and concepts he accepts and embraces. Others he discards. For Zuck it is simply about whether it fits into his vision of the future.

Liked, Disliked, or Just Respected

Even the greatest generational visionaries do not have an award-winning movie made about them until they are near the grave or in it, but that is not true of the Facebook founder. In 2010, a Zuckerberg biopic called *The Social Network* hit the big screen. The movie debuted when he was 27, after only a seven-year run with Facebook.

The opening scene of the film is telling.

In a pub called the Thirsty Scholar, which is just north of Cambridge, Massachusetts, a 19-year-old Zuckerberg searches for the right things to say to his date, Erica, but is not having much luck. Stuck somewhere between narcissism and anxious insecurity, Zuckerberg's attitude becomes more abrasive and condescending as the chat continues, but it is impossible to know if that is his intention because he feels misunderstood, or if he is as awkward and socially inadequate as they come.

Erica thinks she knows; she believes it is his intention to be mean. As she breaks up with Zuckerberg in the middle of the bar, she says, "You are probably going to be a very successful computer person. But you're going to go through life thinking that girls don't like you because you're a nerd. And I want you to know, from the bottom of my heart, that that won't be true. It'll be because you're an asshole."

While it is unclear if a conversation like this actually occurred because Zuckerberg does not approve of the movie, and therefore, does not wish to promote it by talking about it much, it is clearly a representative symbol of Zuckerberg.

The truth of the movie does not even matter to him, and he hopes it does not matter to anyone else either, even the honest parts. "People don't care about what someone says about you in a movie, or even what you say, right? They care about what you build," he told ABC's Diane Sawyer.[17]

While Steve Jobs developed a reputation that helped get him kicked off Apple's main campus because his personality was so abrasive that some did not want to work for him, Facebook's employees take Zuckerberg's Mandate Driven Leadership style much better. It may be that Facebook has grown so fast, makes so much money, and is such an omnipresent piece of culture that most Facebook employees trust Zuckerberg's direction. Another key aspect surely must be that Zuckerberg does not throw fits. Unlike either Bezos or Jobs, Zuckerberg is stoic and calm even in the heat of disagreement. Furthermore, his employees call him an "intense listener," and debate is always allowed.

That being said, Zuckerberg, like most Mandate Driven Leaders, understands the importance of surrounding himself with individuals who fully buy into his vision for the future. And he can make the hard personnel decisions that are needed. In the early years, the top-level leadership of Facebook was somewhat unstable as he booted out a series of senior executives. Some made it no more than 10 days. Things settled when he hired as his COO Sheryl Sandberg, a Google veteran, who brought in a flood of Google employees and executives from eBay and Mozilla.

"He is shy and introverted, and he often does not seem to be very warm to people, but he is warm," Sandberg told the *New York Times*. "He really cares about the people who work here."[18]

In the case of the team who worked on the calendar, no one was upset that Zuck canned the project. "We all sort of viewed Facebook as a manifestation of Zuck's taste, his idea, his vision," the unidentified employee said. "When he made a decision, that was the decision."[19]

Zuck does not win Mr. Congeniality with everyone, however, and we must include the darker side of his character in the story because it is a major contributor to his nearly flawless portrait of success. Several of Zuckerberg's close friends who worked with him from the beginning have left Facebook because they had their own desires in the tech world, and also because it was difficult to work for him. "Ultimately, it's 'the Mark Show,'" one of his close friends said, and it was no hidden secret. In the early days, each page of Facebook was tagged with "A Mark Zuckerberg production."[20]

The most scathing report in recent years might come from former Facebook employee Antonio Garcia Martinez, who wrote *Chaos Monkeys: Obscene Fortune and Random Failure in Silicon Valley*.

According to Martinez, who was fired in 2013 after two years as a product manager, working for Facebook is similar to being in a cult with Zuckerberg as its leader, who is followed by "true believers." He claims that employees were often expected to work 20-hour days, and eat all of their meals in the company cafeteria, during "lockdown" periods.

He also told one story in which an employee leaked key information about a new Facebook product. Instead of dealing with the issue in private, Zuckerberg sent the employee a "chilling" e-mail with the subject line "Please resign," and copied the entire staff. In the e-mail, he excoriated the individual by attacking her "base moral nature."

"The moral to this story, a parable of a prodigal son but with an unforgiving father, was clear," Martinez writes. "Fuck with Facebook and security guards would be hustling you out the door like a rowdy drunk at a late night Taco Bell."[21]

Zuckerberg's friend Chris Hughes, who received Facebook cofounding status, felt the same way, saying, "Working with Mark is very challenging. You're never sure if what you're doing is something he likes or doesn't like. It's so much better to be friends with Mark than to work with him."[22]

The employees at Facebook with million-dollar stock options vested might disagree. And in 2018 Facebook ranked number one in Glassdoor's Employees' Choice Awards as the best place to work in America. Obviously, a Mandate Driven Leader can be well liked—and if not liked, at least respected.

Zuckerberg on Ethics

While some say he has a cutthroat style, Zuckerberg is well grounded ethically and morally with his vision of using technology to bring the world closer. He has had to make many difficult decisions in moving his vision to reality, and they have left some scars. What is obvious is the depth of contemplation, analysis, and torment that comes with many of those decisions. One evening at the Village Pub in Silicon Valley, a 20-year-old Zuck left his friends at the table for a while, only to be found later on the floor of the men's room in a state of distress. The young CEO was bawling, and in between bursts of tears, he said, "This is wrong. I can't do this. I gave my word."

What was the dilemma?

Zuckerberg was troubled over a matter of investment. He was looking for a second round of capital after the initial $500,000 seed funding from angel investors led by legendary venture capitalist Peter Thiel on September 1, 2014. The next round of funding would be the key to fully unlocking the potential of Facebook.

In 2015, Zuckerberg had made it through several presentations to venture capitalists and had agreed upon an investment deal with then–*Washington Post* owner Don Graham worth $6 million for 10 percent ownership. Graham was more than willing to pay the amount and step out of the way of Zuckerberg's machine in order to let the wunderkind perform his magic. Since Graham owned the *Post*, a newspaper that covered the build of Facebook, he preferred to stay to the rear and not interfere. Moreover, he trusted Zuckerberg.

"He was a very unusual 20-year-old," Graham recalls. "He was at that point shy and awkward, but super thoughtful. You would ask him a question and he would pause before answering it. I wasn't entirely sure why he was pausing—I didn't know if I had insulted him or something—but he was thinking, and we in Washington are not used to people thinking when you ask them a question."

As Zuckerberg and Graham hashed out the final details, Accel Partners came sniffing around, unexpectedly. The venture capital firm in Palo Alto needed a fresh score. After years of success in the 1990s with big telecommunication and software ventures, it had not been a major player for a while in the Valley, and the talk was that the company had lost its magic. Accel's comanaging partner Jim Breyer was looking to prove to his investors that his company still had its mojo, and as luck had it for Zuckerberg, at the top of the company's short list of "prepared mind initiatives" was "social and new media applications."

While Zuckerberg had been searching out venture capitalists, Accel was not on his list. Therefore, after careful research, Kevin Efrusy, an Accel principal at the time, found Zuck instead. As Zuckerberg was in the midst of celebrating a major oral agreement with Graham, Accel made calls and sent e-mails, but no one replied. Zuckerberg and crew found Accel irrelevant and was intentionally ignoring it. So, on April 1, 2005, Efrusy showed up at the Facebook office, which was a scattered mess of half-assembled IKEA furniture, multicolored graffiti art on the walls, including nudes, and a smattering of half-filled liquor bottles from a party the night before.

The chaos did not deter Efrusy because the website numbers were there, along with a major buzz around the platform. Millions of students were already addicted to Facebook, calling it the hub of their university experience, so Efrusy went back to his offices to formulate a quick plan with key members of Accel.

A few days later, Efrusy was back at the Facebook office. The Facebook skeleton crew was in the middle of a meeting at the time, and Efrusy interrupted them to slap a deal on the table for $10 million, before saying to the group, "We have full conviction about it. We will move heaven and earth to make this a successful company." Then he left.

The room was aglow except for Zuckerberg, who asked, "What about the *Post?*" No one else cared. That night, in the bathroom at the Village Pub, Zuckerberg was caught up in a moral dilemma. A shift was occurring, as the stakes got higher. He got up off the floor that night, collected himself, and called Graham. "Don, I haven't talked to you since we agreed on terms, and since then I've had a much higher offer from a venture capital firm out here," Zuckerberg said.

Graham was disappointed, surprised, and impressed by the phone call. "I just thought to myself, 'Wow, for 20 years old that is impressive—he's not calling to tell me he's taking the other guy's money. He's calling me to talk it out,'" Graham recalled in *The Facebook Effect.*

However, for Graham, there was no context for raising the investment amount for such a young, small, and relatively unproven company. "Mark, I'll release you from your moral dilemma," Graham said. "Go ahead and take their money and develop the company, and all the best."

Zuckerberg went on to sign an investment deal with Accel that in the end, reached $12.7 million for 15 percent of the company.[23]

While this decision was vital to helping Facebook move forward, it was no less hard on Zuckerberg.

Zuckerberg Saves the World

On February 16, 2017, Zuckerberg released a 6,000-word opus. *Buzzfeed* called it the "Zuck Doctrine" and viewed it as a plan for Zuckerberg to "more actively use his platform's power to intervene in people's lives in real ways."[24] *Recode* called it the "Mark Manifesto." In an interview with *Recode,* Zuckerberg claimed, "No one single event triggered this."[25]

While the Facebook CEO noted the heightened tension of political discourse under President Donald Trump, he said it was not the reason behind his worldview diatribe. "I have been thinking about these things for a long time . . . my views have just become more nuanced."[26]

In the open letter that he wrote himself, he pushed hard on issues he has mostly avoided through the years, and the tone of it all came from a place in which solid ground had shifted. His social plaything had made some real noise as a distributor of media and a political tool in the last few years, particularly during election cycles, and he understood that any stance he takes, along with the self-regulations he puts in place, would influence a world of users, and the world itself. He does not take this position lightly.

Zuckerberg sells "social," and he has become Silicon Valley's most active and earnest leader. His world awareness is a part of his inner being now, and he has grown to realize that his responsibility to society is greater than that of CNN and FOX News, or any news outlet, for he carries all of their newsgathering through shared pages of information across his multibillion-person platform. Good or bad, his invention has become the meeting place where many folks get their daily news fix.

These big-picture issues create agony within him, and they regularly spawn controversy outside of him, and those thoughts came through in his manifesto, which covered fake news, terrorism, polarizing politics, online safety, and even artificial intelligence.

"Everyone who cares about that idea of connecting the world will need to play a bigger role and take some responsibility for making sure that the global community works for everyone," Zuckerberg said from the Facebook campus. "Without that, it is no longer a given that the world will move in this direction on the time horizon that we once thought it would."[27]

While he does not have all of the answers to a world that is currently on tilt, he thinks his mechanism of information dissemination can find a cure, but he is not completely sure.

"The things that are happening in our world now are all about the social world not being what people need and I felt like I had to address that," he said. "One of the ideas I am focused on is common understanding. . . . If I could wave a magic wand and get rid of all misinformation, I would. But people would still use some sets of facts, the true facts, in order to fit whatever bias they have. . . . The idea of connecting the world was not controversial, but now globalization has moved so quickly, many feel left behind and that is picking up in volume. . . . The question is do we come together more or reverse course and separate?"[28]

Zuckerberg leans toward coming together, which includes figuring out ways to align people who come from different worlds and have different worldviews. This is not an easy process.

"We started with friends and family, which is the foundation of society. We always tried to offer that once we got out of the phase as a US college service," he said. "We now have to build a global infrastructure that works for everyone. No matter how good your economic structure, you are going to need a social structure to support you."[29]

For all of its years, Facebook's mission has been to make the world more open and connected through a values-neutral portal. Regardless of Zuckerberg's very distinct beliefs for creating his platform, he has rarely intervened in how people use it. There are sparse community guidelines and a News Feed that he has tweaked for quality, and that has been it as far as censorship goes. However, in his sweeping and extraordinary letter, Zuck signaled that he would more actively use his website's power to intervene in people's lives in a real way—whether by merely providing them with new ideas or by taking serious actions to prevent his users from harming themselves or others. In other words, Facebook is embracing humanity's intended values and incorporating them into his broader technological goal to connect the world.

"A lot of the biggest opportunities, whether it's making sure that everyone around the world has freedom and prosperity or we can eradicate all these diseases or lift people out of poverty," he told *Buzzfeed*. "All those opportunities, and also a lot of the big challenges—like fighting climate change or the fact that a civil war in one country leads to a refugee crisis across continents—these are not only national problems, they're global problems. I do feel like there's this sense that we don't have all the right infrastructure for dealing with that today. That's a thing that needs to get built."[30]

Facebook and the Future

While some people protest the site's embedded place in the culture of humanity, Zuckerberg and his staff are proud of their creation. "It shocks me that people still think this is like a trivial thing," said Facebook engineer Adam Bosworth. "Like it's a distraction or it's a procrastination tool. This is so fundamentally human, to reach out and connect with people around us."[31]

Facebook project manager Sam Lessin looks at the website in an even larger way. "You get at most one—if you're incredibly lucky, two—shots, maybe in your lifetime to actually truly affect the course of a major piece of evolution, which is what I see Facebook as."[32]

Maybe we should let Zuckerberg explain himself in the end, because regardless of how you feel about his character when he speaks, he is forthright and transparent. He has never been caught in a lie as it applies to his values and vision.

"I often say inside the company that my goal was never to create a company," he said. "A lot of people misinterpret that as if I don't care about revenue or profit or any of those things. But what not being just a company means is not being, just that—it means building something that makes a really big change in the world.

"The craziest thing to me in all this is that I remember having these conversations with my friends when I was in college. We would sort of take it as an assumption that the world would get to the state where it is now. But, we figured, we're just college kids. Why were we the people who were most qualified to do that? I mean, that's crazy! I guess what it probably turns out is, other people didn't care as much as we did."[33]

When *Time* made Zuckerberg its Person of the Year, the editors explained their decision in this way:

> For connecting half a billion people and mapping the social relations among them (something that has never been done before); for creating a system of exchanging information that has become both indispensable and sometimes a little scary; and finally, for changing how we all live our lives in ways that are innovative and even optimistic.[34]

From his early youth until the present, Mark Zuckerberg's mind has been based in the distant future. He is constantly pushing innovation that will disrupt the status quo and usher in a better tomorrow. Through mandating these visions into reality, the people of the world are closer.

CHAPTER 9

EFFECTIVE LEADERSHIP STYLES AND THE MANDATE DRIVEN LEADER

Management is doing things right; leadership is doing the right things.
—PETER DRUCKER, Best Selling Author
and Management Consultant

An old man, a boy, and a donkey were going to town. The boy rode on the donkey, and the old man walked. As they went along, they passed some people who remarked it was a shame the old man was walking and the boy was riding. The man and boy thought maybe the critics were right, so they changed positions.

Later, they passed some people who remarked, "What a shame; he makes that little boy walk." They then decided they both would walk!

Soon they passed some more people who thought they were stupid to walk when they had a decent donkey to ride. So they both rode the donkey.

Now they passed people who shamed them by saying how awful to put such a load on a poor donkey. The boy and man said they were probably right, so they decided to carry the donkey. As they crossed the bridge, they lost their grip on the animal, and he fell into the river and drowned.[1]

While we may have heard this story in many different incarnations, each version imparts a valuable message about the risks of overreacting to the opinions of others. Sure we want to listen. Often, we'll give those opinions consideration. On some occasions, we'll even realize we need to change our actions. What we don't want to do, however, is panic when we hear conflicting opinion and constantly change our vision and strategies, often in ways that don't make any sense. A clear sign of effective leaders is that they take input but ultimately understand the decision is ultimately theirs to make and own.

So how do we know what effective leadership looks like? To gain some insight, just pick up a copy of the *Harvard Business Review*. Rarely does an issue pass without an article on leadership. One of the more interesting articles in the past few years comes from Kevin Sharer, who was the CEO of Amgen for more than a dozen years. For those not familiar with Amgen, it is a large pharmaceutical firm that has shown significant growth over the past decade. Sharer points out that he expected leaders at Amgen to act as role models, deliver results in the *right* way, empower diverse teams, and *motivate others with a vision*. One thing they should not do is imitate some flavor-of-the-moment leadership trend that may or may not have any value. Far from being a momentary trend, Mandate Driven Leadership has been proven effective in many varying leadership styles.

Mandate Driven Leadership Relative to Established Leadership Models

When we think about Mandate Driven Leadership, how does it fit with a servant and transformational leadership approach used by someone like Dr. Martin Luther King? How might it be integrated into a directive leader like Jack Welch? I would provide some examples of great consensus-driven leaders, but to be honest, there don't seem to be too many specific examples of those.

Profiled later in this book is Bill Gates, founder of Microsoft. He was clearly a Mandate Driven Leader. Microsoft at its birth was singularly focused on transforming how society can use technology, specifically the desktop PC, to transform and better the world. This was not only Bill Gates's vision, but also his mandate. And during these early days, Gates was unrelenting in driving this vision forward. As time has gone on and he has been able to let Microsoft run without him, Gates has transferred this Mandate Driven Leadership approach to his charitable work.

The Bill & Melinda Gates Foundation is by far the largest philanthropic organization in the world with an endowment exceeding $45 billion. The focus is on "improving people's health and wellbeing, helping individuals lift themselves out of hunger and extreme poverty." It is their belief that education coupled with technology enablers plays a critical part in this objective. The Foundation now spends more each year on health issues than most individual countries of the world. However, some academics have questioned the spending priorities of the Foundation. Researchers from Oxford published an article in 2008 questioning whether the Foundation was prioritizing spending on infectious diseases affecting highly developed countries over the chronic health problems of the poor. An often-cited example is the Foundation's funding for the eradication of polio and whether this "was really a priority of wealthy nations and not necessarily developing ones, many of which were more preoccupied with battling illnesses that created a far greater health burden in their nations." While the critics have their say, as he did at Microsoft, Gates continues to propel his vision for the Foundation forward without being distracted by the naysayers.

This focus on what needs to be done without getting bogged down in what the critics say makes Bill Gates a Mandate Driven Leader. A fair question, however, is, is Gates also a a servant leader? Or is Gates a directive leader or an authoritarian leader? What about a transformational leader? Or does his habit of poring through lines of code even at the CEO level during his Microsoft days make him more of a transactional leader? Do any of those classifications even matter? The answer is yes and no because these different leadership styles all have a place depending on the situation. And different leadership styles can live in harmony with a Mandate Driven Leadership style. Mandate Driven Leaders understand that they need to balance between different styles of leadership to get to the desired outcomes.

This, of course, leads to the question of whether you can be a Mandate Driven Leader within many of the accepted leadership styles. Does it align best with servant leadership or transformational leadership? Does it support transactional leadership or authentic leadership? Or is Mandate Driven Leadership just a nicer way of saying autocracy? The simple truth is that Mandate Driven Leadership enables and enhances most leadership styles and helps us avoid autocracy because it keeps the leader focused on the vision.

Full Range Model of Leadership

When we look at business articles and textbooks, three of the most popular leadership styles are transactional, transformational, and laissez-faire. These are part of what is sometimes referred to as the Full Range Model of Leadership. These three styles conceptualize how leaders engage with their teams and those in their organization. For the most part, Mandate Driven Leaders can use any of these styles, depending upon the needs and culture of the organization they are working in.

As most high school French students can tell you, *laissez-faire* roughly translates to "letting things take their own course without interfering," as in "let the people do what they want to." Some consider this an absence of leadership, and leaders who exhibit this as avoiding responsibility. For the most part, teams and employees are left to themselves, and there is a notable absence of fixed rules and processes. It is very rare to see a Mandate Driven Leader using this style. The exception is Mandate Driven Leaders who have extreme trust in their management. Many Mandate Driven Leaders have trusted lieutenants, individuals in whom, through experience, they can have absolute trust for bringing to reality the desired outcome. In such a case, Mandate Driven Leaders will not only monitor the outcomes but will also be laser-focused on making sure they select the right people for the team. Everything in between is left alone, and it can be very risky.

Transactional leadership is focused on the interactions between a leader and followers, as well as the transactional execution of workplace processes. Transactional leaders promote compliance through rewards and punishments. These leaders use more of the traditional carrot-and-stick approach that is always popular. They are what some people like to call operational managers because transactional leaders are focused on keeping the ball moving forward.

Given that many of the Mandate Driven Leaders we are discussing here have made major disruptions in their given industries, how can a transactional leader do this? Here's the thing: you can't disrupt an industry if you can't keep the lights on long enough to make an impact. As we discussed earlier, Mandate Driven Leaders have to make decisions that will maintain the organization as an ongoing concern. If we look back to the original Internet bubble, that landscape is littered with stories of visionary leaders who spent more time building consensus than executing on operational imperatives and ended up burning through their venture capital before anything got accomplished. Mandate Driven Leaders know that you can't transform if you can't transact.

This, of course, brings us to transformational leadership, which is much more about the leader creating a need for change than about inspiring and empowering their followers to achieve next-level performance. Some transformational leaders break new ground in the world of business; others promote social good. While there are varying definitions of what (and even who) is a transformational leader, the common denominator seems to be that they create loyal and high-performing followers. They are also known for having a lasting impact. The generally accepted view is that transformational leaders develop these loyal followers through four key components, commonly referred to as the 4Is:

- ▶ Idealized Influence (II). Leaders act as a role model for what their followers want to be.
- ▶ Inspirational Motivation (IM). Leaders inspire and motivate their followers.
- ▶ Individualized Consideration (IC). Leaders demonstrate genuine concern for those around them.
- ▶ Intellectual Stimulation (IS). Leaders challenge their teams to be innovative and creative.

The importance of IC and IS cannot be understated because these are part of the characteristics that differentiate a transformational leader from someone who is just charismatic. Where this tends to get misapplied, however, is with the idea that transformational leaders should focus on each and every individual's needs and wants. This misunderstanding is also why a Mandate Driven Leader with a transformational style will be much more effective than just someone who claims to be a transformational leader. Mandate Driven Leaders know that that individual consideration and intellectual consideration must serve the needs of the organization. To paraphrase Mr. Spock, the needs of the many do indeed outweigh the needs of the few, and Mandate Driven Leaders accept this.

Servant Leadership

This "needs of the many" idea brings us to another leadership style that is greatly enhanced by a Mandate Driven Leadership view, and that is servant leadership. Popularized by Robert Greenleaf, servant leadership grew out of his Christian worldview, to see the leader as someone who serves, rather than just someone who directs. It views leaders' role as taking care of others rather than just enhancing themselves. This focus on others has created a common misconception that servant leaders are only focused on the needs of the people who work for them. While servant leaders do consider their followers' needs and wants carefully, that consideration is in the context of the organization serving a greater good for society as a whole.

Let's say for example someone sees herself as a servant leader and sees an opportunity for developing some new and improved widget that will help feed underprivileged people. Taking the organization in that direction, however, would make things more challenging for the people in the organization, at least in the short term. Someone with only a surface-level understanding of servant leadership might assume that a servant leader would forgo that direction because she is taking care of the people in the organization first. A true servant leader, however, would make the hard choice to go toward the greater good, despite the complaints from the employees, because she knows that is the best thing to do in the long run. You don't get much more mandate driven than that.

Authentic Leadership

Another idea that is starting to get more and more academic thought is something called authentic leadership. This is a relatively nascent concept that is centered around honest relationships and leading from an ethical foundation. In fact, it is such a new concept that it has only recently begun to be included in textbooks. While particular definitions may vary, the most common conceptualizations center around four key constructs:

- ▶ Self-awareness. An ongoing process of reflection and reexamination by the leader of his or her own strength, weaknesses, and values.
- ▶ Relational transparency. Open sharing by the leader of his or her own thoughts and beliefs, balanced by a minimization of inappropriate emotions.
- ▶ Balanced processing. Solicitation by the leader of opposing viewpoints and fair-minded consideration of those viewpoints.
- ▶ Internalized moral perspective. A positive ethical foundation adhered to by the leader in his or her relationships and decisions that is resistant to outside pressures.

The first three of these constructs are about leaders being honest with themselves and others about what they are doing and why. The fourth construct is about not bowing to outside pressure when the leaders know they are right. These constructs actually work well for Mandate Driven Leaders because when a leader is focused on doing what is right rather than what is popular, there is no reason to be anything but authentic. You can say this is what we're doing, and this is why we are doing it. There is no time wasted trying to drag along the contrarians because you have a job to do. If the mandate is authentic, then the leader will be too.

Authoritarian Leadership

The last leadership style we will discuss is authoritarian. While this style has become much less popular in the modern discourse, it is still an important consideration for several reasons. The first reason is that even though many sophisticated leaders preach that this style is outdated and obsolete, quite a few of them will revert back to it when things get tough. The second reason is that there are some industries and cultures where having a more authoritarian style is not only accepted but necessary. As such, understanding when and where it is appropriate is an important part of the leadership development process. The final reason to cover it here is that we suspect that when some people hear the term Mandate Driven Leadership, they will assume it is just a repackaging of the authoritarian style for leaders who lack empathy and are totally self-absorbed. In fact, according to recent research from Brigham Young University, when we see leaders who have that kind of outrageously high narcissism, and they mix it with a little bit of humility at the right times, followers tend to perceive these same behaviors as confidence and charisma.

The authoritarian style of leadership is generally considered to be synonymous with an autocratic or dictatorial style where the leader directs all policies and procedures. The goals are set, and the decisions are made with little input (if any) from subordinates. While some sources will say that an authoritarian leader has a vision in mind, that is not always the case. In our experience, many of the most truly authoritarian leaders lack a clear vision and default to this style out of fear or self-interest. This is one of the first ways that a Mandated Driven Leader is different than an authoritarian leader. Mandate Driven Leaders always have a clear vision of where they want the company to go, and they are open and honest (authentic) about what those goals are. When we talk about Mark Zuckerberg, there was never any question in anyone's mind of where he wanted to take Facebook or what outcomes he wanted to drive.

Another defining characteristic typically associated with authoritarian leaders is lack of input from subordinates and team members. What little input they do allow comes from the "yes" crowd; they don't ever actively seek opposing views but enjoy their echo chambers. Mandate Driven Leaders, by comparison, look for different views and listen to them. Once they make a decision, however, they do not let the naysayers second-guess the direction, and they keep the organization laser-focused on its goals. Even when the goal is some crazy idea like streaming movies over the Internet.

The Mandate Driven Leadership Diamond

What makes Mandate Driven Leadership unique is that it is not just another leadership style or theory. It is a new way of understanding how successful leaders decide what agendas to pursue and then how to take the agenda to reality. It is more what some researchers might call a leadership ontology, meaning that it is about understanding how and why leaders push their organizations to reach new heights. In truth, Mandate Driven Leaders can use almost any style of leadership, as long as they are driving toward the necessary vision.

While leaders may be using many types of leadership styles, a Mandate Driven Leader exhibits the characteristics summarized by having a vision, driving to an outcome, and being unrelenting until it is accomplished. Within some of the more prolific leadership models previously discussed, a Mandate Driven Leader is always focusing on a balance between the aspects of People, Process, Outcomes, and the Vision as illustrated in Figure 9.1.

When we consider Figure 9.1, a few things become very apparent. The first is that outcomes are at the top. This is because at the end of the day those outcomes are what Mandate Driven Leaders truly care about. The rest is secondary. Sure we don't want to burn out our people and take a scorched-earth approach to our business, but Mandate Driven Leaders understand that subordinating the outcomes to other concerns is a short-term fix. As we'll discuss shortly, Mandate Driven Leaders know that they sometimes

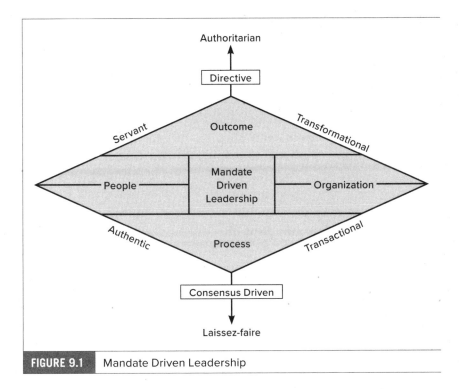

FIGURE 9.1   Mandate Driven Leadership

have to make hard, possibly unpopular, decisions to disrupt the markets for the common good.

The next thing we'll notice in this model is that People and Organization are on opposite sides of the spectrum. This is because a Mandate Driven Leader is having to constantly rebalance the needs of the organization with the needs of the individual people in it. As stated before, Mandate Driven Leaders are not heartless ogres who don't care about anyone. Quite the opposite, in fact. It is their caring about people that makes the mandate so strong. They realize and accept, however, that you cannot please everyone all the time, and there will be times when you'll have to do things that other people don't like. If the organization doesn't succeed, then no one has a job. This not only impacts the people in the organization but the people who are supported by those employees. Not only that, but if an organization with a social mission fails to consider the organization's survival as the primary concern, then the needs of the people the organization services will never be met. It is an awesome responsibility when we consider it, and one that Mandate Driven Leaders take seriously.

To illustrate this point, I'll share the story of a CEO of a financial services organization. For confidentiality, I'll refer to this person as John and won't share too much about exactly what the organization did other than that they acquired distressed assets of existing organizations and sold them at a profit. They also provided social good to help make the world a better place by doing some pretty unique things that brought capital to those who needed it. Like most organizations, however, this firm had ebbs and flows in its business. During some of those ebbs, layoffs were required. Every single layoff was gut-wrenching for John as he is a man of faith and the kind of leader who truly cared about every single person in his organization. He knew, however, that he had to put the needs of the organization first, before the needs of the individuals. If he didn't, before long there would be no organization.

Knowing that taking these unpleasant steps was critical to the long-term success of the organization didn't make these decisions any easier. Each decision to terminate someone was difficult. The most difficult one was when he had to dismiss his own brother-in-law. He didn't want to do it, but the numbers demanded it. He knew he was going to hear about it later, but Mandate Driven Leaders know that they have to make the best decisions they can and trust the process, even if they won't be popular or appreciated in the short term.

Speaking of process, you'll also notice that Process is at the bottom of our illustration. Mandate Driven Leaders are less concerned with how their teams get there, as long as they get there, within reason of course. As we mentioned in a previous chapter, Mandate Driven Leaders delegate the process but micromanage the outcome.

This perspective applies not only to the business process (accounting, customer service), but also for the interpersonal process (meetings, personal interaction). Many times, Mandate Driven Leaders will leave things alone and trust the people to get the job done. However, if there are things that can be done to help that along, a Mandate Driven Leader takes swift and decisive action to find the resources the team needs to move the ball forward.

What Mandate Driven Leaders do not do is let the organization fail at the altar of process, group dynamics, and consensus building. Mandate Driven Leaders accept that not everyone will be happy with every decision. As long as progress is beneficial to the organization, a small amount of momentary dissatisfaction is OK. Yes, Mandate Driven Leaders see the obvious value of team cohesion, progressive discourse, and loyalty, but by the same token, they also refuse to tolerate groupthink and counterproductive debates. At some point, you have to call the play and execute.

Some of my favorite examples of this are the stories after stories of great NFL quarterbacks showing appreciation for, and getting the input from their teams during practice and before and after the season and game. They solicit input, they watch tape, and they listen to what the backs and the line have to say. They use this input to help decide how to run the team and the plays. What you never hear, however, is about great quarterbacks asking the team what they should do *during* the game. *Should we run or throw?* Because during the game it is time for debate to be over and execution to begin. The same is true of great generals in battle situations. Most great generals will solicit the views of their lieutenants during the planning; they'll also ask for After Action Reports. Once the enemy is engaged, however, it is time stay on task. This is true no matter what business you are in or what style of leadership you are exhibiting.

Perhaps one of the more difficult concepts to discuss is how Mandate Driven Leadership does not exist in a vacuum of leadership styles. As stated before, it is more of an ontology—a set of leadership concepts and traits and relationships between them. Individuals can exude Mandate Driven Leadership whether they work within a servant leadership model or a directive one. Yes, there have been some Mandate Driven Leaders who may have strayed too close to an authoritarian model. However, most Mandate Driven Leaders recognize that while the leadership model to use may be situational, the foundational principles of Mandate Driven Leadership are more constant.

CHAPTER 10

REED HASTINGS OF NETFLIX: INNOVATION WITHOUT WALLS

*Most entrepreneurial ideas will sound crazy, stupid, and uneco-
nomic, and then they'll turn out to be right.*
— REED HASTINGS, Cofounder and CEO, Netflix

N etflix cofounder and CEO Reed Hastings has redefined television
watching in merely a decade. Much of today's current video entertainment is built around a service that he built, which allows viewers
to watch almost anything they want when they want, and as often as they
want. His mail-order DVD operation evolved into the world's leading source
for movie streaming while completely dismantling a video rental industry
within a decade and pushing the world's biggest retail giant to the side. These
days, there is even mainstream jargon affiliated with a Netflix night—"binge
watching" has become a household staple, and people count the days before
a new Netflix series premiere.

When you discuss the origins of Netflix with Reed Hastings, it is difficult
to pin him down on what exactly was the genesis moment for Netflix. He
has several stories that all sound authentic.

First is the "late fee" story—one that each of us can understand. In 2006
Hastings related to the *New York Times* that he started Netflix after getting
charged an exorbitant fee by Blockbuster for an overdue video:

> I got the idea for Netflix after my company was acquired. I had
> a big late fee for *Apollo 13*. It was six weeks late, and I owed the

video store $40. I had misplaced the cassette. It was all my fault. I didn't want to tell my wife about it. And I said to myself, "I'm going to compromise the integrity of my marriage over a late fee?" Later, on my way to the gym, I realized they had a much better business model. You could pay $30 or $40 a month and work out as little or as much as you wanted.[1]

Then, there is Hastings' "math" version of the genesis of Netflix. During a session at the Mobile World Congress in Barcelona, Spain, in February 2017, Hastings said that the Netflix idea stemmed from a math problem he learned while a Stanford graduate student. The problem required him to figure out the bandwidth of a "station wagon" loaded with data tapes. To calculate the answer, Hastings had to figure out how many tapes could fit in a station wagon, the amount of data on each tape, and the speed at which the station wagon could get to a particular destination. Later, he applied the math problem to digital distribution.

A friend told me about DVDs, and I realized, well, that's five gigabytes of data, and you can mail that very inexpensively," Hastings said. "I realized that that is a digital distribution network. And from that original exercise, it made me think, we can build Netflix first on DVDs and then eventually the Internet would catch up with the postal system and pass it.[2]

While Hastings tells these genesis stories with much aplomb, the real genesis moment is much more complex.

Visionaries in Cars Drinking Coffee

The way that Netflix actually began is different from the numerous stories Hastings has told over the years. That might not seem essential to understanding Hastings as an entrepreneur and leader, but it is a crucial element, as you will see.

Netflix cofounder Marc Randolph—who gets nary a mention these days when Hastings offers the Netflix origin story script to the media outlets that print it—has a different recollection of the days that spawned Netflix. Randolph, the original Netflix CEO, who held the title until he left in 2004, discussed Netflix's beginnings with Jon Xavier of the *Silicon Valley Business Journal* in 2014.

> These founding stories are just that—they're stories. They're constructs that we come up with to take what's a very messy process with input from many, many people, and condense it into a story which you can get across in a sentence or two. Quite frankly, with apologies, most press, that's all they want. That's the very quick bit. We morph into a story that resonates. And it's a good story, and Netflix is a story, so I'm okay with that. But you're correct if you're digging in and asking what really happened. It's a pretty far cry from what the story is.[3]

Randolph retells the story in an affable manner without a single demeaning word regarding Hastings, even though Hastings's stories are not true. There is no bitterness or animosity, even though Hastings never mentions Randolph when discussing the founding of Netflix. In fact, Randolph calls Hastings "brilliant."

Randolph describes a plane ride to Boston while he worked with Hastings at Pure Atria, a software debugging company, which Hastings founded.

"Before your seat belt's even on, Reed's leaning in," Randolph said of Hastings, who was the CEO of Pure Atria, while Randolph was VP of corporate marketing. "Then, begins his intense discussion, and tutorial, and exploration of ideas that pretty much continued unrelentingly for five hours and forty minutes. And I'm going, 'Holy shit, this guy has unbelievable capacity, and range of curiosity, and ways to create ideas and assimilate them in different ways.'"

Randolph realized that Hastings was going to create something huge, and the two worked together well as individuals within Pure Atria because they both had analytical minds. When the company was acquired in 1996, and the acquisition left them both without a job, they became close friends. At the time, the two were, basically, on loan to the acquiring company as the keys were being passed, so the two carpooled to the office every day because they lived close to one another in Santa Cruz.

During those car rides, Hastings discussed going back to college to get another degree, but Randolph had different plans for him going forward. On those trips to work through Silicon Valley, Randolph discussed e-commerce ideas with Hastings, a relatively new notion in 1996 but a booming market.

"We used that commute time to brainstorm what might work. And these were very wide-ranging sessions and they basically started by one of us getting in the car and saying, 'What's the criteria for something that is going to be successful?' or 'What's a trend that we could leverage?'"[4] Hastings and Randolph would discuss far-reaching ideas and vision about how this new digital landscape that was rapidly growing could be used to disrupt an industry. They had heard a recent venture, Amazon, was growing exponentially selling books online, and Hastings and Randolph, at least in the car during this commute, wanted to identify a concept that had equal potential.

They stayed away from commoditized business ideas like selling music or videos, but they liked the idea of creating an e-commerce site based on video rentals. However, at the time, VHS tapes were the medium of delivery, which created numerous logistical challenges in terms of shipping. The tapes weighed too much and would require extravagant postal fees to get them from a distribution center to the customer and then back to the original hub. After toying with this concept over several months of commuting, the distribution hurdle seemed too great, so they shelved this idea.

Then, in the summer of 1996, Hastings and Randolph began reading about DVD technology. This new format for video distribution was more compact, lighter, and flexible, and it held more data at better qualities than the VHS format. The DVD format was already being test-marketed in quite a few cities with plans for mass distribution in the works. Hastings and Randolph's intuition was that the DVD format had an obvious competitive edge over VHS, and they began discussing the opportunities if DVD became the default standard for video playback.

They tested the idea of sending DVDs through the mail and found that it could be a viable business model, and not only that, an idea that could disrupt the rental market if they could get in front of the competition because DVDs were a brand-new notion in the marketplace at the time.

> One of the founding myth stories that is actually very true is the fact that Reed and I did go down to Logo's in Santa Cruz and bought a used CD, and then went to one of the little gift shop stores on Pacific Avenue. We bought ourselves one of those little blue envelopes that you put the greeting cards in and we mailed a CD to Reed's house. We go up the steps to the Santa Cruz Post Office and dropped it in with a single first-class stamp and by the next day when he came to pick me up,

he had the envelope in his hand. It had gotten to his house with the unbroken CD in it. That was the moment where the two of us looked at each other and said, "This idea just might work."[5]

Netflix launched on April 15, 1998. Two decades later, video streaming on Netflix is much more prevalent, but the firm started as a mail-order DVD rental company with 30 employees and 925 DVDs. It moved to a subscription service in 1998. Today, Netflix, with more than 139 million subscribers, is the preeminent content distribution company that now produces its own award-winning content.

To set the record straight, sandwiched between the various origin stories, there was a moment when Hastings told the truth to *Inc.* magazine in 2005, almost.

> Netflix was originally a single rental service, but the subscription model was one of a few ideas we had—so there was no "Aha! Moment." Having unlimited due dates and no late fees has worked in a powerful way and now seems obvious, but at that time we had no idea if consumers would even build and use an online queue. It was still a dial-up, VHS world and most video stores didn't carry DVDs, so we were able to sign up early adopters. By the time there were enough DVD owners, we had gotten better and better, and broadband had grown.[6]

What started as visionaries in cars having coffee is now a company worth $155 billion, and Hastings has a net worth exceeding $2 billion.

The more you learn about Hastings, the more you will find that even though he has a mathematics degree and a master's in engineering, he is mostly a psychologist and a politician, with a list of numerous paradoxes. That is why he chooses certain Netflix myths from an endless cache, according to the audience before him, telling them what they want to hear, in order to recruit customers and investors.

In Hastings, you will find a Mandate Driven Leader, but not in the style of Jobs or Bezos or Zuckerberg. Yes, Hastings, as with all Mandate Driven Leaders, had a vision and drove to an outcome. However, unlike Jobs, Bezos, or Zuckerberg, Hastings will readily admit that he is not *The Product Guy*, mandating specific visions of product development and propelling them to reality. He gives his teams wide latitude in product development. "There's this whole motif that to be a great CEO you have to be a great product person," Hastings has said. "That's intoxicating and fun, but you build in incredible amounts of dependence on yourselves. You're much stronger building a distributed set of great thinkers." However, make no mistake, Hastings is the holder of the strategy and propelling that strategy forward to the outcome. In fact, Netflix was so named because Hastings knew that content distribution would eventually be streamed over the "Net" even before the technology was there to make that happen.

Hastings also claims that as a CEO, he chooses to make as few decisions as possible and gives his employees unlimited freedom, but it is all a wily subterfuge, as you will see. Hastings uses his Mandate Driven Leadership style to mandate a culture that is the heartbeat and the head of Netflix. He is a spin doctor who has figured out a way to gently manipulate the minds of his employees into becoming near clones of himself. This culture results in the key characteristics and personality traits important to Hastings being ingrained into the rank and file of Netflix.

In other words, if Hastings is not mandating directly, his culture is. And, this successful style took some time to polish.

From Boston to Africa to California

Wilmot Reed Hastings was born in Boston, Massachusetts, on October 8, 1960, and grew up in the nearby suburb of Belmont in a close-knit family of five. His mother, Joan, was a philanthropist and volunteer for numerous nonprofit organizations, and his father, Wilmot, was a lawyer who worked in President Richard Nixon's administration within the Department of Health, Education, and Welfare.

Hastings graduated from a private high school in Cambridge, Massachusetts, in 1978. The school, Buckingham Browne & Nichols, educates children from kindergarten to twelfth grade. It is one of the most expensive schools in the country, ranked ninth costliest by *Forbes* in 2006, and in 2007, the *Wall Street Journal* listed BB&N as one of the 50 best schools in the world for its curriculum that prepares students to enter top universities. However, Hastings was not compelled to pursue higher education or do anything extraordinary at the time of his graduation, choosing to be a salesman instead.

"I took a year off between high school and college and sold Rainbow vacuum cleaners door to door," he told the *New York Times*. "I started it as a summer job and found I liked it. As a sales pitch, I cleaned the carpet with the vacuum the customer had and then cleaned it with the Rainbow."

After a year, Hastings left the trade to attend a small liberal arts university, Bowdoin College in Maine, to study mathematics because he found math's "abstractions beautiful and engaging." He was also the head of the school's "Outing Club," where he organized student rock climbing and canoeing expeditions, and he joined the school's Marine Corps Platoon Leaders Class with the objective of becoming a military officer upon graduation. However, after a summer of rigorous Marine Corp training at Officer Candidate School in Quantico, Virginia, he reconsidered.

"I found myself questioning how we packed our backpacks and how we made our beds," he said. "My questioning wasn't particularly encouraged, and I realized I might be better off in the Peace Corps. I petitioned the recruiting office and left the Marines."

The attempt to enter the Marines came from Hastings's deep desire to serve, as his parents did for much of their lives, so he became a Peace Corps volunteer in rural Africa on the day of his college graduation. His base became Swaziland, a landlocked monarchy between South Africa and Mozambique. He taught geometry, algebra, and differential equations to 800 high school students. "Either that developed my risk tolerance, or it was symptomatic of it," he told the *Times*. "We had no electricity and cooked with propane and wood. Corn was our staple. I lived in a thatch hut and slept on a cot."

During the three years, he only went home once to attend his sister's wedding. He holds fond memories of his African high school students graduating in a colorful and traditional ceremony, and considers his experience in Africa extremely satisfying, saying, "Taking smart risks can be very gratifying. Guessing right is a skill developed over time. Not all smart risks work out, but many of them do."

In 1985, Hastings took a two-hour bus trip to Mbabane, the capital of Swaziland, to take the Graduate Record Examination (GRE). After failing to get into the Massachusetts Institute of Technology (MIT) in an attempt to go to school near his family, he applied to Stanford and was accepted.

"I had never been to California and arrived in late summer," he said. "Driving up to the campus I saw palm trees. It was dry and brown. I asked myself, 'Where's the ivy?' Within a week I had fallen in love with California."

According to *USA Today*, he sent word back to his parents, "You'll never see me again. I've found nirvana."[7]

Underwater and Over His Head

After Hastings finished graduate school in 1988, he worked for Schlumberger Palo Alto Research, a technology lab, but it closed a few months later. Then, he moved over to a company called Coherent Thought, where he debugged software, but after a year there, he was unfulfilled, right as he turned 30. It was time for him to take a risk and put together his own start-up.

"Once you have hitchhiked across Africa with ten bucks in your pocket, starting a business doesn't seem too intimidating," he commented.[8]

Hastings's vision for his first start-up was to be the source of tools to help engineers debug software. Many counseled him that he had no breakthrough software idea and he would be competing against many established players. Like most Mandate Driven Leaders, Hastings had a vision to grow a portfolio, and he was not going to shy away from the challenge. He launched his company, Pure Software, in 1991. The company grew fast through acquisitions and mergers, and in 1996 it changed its name to Pure Atria, after its biggest merger with a company called Atria. The most difficult challenge for Hastings was the clash of cultures. Over the years the acquisitions and fusing of employee bases created chaos, and the young entrepreneur had little experience as a leader to draw from in an attempt to right the ship.

> "As the company grew from 10 to 40 to 120 to 320 to 640 employees, I found I was definitely underwater and over my head," he told the *New York Times*, and in *Inc.*, he said, "Management was my biggest challenge; every year there were twice as many people, and it was trial by fire. I was unprepared for the complexities and personalities."[9]

Regardless of the anxiety Hastings felt as he rapidly moved from an engineer to a CEO, the company had a stellar offering, going from a niche item to a broad portfolio of offerings, and revenue doubled every year. While others concentrated on research and development and new product launches, Hastings continued mandating acquisitions to broaden and deepen the portfolio. In 1997, Hastings's company was too big to ignore, and the hunter became the hunted. In 1997, Hastings was approached by rival company Rational Software, which purchased Pure Atria for $750 million. Hastings was now a rich man and ready to move to his next challenge. He had the money he needed to start Netflix, but he didn't make that move right away or take the lead. Initially, Randolph took the reins at Netflix while its business plan came into fruition as the two carpooled together for several months after the acquisition.

Start-Up Netflix Takes Down a Giant

Marc Randolph was a seasoned professional when he first met Hastings. Within a year of graduating from Hamilton College in Clinton, New York, in 1981, he began a career in marketing, rising quickly to become the VP of marketing for software company Borland International in only five years. Basically, Randolph provided the company's voice to consumers from a non-technical point of view, not something the engineers who ran Silicon Valley could do very well. In 1996, he ended up with Hastings at Pure Atria after the merger but wasn't there long before the company was swallowed up.

Hastings's desires were clearly in education at the time that Pure Atria was acquired. He returned to Stanford to work on a degree in education, assisted the California State Board of Education with passing new education legislation, and eventually becoming the president of the California school board. On the other hand, Randolph focused on the idea that became Netflix.

"I plunged into this period of most of the summer, working through the details," Randolph told Xavier. "If we're going to do this, how would it work? You get to this point—and of course, I was mostly doing this work by myself—but Reed, every morning and evening on the car ride, he checked in on how it was going with ideas, costs, how to overcome certain things."[10]

Randolph got to a point where all the research had been done and no more plans could be made, so there was only one last step: to launch. It was the hardest step, though, because launching often leads to failure, and if failure comes, it is not only costly, but it becomes a part of a person's legacy.

Hastings was a man of action, not words. He was not going to take the helm at Netflix and mandate the vision to outcome, but he was going to mandate Randolph do just that.

"The only way to do it is to jump," Randolph recalls Reed telling him. "And Reed is phenomenal. I considered myself a pretty good entrepreneur, and he is a phenomenal entrepreneur. And he is going, 'The only way to figure this out is to do it,' and he wrote that first big check. He was the first angel. So at that time, the idea is that I'd go off, I'd run this company, and he'd be the chair and the angel. And he'd be able to dabble. He'd be the education guy, and occasionally he'd be able to drop in and see how things were going."

Hastings tells a different story, one that is simplistic and gets to the point. Well, he tells numerous simple creation stories as has been discussed, but more curiously, he never mentions Randolph in any of them, while Randolph extols Hastings's greatness at great length. For example, when Hastings told the following story to *Fortune* in 2009, the "friend" is his partner, a founding member of Netflix, Randolph, who did much of the work while Hastings flung himself into education from a distance.

"I started to investigate the idea of how to create a movie-rental business by mail," Hastings said. "I didn't know about DVDs, and then a friend of mine told me they were coming. I ran out to Tower Records in Santa Cruz, California, and mailed CDs to myself, just a disc in an envelope. It was a long 24 hours until the mail arrived back at my house, and I ripped them open, and they were all in great shape. That was the big excitement point."[11]

Hastings and Randolph founded Netflix in 1997 and launched it a year later, at a time when people dropped by a video store whenever they wanted to watch a movie at home. The process involved membership and late fees, and usually involved the name Blockbuster, which at its peak had 9,000 stores and 60,000 employees.

Hastings and Randolph's vision was not universally accepted. There was no rush to further fund their enterprise, nor did every tech-savvy engineer come knocking at their door. At the time, the cofounders presented an easier approach to video rental. DVDs weighed next to nothing, so the cost to ship them was minimal. They figured that people could save time and money by renting movies online and receiving their rentals in their home mailbox. However, few homes had DVD players yet, and going down to the neighborhood Blockbuster for your weekend video rentals was almost a way of life.

"They had a big advantage, were 15 times our size, and if they started a mail-order business model two years sooner, they probably would have won," Hastings told *Insights*.[12] However, with Randolph at the helm Hastings was mandating he move their strategy forward.

Initially, Netflix charged a fee per movie rental, using Blockbuster's model, but it wasn't popular and would never bring Netflix to a position of power in the video rental industry.

"I remember thinking, God, this whole thing could go down, and we said, 'Let's try the more radical subscription idea,'" he told *Fortune*. "We knew it wouldn't be terrible, but we didn't know it would be great."[13] Many advisors, friends, and even employees told Hastings that the subscription model would prove disastrous financially. Customers were not use to subscription in this industry, so they would not subscribe. Ones that did would overuse the service, resulting in negative operating profit. However, Hastings felt the industry was ready for a threefold disruption: shift from VHS to DVD, shift from per rental to subscription, and implementation of a costly, monthly free trial program. Throwing caution to the wind, Hastings mandated all three.

On September 23, 1999, as the company floundered, the subscription model went into action. Hastings offered a free trial for a month, and 80 percent of the free trial participants moved from the free service to a paid membership after a month. The tide had turned.

In 2003, on a rainy day in Arizona, Hastings was visiting a distribution center when he received good news. "My umbrella wasn't working, and as I walked the half mile from the distribution center to the hotel, I got the message on my BlackBerry that we hit a million subscribers that day while I was walking in the rain," he said. "It was this beautiful moment where I was just so elated that we were going to make it, and that was also the first quarter that we turned profitable. It was a magic walk. Don't be afraid to change the model."

Meanwhile, the battle with Blockbuster was on, and there isn't a more clear case of disruption as Netflix moved fast and never slowed down, crushing its rival in the end. In 1999, the year that Netflix began its subscription service, Blockbuster had a value of $4.8 billion. The next year, Hastings offered Blockbuster a 49 percent stake in Netflix for $50 million. Blockbuster declined several times, and it fired Hastings up. He knew at that point that Netflix would set its own destiny by sticking to its vision.

In 2002, two major things happened for Netflix. First, it began opening regional distribution offices to reduce shipping times. Again, the prognosticators could not understand why Netflix would open up regional distribution centers. Netflix's business model was working, so why go through the expense of regional distribution to save one or two days of mail time? Hasting understood what others were not seeing. The "Net" was pushing customers to real time. While the technology for real-time streaming was not quite there yet, Netflix was positioning itself as the place for the fastest distribution of video content. If Netflix could improve content distribution by one or two days through regional distribution centers, great. Hastings mandated the change.

"Overnight delivery is so exciting to our customers, and we were getting way too many complaints from subscribers that they had to wait too long," he told *Inc.* "I learned from our mistake. We now have 36 warehouses spread out around the country."[14]

Next, in 2002, Netflix went public, opening at $15 a share and raising $82.5 million. That same year, Blockbuster bought a Super Bowl advertisement in a desperate move to drum up business, but it failed. It lost $1.6 billion in 2002.

"We erroneously concluded that Blockbuster probably wasn't going to launch a competitive effort when they hadn't by 2003," Hastings said. "Then, in 2004, they did. We thought, 'Well, they won't put much money behind it.'"

He was wrong. Blockbuster spent $500 million to compete against Netflix, which caused Hastings to tell analysts in an earnings call, "Blockbuster has thrown everything but the kitchen sink at us." The next day when the mail arrived at Netflix's headquarters, it received a kitchen sink from Blockbuster. It still was not taking Netflix seriously.

In 2006, Netflix had 6.3 million mail-order subscribers and Blockbuster had 2 million, but the video giant wouldn't maintain them. Blockbuster's numbers steadily declined, and then, when Blockbuster was met with competition from another upstart, video kiosk rental company Redbox, it was done. In 2010, Blockbuster lost $1.1 billion and was valued at $24 million. When *Fast Company* asked if its woes were because of Netflix, Blockbuster CEO Jim Keyes replied, "No, I don't know where it comes from."[15] Truly, this is perhaps the single greatest statement showing a leadership team being out of touch with reality. Blockbuster filed for bankruptcy that year and sold the company to Dish Network in 2011.

Where Hastings shined as a Mandate Driven Leader in building Netflix was truly understanding everything that was occurring in the technology and consumer realm related to video content distribution and building that into a strategy and vision and not wavering until the outcome was achieved.

"The most difficult thing is anticipating the threats ahead of time," Hastings told *Inc.* "We've got a great head of steam, fast growth, big earnings, customer growth, all kinds of good things, but we've watched a lot of companies rise and then fall, especially in Silicon Valley. So we work very hard to kind of game-theory it out: what could happen if all of these things happened, how we'd react in that scenario, strategic planning, anticipating what will come up."[16]

Radical Change to Stay Ahead

Netflix was founded in 1997 and named Netflix in anticipation that eventually consumers would stream video content over the Internet. In the era when VHS was the predominant distribution vehicle, Netflix's strategy was to move consumers from VHS to DVD and then to streaming. Hastings's and Netflix's strategy and vision were uncompromising on this bet.

In 2007, 10 years after the founding of Netflix, Netflix introduced video streaming, which allowed its customers to watch a small selection of television shows and movies from their computers. In 2008, they advanced the streaming model to include Xbox, Blu-ray, and TV set-top boxes so that customers could watch this content on their television sets. In the following years, the streaming technology advanced to become more accessible, and new markets became available in Europe. As streaming became more available, Hastings mandated one of the final phases of his strategy: focus solely on streaming.

In 2011, Netflix made a radical change in its business model, separating its mail-order DVD rental platform from its streaming service plan, and the change came with a 60 percent price increase. The DVD rental option was pushed to another website called Qwikster, and a backlash immediately occurred. Customers and investors despised the change in structure and price, but it was a gamble that Hastings was willing to make at the time in an attempt to not fall behind in the market and dissolve into one of many past relics of the technology age.

"We were so obsessed with not being the next Kodak, the next AOL, about not being the company that clung to its roots and missed the big thing," Hastings told *Insights*. "We said if there's a bias, we should be more aggressive; we have to be so aggressive it makes our skin crawl."[17]

It is here, Hastings now admits, where mistakes were made. Mandate Driven Leadership is not practiced in a vacuum. While he was mandating the correct strategy where DVD distribution would eventually be replaced by streaming, he forgot many other key leadership lessons. Hastings went rogue when making the decision to split the services and increase the rates. Within 72 hours of presenting the plan to executives and board members, Hastings had hired a CEO for Qwikster, as he looked for a way to distance Netflix from DVD rentals and focus more on streaming, and it did not require debate as far as he was concerned. Stunned employees quickly transitioned, and people involved in the DVD side were moved out of the Netflix headquarters to a new location. Even Andy Rendich, the new CEO of Qwikster, tried to talk him out of some aspects of the change, such as announcing the new structure via a casual YouTube video, but Hastings would not hear any of it.

CNET reported, "As Netflix's business blossomed and as Hastings was personally applauded in the press, he had grown much more confident in his own decision making, less receptive to taking advice from his senior management team. What's more, few of the people who could persuade Hastings or tell him he was making a mistake were around anymore,"[18] referring to the resignation of several top executives in the previous years, including CFO Barry McCarthy, who left because of conflicts with Hastings, and Ken Ross, head of worldwide communications.

Netflix immediately lost a million customers, stock shares plummeted from $300 to $155, and the adverse reaction became so huge that Reed Hastings and Netflix were parodied on *Saturday Night Live*, which mocked Hastings's decision as confusing and absurd.

Mashable asked in a headline, "The Worst Product Launch Since New Coke?," and the article went on to rip Hastings after he released the ill-advised down-home YouTube video, "I first interviewed Reed Hastings 10 years ago . . . he is one of the smartest and most amiable minds I have ever met. He predicted his company's transition to Internet streaming 10 years ago, hence the name Netflix. His incredible foresight and drive helped bring Blockbuster, once an impossibly large rival, to its knees. But the Hastings in the video is not the Hastings I knew. He seems spooked . . . he fluffed one of his lines . . . he compounds the poor communication. The whole thing leaves an impression of haste, of someone being reactive rather than proactive."[19]

In a blog, Hastings issued an apology for the debacle, writing, "I messed up. I owe everyone an explanation. It is clear from the feedback over the past few months that many members felt we lacked respect and humility in the way we announced the separation of DVD and streaming and the price changes. In hindsight, I slid into arrogance based upon past success. We have done very well for a long time by steadily improving our service, without doing much CEO communication."[20]

The new model lasted three weeks. Hastings withdrew the idea, and the move was praised by the media. The *HuffPost* wrote, "The embattled CEO of Netflix has done a good, smart, honorable and difficult thing by axing Qwikster. He has shown he is not insensitive to the demands and grievances of his customers, and that he is not afraid to admit, in public, that he made a mistake."

In the aftermath of the 2011 disaster, Hastings learned a lesson about Mandate Driven Leadership and stepping outside of consensus. It didn't work for him at that moment because he applied mandates where they were not needed. His mandates were not about moving a vision to an outcome, they were about tactics of transition where he was ill informed. He stopped listening, stopped learning and stopped communicating, a lesson he would not forget. He issued the statement, "Consumers value the simplicity Netflix has always offered, and we respect that. There is a difference between moving quickly, which Netflix has done very well for years, and moving too fast, which is what we did in this case."[21]

However, he certainly was not going to give up control of the company he had built. In fact, he would spin a way to gain more control by owning the entirety of its culture, while making his employees believe they were the ones in charge.

"Making as Few Decisions as Possible"

In 2012, Netflix made the decision to begin creating original content. Hastings was now having his team move to the final phase of his strategy: creating original content for streaming distribution. As with many of the decisions made prior, there were many loud naysayers. Why take on another established industry—license the content like everyone else. Hastings knew better—as the world shifts to the streaming, subscription model created by Netflix, a key differentiator would be original content.

His mandate to move forward with this vision was clear. However, Hastings knew that long term Netflix must be powered by a vision and unrelenting drive to an outcome culture more than driven by one man. This is where Hastings begins to differentiate himself from some of the other Mandate Driven Leaders. His successful efforts in mandating a distinctive culture at Netflix is in many ways his proxy for being the single holder of that vision.

One of the first meetings to affirm the move into original content occurred in 2011. *House of Cards* was the debut of original content for Netflix, making its premiere on February 1, 2013. The meeting that took place to present the idea of taking the show to production lasted only 30 minutes before Hastings gave the green light to proceed with the series. He was immediately satisfied with the groundwork that had been laid by his team, and he did not want to muddy the waters by flexing any muscle just to say he played a part in its final development.

"I take pride in making as few decisions as possible, as opposed to making as many as possible," Hastings told *Insights*. "It's creating a sense in your employees that 'If I want to make a difference, I can make a difference.'"[22]

Along with the freedom that Hastings purposefully gives to his employees comes the rigors of responsibility, which demand the highest level of performance on a daily basis. There is no room for mediocrity on his staff.

"Adequate performance gets a generous severance package," he continued. "We turn over a lot of people."

Before Netflix, when Hastings was the CEO of his start-up company, he claimed that he was at times an ineffective executive officer in the area of culture and development and that lack of effectiveness brought chaos with it. It was the first time that he had been the leader of anything, and he failed to provide honest critiques to his failing employees for fear that he might inflame a situation or hurt someone's feelings.

"I was uncomfortable about being honest with people because I valued kindness and consideration," he said during a Q&A session at *The New Yorker*'s TechFest in 2016. "And those are good values too, but honesty is really important at work. I'd be frustrated with my employees, but I wouldn't really tell them, and it would, of course, manifest itself, and it took me a long time to have the courage to be completely honest with them."[23]

Blunt communication isn't an issue at Netflix, where the truth is told out of obligation. The company is also well known for its high standards and quick trigger when it comes to removing employees who do not contribute.

"Netflix is definitely more cutthroat about firing 'dead weight' than every other company I worked for," a Netflix employee wrote in a 2016 Reddit AMA (ask me anything). "If you're not working out for whatever reason, there's no reason to keep you."[24]

This outcome driven culture at Netflix has been created through the Mandate Driven Leadership style of Hastings. He has taken traits, characteristics, and philosophies he believes are critical to Netflix's success and, through mandate, institutionalized them within the organization.

A released 2009 PowerPoint slide deck that Hastings used to summarize the management style at Netflix reveals the importance he places on "seeking excellence" in all things that are produced by employees at his company. The nine behaviors and values he holds dear are not the typical collection of broad value statements that many companies circle their wagons around, such as integrity, communication, respect, and excellence. Netflix has a list of "behaviors and skills" that its colleagues must abide by to get hired, maintain a job, and get promoted, and Hastings himself directly details the nine values so that there is no disconnect:

Judgment

- You make wise decisions (people, technical, business, and creative) despite ambiguity
- You identify root causes and get beyond treating symptoms
- You think strategically, and can articulate what you are, *and are not*, trying to do
- You smartly separate what must be done well now, and what can be improved later

Communication

- You listen well, instead of reacting fast, so you can better understand
- You are concise and articulate in speech and writing
- You treat people with respect independent of their status or disagreement with you
- You maintain calm poise in stressful situations

Impact

- You accomplish amazing amounts of important work
- You demonstrate consistently strong performance so colleagues can rely upon you
- You focus on great results rather than on the process
- You exhibit bias-to-action and avoid analysis-paralysis

Curiosity

- You learn rapidly and eagerly
- You seek to understand our strategy, market, customers, and suppliers
- You are broadly knowledgeable about business, technology, and entertainment
- You contribute effectively outside of your specialty

Innovation

- You re-conceptualize issues to discover practical solutions to hard problems
- You challenge prevailing assumptions when warranted, and suggest better approaches

- You create new ideas that prove useful
- You keep us nimble by minimizing complexity and finding time to simplify

Courage
- You say what you think even if it is controversial
- You make tough decisions without agonizing
- You take smart risks
- You question actions inconsistent with our values

Passion
- You inspire others with your thirst for excellence
- You care intensely about Netflix's success
- You celebrate wins
- You are tenacious

Honesty
- You are known for candor and directness
- You are non-political when you disagree with others
- You only say things about fellow employees you will say to their face
- You are quick to admit mistakes

Selflessness
- You seek what is best for Netflix, rather than best for yourself or your group
- You are ego-less when searching for the best ideas
- You make time to help colleagues
- You share information openly and proactively[25]

Let's be clear, these nine "behaviors and skills" are mandates. While, Hastings allows "freedom" and "makes few decisions" and eschews "processes" over action, his collection of ideas across these nine values alone represent the heart of Hastings. Also, consider that these nine slides are only a small portion of the 125 densely populated slides that cover every aspect of company culture. These slides are critical for new and existing employees, essentially becoming orders that, if not abided by, result in rapid extraction.

From the initial interview of prospective employees, Netflix seeks a particular type of person, according to the Reddit AMA, in which the Netflix employee said, "About 40 to 50 percent of the interview is about making sure your personality is compatible with our company culture. The rest is about making sure you're technically capable. They flew me out and interviewed me for eight hours. It seemed really easy at the time, but I now realize that a lot of the questions were checking that my personality was a fit for the company."[26]

Nothing else matters beyond technical capability and culture fit. That might seem like the criteria for every company, but large companies usually can't monitor for culture fit because it is difficult enough to find a good technical fit—and consider what else the employee told the Reddit audience, which is very different from most companies:

1. Education has no weight in the hiring process. "I'm a college drop-out. I haven't heard a single person discuss education or degrees," the employee wrote. "When you're working with people who have 5, 10, or even more years of experience, education doesn't matter anymore. It's all about what problems you have the knowledge to solve."

2. There are no entry-level positions, according to the employee. Netflix is not trying to save a dollar by looking for young talent. It will take whoever qualifies and is a good fit regardless of age.

3. There are no hierarchies, no "orders," only "context," she continued, abiding by the company notion that Hastings has a no-procedures company culture.

As you read through the details of Hastings's nine values for Netflix employees, you quickly see the traits of a Mandate Driven Leader embedded in them. One detail of the nine values is "You think strategically, and can articulate what you are, *and are not*, trying to do." Mandate Driven Leaders embrace vision and change that propels that vision forward. They demand that individuals think and understand strategy, not just process. Hastings also says that he avoids creating company SOPs (standard operating procedures) and other business processes that he believes limit intellectuality, curiosity, and creativity. "People tend to think that they need a process for everything, and once in a while you hear, 'We're going to dummy-proof it.' But if you dummy-proof the process, you only get dummies to work there,"

Hastings says. "That's why we're so opposed to that and focused on giving people great freedom. They'll make mistakes, of course, but you'll get a lot of great ideas."

Another detail under the nine values is "You exhibit bias-to-action and avoid analysis-paralysis." Mandate Driven Leaders are outcome oriented. Outcomes are more important than style or status quo. Then, there is the value of "You are tenacious." Mandate Driven Leaders are unrelenting in their drive to propel the vision to reality. Phrases like "can't be done," "not realistic," "not enough time" are not heard or accepted by Mandate Driven Leaders.

Hidden within these slides, we see that Hastings, with little doubt, pushes mandates down a funnel to his staff with the grace of a hypnotist. He manipulates his employees' minds into believing that there is freedom in each decision. While these 125 slides act as an employee culture handbook, they read more like a manifesto from a directive leader.

In many of the slides, there is the discussion of "high performance" and "severance" if high levels are not reached. There are other ideas as well. In one of the slides, employees find a definition for the office environment: "Great workplace: stunning colleagues . . . great workplace is not espresso, lush benefits, sushi lunches, grand parties, or nice offices."[27]

Another slide asks, "Which of my people, if they told me they were leaving for a similar job at a peer company, would I fight hard to keep at Netflix?"[28]

Additional slides remark that they are not interested in "Brilliant Jerks" and that people who "value job security and stability over performance" will realize quickly Netflix is "not right for them." Described another way, Hastings used a sports analogy, telling the *Financial Times*, "If you want job security, you don't get into sports, and you don't join Netflix."[29]

The slides discuss chaos and complexity and shrinking talent pools as a company grows, and the way to combat it is to throw out the rules and kick out low performers with them. On slide 59, employees find out that their freedom is not absolute, so there are some rules, and on slide 62, "good" versus "bad" processes are explained, although it has been previously celebrated that outcomes are more important than process at Netflix. On slide 72, employees are told to "Act in Netflix's Best Interest." Then, there are 57 more slides discussing how to do that.[30]

Psychology and manipulation are involved in all aspects of Netflix's company culture, which Hastings described as "pockets of fear," while the

Financial Times described the CEO himself as a "breezy and relaxed" chief executive who delivers "chilling statements with unnerving warmth."[31]

In 2004, Hastings gave his employees unlimited vacation days. In addition, his staff can choose the hours they wish to work and are in control of the amount of time it takes them to finish a project. Just recently, Netflix also gave its employees unlimited maternity and paternity leave.

The psychological ploy to "give" these unlimited days ultimately leads to employees taking fewer vacation days and producing more output than if they were given a set number of days. Travis Bradberry, the cofounder of consultancy TalentSmart, wrote in *Entrepreneur* magazine, "Freedom gives people such a strong sense of ownership and accountability that, like business owners, many end up taking no vacation at all."[32] An article in *New York* magazine agreed, saying, "While you'd expect an unlimited policy would result in more days off, it can sometimes do the very opposite, resulting in few vacation days, especially for the employees with the biggest work loads."

Adaptation Through the Years

Regardless of Hastings's psychology play, and his backdoor mandates instead of consensus, he does rely more heavily on those around him to make decisions that are not his strengths, which he understands better now after the 2011 Qwikster disaster. He has at least figured out his weaknesses through failures. For the most part, Hastings quietly propels Netflix to higher performance each year by both sticking to his vision and relentlessly enforcing the Netflix culture.

"Most good management isn't day to day," Hastings said. "It's a lot of investment in things, investments in relationships, in management. So most of my time is spent making sure that the day-to-day urgent doesn't take over for the important. If you keep working on the important, you'll have to do some of the urgent, but as little as possible."

By all accounts, Hastings's Mandate Driven Leadership style is a success. In 2013, Netflix surpassed HBO's subscription base of 29 million, the company it identifies as its biggest rival. And, it did not slow down; Netflix has just recently exceeded 139 million members, leaving its closest rivals, Amazon Prime with 30 million subscribers using video and Hulu with 32 million, significantly behind.

By Hastings mandating a very distinctive culture within Netflix, he has eliminated the need for him to micromanage the organization. In the end, he has created a culture defined by him so that he could step away and watch his company evolve as he would have evolved it if he were every employee in the company. He has established a culture that itself ensures the core values of Mandate Driven Leadership are followed.

"Being an entrepreneur is about patience and persistence, not the quick buck, and everything great is hard and takes a long time," he told *Inc*. "If we can transform the movie business by making it easier for people to discover movies they will love and for producers and directors to find the right audience through Netflix, and I can transform public education . . . that's enough for me."[33]

CHAPTER 11

CREATING A MANDATE DRIVEN CULTURE

We try to have the kind of a culture that doesn't value excuses in the sense that when you're supposed to accomplish something, and you're at a high level, then your job is to accomplish it, in spite of difficulty. And you're rewarded for dealing with that.

—PHIL LIBIN, Cofounder, former CEO of Evernote

There is a story of an executive who was working for a firm during a change in CEOs. On the day of the CEO change, the executive arrived at work early to find building maintenance removing all of the assigned parking spot signs for the executive team. When queried, building maintenance said the new CEO had requested that reserved parking for senior executives be eliminated. He had told them, "If you want a good parking spot, get in early." However, the executive noted that the CEO's car was still in his assigned spot.

While this anecdote in many incarnations is often used to cite the old adage "practice what you preach," it clearly has relevance to corporate culture. There is a saying that "culture eats strategy for breakfast." The meaning of this statement is that no matter what high ideals you put out there for your organization, the people in that organization will default to their collective habits, whether you want them to or not. As such, leaders must understand and be able to influence their culture if they want their vision and their strategy to be successful. If not, you are bound to have a major mess on your hands.

The idea that culture wins in a head-to-head battle with strategy over which will have a greater impact on an organization is not hard to understand. The reason for this is that vision as defined by the strategy is about creating a sustainable competitive advantage that allows an organization to outperform its competitors. Strategies set the foundation for the goals that the organization must meet and the plans that must be implemented to get there. The strategy is often formally defined, and its success is determined by how well the organization meets its measurable objectives.

Culture, on the other hand, is closer to the DNA of the corporate being, so to speak. It is the shared norms that drive how people perceive, think, feel, and ultimately act within an organization. This, of course, is just one of the various definitions, but the commonalities across these definitions always come down to culture manifesting in the common habits, shared norms, and consistent behaviors of the people in that organization. When you embrace the definition and understanding of culture, it is easy to understand how a company may have a vision and strategy that is ideal, however, culture can easily prevent that organization from ever achieving the outcome of that vision.

This is precisely why leaders like Reed Hastings instill cultures in their organizations that are supportive of the principles of Mandate Driven Leadership.

While there might be a number of views as to how to formally define a company's culture, there is much more agreement that culture is a tricky concept to measure or change. While financial metrics like return on capital or production metrics like widgets per hour are fairly consistent across most organizations, the assessment of culture is still evolving. Academic articles abound on various methodologies or tools to measure culture. One widely used tool is the Organizational Culture Inventory (OCI) developed by Robert A. Cooke and J. Clayton Lafferty. The OCI measures the attributes of organizational culture most closely related to the behavior and performance of individuals in the organization. It reveals what members collectively believe is expected of them and how those behavioral norms influence their engagement and effectiveness.

Another tool is the Organizational Culture Assessment Instrument (OCAI) developed by professors Kim Cameron and Robert Quinn. They developed the model of the Competing Values Framework, which consists of four competing values that correspond with four types of organizational culture. Their thesis is that every organization has its own mix of these four types of organizational cultures. This mix is determined by completing a concise survey. The OCAI is used by over 10,000 companies worldwide.

McKinsey & Company offers an Organizational Health Index (OHI). The OHI benchmark provides leaders with a detailed picture of their organization's health compared to peers. With over 1 billion data points across geographies and industries, it offers a global standard to measure and manage organizational health. Rightfully, the assessment of an organization's culture is heavily embedded in the OHI.

While these tools are great, and I've used them myself from time to time, the tool you use to understand an organization's culture is less important than simply understanding it. Continuing the DNA analogy, leaders can put forth or even mandate a phenomenal vision, but a vision alone is not going to make a turtle run faster. Mandate Driven Leaders understand that corporate culture can kill unrelenting implementation of a vision unless the culture is understood, acknowledged, and many times even changed.

Getting a quick and dirty assessment of a culture often requires a much less formal approach. One of the best ways to informally assess an organization's culture is to look at what the people in that particular organization take for granted. This can include everything from the expectation that meetings begin on time, abiding by corporate rules and governance, employee accountability to metrics, and how people are expected to address each other in the office. All these things tell us very important aspects of the organization's culture.

Let's say we are talking to someone who works for a company that makes television sets. Now let's say this is a place where it is taken for granted that quality control and focus on details is only the responsibility of manufacturing. Customer service, sales, marketing, and many other business units may have feedback streams directly related to quality, but since quality is not in their metrics, they may rarely use their business unit's data in a feedback loop for quality assurance. In other words, this is a culture where it is permissible for certain business units to ignore manufacturing quality. How do you think this affects this company's culture? If the company's published and promoted core competency is manufacturing quality excellence, do you think this desired core competency will find its way into corporate culture? I would not be surprised to see that a quantity of those televisions get assembled and boxed up incorrectly.

Now let's imagine that we are working with an organization where embedded in the DNA is an understanding that *everyone* is responsible for quality. Quality is the hallmark and heritage of the company. Here, it is assumed that if anyone sees a quality issue, they must bring it to the attention of someone who can fix that issue immediately. In such a culture, it is much more likely that a zero defect environment will be obtained. This would be a great place for a Mandate Driven Leader who is trying to disrupt a market based on a quality vision.

Mandate Driven Leaders must look at the culture within their organization relative to things like innovation, outcome versus process, roadblocks, and tenacity. Seth Godin, former head of marketing at Yahoo, once said, "This notion that it is up to each person to innovate in some way flies in the face of the industrial age, but you know what, the industrial age is over."[1] This is absolutely true, but most cultures when honestly analyzed do not support innovation. Leaders must truly understand all aspects of the existing culture to determine what parts of the culture are supportive of the vision and where the culture could kill the vision.

Let me give you more of a real-world example. I spent many years at Hewlett Packard (HP). This is an iconic company that was at the heart of the technical revolution that drove our economy in the twentieth century. It truly was a privilege to work for HP. Deeply entrenched in HP's DNA was a culture of engineering and a culture of consensus management. When problems arose, whether product or financial, HP could harness large swaths of the management team to set up processes to gather data, analyze, assess, and report out on the problem. A well-thought-out 200-slide PowerPoint presentation would be produced and, through consensus, would be agreed upon by various business units and management layers identifying the 20 very specific root causes of the issue at hand. "Here is why we missed our revenue and profit targets in Q2." Now well into the next quarter, senior leadership would agree to the issue assessment and would begin an equally impressive process to determine detailed action plans, which through consensus would be agreed upon by all business units and levels of management to address the issues that resulted in the Q2 miss.

Of course, we would now be well into the following fiscal year.

HP had a culture rooted in engineering and process and consensus as opposed to a culture rooted in agile decision making and financial performance. When HP entered the software and technology services business where fast innovation, agility of decision making, and financial performance is key, the result was deteriorating market share, failed acquisitions, and poor financial performance. Culture ate strategy.

So why does this matter to a Mandate Driven Leader? Mandate Driven Leaders understand that they want to avoid the *Field of Dreams* fallacy. This is the erroneous belief that "if you build it, they will come." Mandate Driven Leaders understand that you can't just throw an idea out there and expect people to embrace it. No leader disrupts the market alone, and you have to create a compelling vision for people to follow and create an environment that enables them to do that. And given that Mandate Driven Leaders do not micromanage processes, they have to create a culture where everyone accepts the mission and socially motivates others to do the same. All members of the organization must realize that they only have two choices: get in the boat and row, or get out and swim to a different shore. The question, of course, is how do you create such a culture? How do you drive everyone to buy into these efforts? As with all things related to Mandate Driven Leadership, that is a bit tricky but very doable.

To begin to answer this question, we'll go back to a daylong symposium I attended in 2006 with speaker Edgar Schein. For those not familiar with Dr. Schein, he spent several decades as a professor in the MIT Sloan School of Management. His work included major contributions to the topics of group processes and organizational culture. He also served as a consultant to Digital Equipment Corporation (DEC) during its rise and subsequent fall. These experiences provided him with unique perspectives on how leaders lead and how organizational culture impacts an organization's success.

The Q&A for this particular session started in the midafternoon, and one of the first questions was, how do we change an organization's culture? Dr. Schein's reply drew from his experience at DEC and several other organizations, and I could probably not do it justice other than to say that the overall instructions went something like this: define the culture you want, put programs in place that support that culture, then force people to use those programs until they become the habits and shared assumptions of the organization.[2] In other words, *force people to use those systems and be held accountable on those metrics until they become the habits and shared norms of the organization*. Individuals who never really bought into the vision (or culture) will be forced out by the management system. New talent will be added who only experience the new norm. Culture will quickly switch to be in synch to the vision and the strategy.

Mandate Driven Leaders understand and accept that at least some of the people in that organization are not going to like change and may need to leave. I've been in many meetings with leaders who hear that fact and decide that it is unacceptable. They believe time and programs need to be put in place to change the beliefs of these naysayers. What they fail to recognize is that if people are in the organization now, it is because there are things about that space that they like. If we change those things to processes or vision with which they disagree, the people will not want to stay. Or, worse, they create institutional blockage to achieving the vision. Mandate Driven Leaders accept this because they know they can't create positive impact with people who don't want to be there and don't embrace the organization's goals.

Obviously, this is very different from the consensus-driven approaches often promoted that say something like "ask the team what they think," "get everyone on board," and so on. Mandate Driven Leaders know they are working against time, and while no culture changes overnight, you must change behavior if you are going to change the culture. And if you want to change behavior, start by changing management systems inclusive of processes, metrics, and accountability. It is this ability to force culture change that is critical to a transformative Mandate Driven Leader.

As mentioned earlier, Ed Schein had a front-row seat for the rise and fall of DEC. He witnessed firsthand what can happen when a company loses sight of its mandate and its culture. In the early days, DEC did have what could be described as a Mandate Driven Culture with Ken Olsen's early focus as a scientist trying to harness the power of computer technology to help businesses. As time when on, however, the company grew, got comfortable, and became less concerned about the burning platform advancing the way people used computers and more concerned with maintaining the status quo. When an organization starts feeling comfortable with the status quo, that's when groupthink is given an inroad.

One of the most important things Mandate Driven Leaders do is to develop a culture that opposes and prevents groupthink. Groupthink is where people put constancy with the group as the highest priority. Some people confuse this with group cohesion, but in fact, it is very different. The difference is that in groupthink, maintaining group cohesion becomes more important than making good decisions. The fact that the term originally came from George Orwell's novel *1984* should be a pretty good indication that it is something to be avoided.

Two of the most popular examples of groupthink are the *Challenger* disaster of 1986 and the Bay of Pigs fiasco in 1961. In the space shuttle *Challenger* disaster, individuals had concerns over several design issues in key systems. Specifically, "There was a fundamental design flaw in the joint that engineers had grown accustomed to and had learned to live with."[3] A *groupthink* atmosphere, which is different from outright pressure, resulted in these observations not being given the priority they deserved. A root cause analysis shows that the design flaw resulted in a seal failure ultimately resulting in the *Challenger* explosion. In the Bay of Pigs fiasco of 1961, multiple individuals and agencies saw fundamental flaws in the operational plan prior to its execution. The White House believed the US-trained and armed guerillas would be successful without requiring direct US military intervention. The CIA Directorate for Plans believed that the White House would commit direct US military intervention once the guerillas had landed if needed. Other CIA agencies were firm in knowing that the White House had no such inclination; thus "an analogous misunderstanding within CIA itself hampered planning for the invasion and contributed to the communications breakdown with the White House."[4] The invasion resulted in over 100 deaths, more than 2,500 guerillas taken prisoner, and a major black eye for President Kennedy and US foreign affairs.

In both cases, many people were not comfortable speaking up in opposition to the group, and those who did were quickly silenced for the sake of group consensus and cohesion. One of the advantages of a Mandate Driven Leadership approach is that we encourage discourse and dissent when it helps drive the organization to the vision.

This focus of a Mandate Driven Leader may fly in the face of the increasingly popular notion of "wisdom of crowds." The idea of the wisdom of crowds is an illogical extension of the idea that the opinion of a group of individuals is more reliable than the views of a single expert. The problem with this notion, however, is that the term *crowd* is often taken to mean something like "a group of people amassed by an open call for participation." In other words, it is the amalgamation of everyone's "two cents' worth," informed or otherwise, innovative or stale. Even if we were to take this notion and apply it to a "crowd" of experts, the crowd may be more informed, but may still be rooted in old processes and paradigms. I would challenge anyone to find the disruptive company founded on a vision "from the crowd."

So what kind of culture should Mandate Driven Leaders create? It depends on what kind of culture they want to create. As you read through the leadership profiles and case studies in this book, you'll see that the culture at Facebook is very different from the culture at Netflix or Amazon. It is also a pretty good bet that the culture at Apple is nothing like the culture at Airbnb. All of these cultures are aligned to the strategy that the organization wants to execute and the vision the leader is mandating to fruition. It may be a culture of sheer innovation or a culture of agility or a culture of competitiveness. And if there is one thing that all Mandate Driven Leaders know, either you manage the culture or the culture manages you.

If you let it manage you, culture will eat leaders.

CHAPTER 12

BRIAN CHESKY OF AIRBNB: THE SLEEPER

A consensus decision in a moment of crisis is very often going to
be the middle of the road, and they're usually the worst decisions.
—BRIAN CHESKY, founder and CEO of Airbnb

Airbnb's headquarters is located in the San Francisco neighborhood of SoMa, an expansive community that is "South of Market" Street and is a mixture of art conservators, beatnik-inspired philosophers, and technology leaders.

The President's Room inside the Airbnb headquarters of the online home-sharing platform has leather chairs, wood paneling, and a model of a ship on a circular coffee table. Above the lounge chairs dangles a dainty light fixture that slides into a dark teal ceiling. The teal runs to the upper edges of the walls, which sport an ornate white trim. There is a black marble–framed fireplace in the quarters, and a large rug occupies the wood floor. When Airbnb cofounder and CEO Brian Chesky moved into the building in 2013, he restored the room to its 1917 version, when it housed a battery company. It has the feel of a men's club, not an office, and surely there are cigars and cognac hidden somewhere in the handcrafted wooden cabinets.

The model ship that sits on the coffee table, a nineteenth-century sailing yacht, is the key to the President's Room, and maybe the backbone of the Chesky operation, for the sailing vessel works as a metaphor for Chesky's leadership style.

"If you think about it, Airbnb is like a giant ship," Chesky told *Fortune* magazine. "And as CEO I'm the captain of the ship. But I really have two jobs: The first job is that I have to worry about everything below the water-line, anything that can sink the ship. Beyond that, I have to focus on two to three areas that I'm deeply passionate about—that aren't below the waterline but that I focus on because I can add unique value, I'm truly passionate about them, and they can truly transform the company if they go well."[1]

For Chesky, those three focus areas that are above the waterline are the product, brand, and culture, which are the crucial components beyond the technical aspects of an Internet operation. It is in these three areas that Chesky shows his Mandate Driven Leadership style.

"I'm pretty hands-on with those three," he says. "And with the others, I really try to empower leaders and get involved only when there are holes below the waterline."[2]

Chesky understands that his role as captain of that ship is to establish the destination, chart the course, and propel the ship to that destination. Captains do not sail a ship by consensus. As the captain, Chesky under-stands that propelling an organization to achieve a vision requires directive stewardship.

The Beginning

Chesky grew up in Niskayuna, New York. Both of his parents were social workers, and his little sister by five years grew up to become the fashion edi-tor and editorial director of digital at the "Gen Z" lifestyle publication *Tiger Beat*. As Chesky grew up with nurturing and loving parents in a peaceful home, he became obsessed with anything he found interesting. His mother Deb Chesky told *Fortune*, "From a very young age, you could see that he didn't just dabble in something."[3]

When Chesky received his first set of hockey gear, including helmet and pads, he slept in them, and he worked relentlessly to become a skilled player. "I was captain of some of the hockey teams I was on, and that taught me a fair amount about leadership," he told the *New York Times*. "My dad also taught me a lot about setting a good example for other teammates and trying hard."[4]

In addition, Chesky liked to draw and design as a teenager and spent hours in art museums attempting to master the techniques of great artists by drawing reproductions of their paintings. He also redesigned the world around him inside of drawing tablets.

"Most kids would ask Santa Claus for toys because they wanted to actually play with them," Chesky continued telling the *Times*. "I would ask Santa Claus for badly designed toys so I could redesign them."[5] Like most Mandate Driven Leaders, early on Chesky showed his knack for looking at the status quo and determining that it could be better.

When he graduated high school, those things carried over into young adulthood. He was the captain of his hockey team at Rhode Island School of Design where he studied industrial design. Chesky has stated that he was slightly lost in college. However, industrial design allowed him to continue his passion for making the *existing* better.

Joe Gebbia, whom Chesky met in college, made a prediction to Chesky after their RISD graduation commencement, saying, "Before you get on the plane, there's something I need to tell you. We're going to start a company one day, and they're going to write a book about it."[6]

Gebbia could see the future. The future included two unemployed graduates hatching a billion-dollar plan in order to pay rent. Chesky and Gebbia were broke and unemployed roommates in 2007. "After I graduated, I worked in an industrial design shop in Los Angeles," he told the *New York Times*. "But a year in, I realized this isn't what I should be doing for the rest of my life. Part of it was that I was working with entrepreneurs on small projects, and I started to think, 'Why are they doing that and not me?' I realized the difference is that they took the chance and I didn't. I needed to take the risk, too."[7] Undoubtedly, this helped Chesky understand the importance of leaders having an unrelenting drive to their vision.

To make money to pay their upcoming bills the roommates sold their apartment space to attendees of a design trade show because the hotels closest to the show were all booked. In a pivotal e-mail from Gebbia to Chesky on September 22, 2007, he wrote, "I thought of a way to make a few bucks—turning our space into 'designers bed and breakfast'—offering young designers who come into town, a place to crash during the four-day event, complete with wireless Internet, a small desk space, sleeping mat, and breakfast each morning. Ha!"[8]

Chesky and Gebbia's only option for beds for their three guests were air mattresses, so they called their little weekend operation "Air Bed and Breakfast." The clever name required the two friends to come up with a morning meal, so they gave untoasted Pop-Tarts to their visitors.

"I think there was a lesson there," Chesky has stated. "One of the things I always tell entrepreneurs is to solve your own problem. A lot of people are way too academic about what they're trying to create. But everyone has their own itch—something they're trying to solve. For us, our problem was we didn't know how to make rent, we had this extra space, and we wanted to meet people. So we created this idea."[9]

After the successful weekend, they pushed the idea further. A few months later, their engineer friend Nathan Blecharczyk hopped on board the BNB train to help build a website focused on assisting people to rent out space in their home. In August 2008, the three founders launched Airbedandbreakfast.com. Each of the three gravitated toward their strength. Gebbia focused on design, Blecharczyk took on the technical aspects of the online platform, and Chesky became the leader.

LinkedIn cofounder Reid Hoffman would later say about the beginnings of Airbnb, "It's the old adage about jumping off a cliff and assembling the airplane on the way down."[10] Reid personally invested in Airbnb in 2010 and is one of a number of people Chesky has met with about leadership over the years.

Investors didn't immediately see the genius behind the platform. In the summer of 2008, Chesky met with more than 20 angel investors and a few venture capitalists.

"I met a guy named Michael Seibel [CEO and partner at Y Combinator]. And Michael Seibel says there are people called angels, and they will give you money. The first thing I thought is I can't believe this guy believes in angels. That's how naïve I was," Chesky told *Fortune*. "People mostly ran away from—well, everyone ran away from the idea. The first reason was Joe and I were designers. And as far as they were concerned, designers don't start companies. The bigger problem was a simple idea: People did not think strangers would stay with other strangers. They thought it was crazy. One person said, 'Brian, I hope that's not the only idea you're working on."[11]

During that time, Chesky racked up $25,000 in credit card debt in order to keep his idea afloat, refusing to give up even after several instances in which his investors chastised his ego and sent him down the road. There was no more room on his credit cards, and no one would issue him another one, but he believed in the product and continued to meet with people.

Chesky's patience coupled with tenacity eventually paid off just enough to keep him moving forward with his idea. In January 2009, venture capitalist Paul Graham accepted Chesky and his team into the Y Combinator incubator and gave them a seed fund of $20,000. The founders changed their name to Airbnb and developed their platform to include all properties, from castles to tree houses.

Three months later, Sequoia Capital and Y Ventures invested $600,000 in their product. Then, in November 2010, Greylock Partners and seven other venture capitalists including actor Ashton Kutcher unloaded $7.2 million into the start-up.[12]

On May 31, 2017, Chesky posted his high school graduation picture on Instagram. The snapshot from his yearbook included a quote below it that he attributed to Jerry Seinfeld: "I'm sure I'll amount to nothing." He recalled his father yelling at him right after he saw the quote for the first time, "Nothing?! Nothing?!" Chesky found it humorous. His dad? Well, not so much. The post continued and informed his Instagram audience that his dad was happy to find out that he would be the commencement speaker at both his high school and university in the spring of 2017.[13]

A key characteristic of the Mandate Driven Leader is the unrelenting drive to the outcome. Chesky and his partners simply would not take no for an answer in order to establish their vision. While unrelenting drive might be easy to state, Chesky understands it is harder to embrace. "I think a lot of people who try to do what we did, or try to do other things, they quit, they stop short."[14]

In 2008, Chesky had maxed out his credit cards in order to get Airbnb off the ground. As of January 2019, Brian Chesky's estimated net worth is over $3.7 billion.[15]

Mandate Driven Leaders Value Learning

Chesky's role in Airbnb was his first business leadership position of any kind. Chesky reached out to George Tenet, Distinguished Professor at Georgetown University, for a meeting after acquaintances introduced the two. Tenet was the director of the CIA from 1997 to 2004 and is also currently a managing director at Allen & Company, an investment bank. Chesky wanted Tenet's advice on how to run his home-sharing company. Along with the boat metaphor, Tenet provided Chesky with tips on how he could achieve a transparent and open business environment and how to be visible and create bonds with his staff through handwritten notes and meaningful conversations with random groups of employees during lunch in the company cafeteria.

Tenet isn't the only person from whom he has sought advice. Chesky wants business knowledge from as many worldly luminaries as possible. It has become Chesky's style: he petitions people for guidance, and those people who supply his leadership intelligence span far beyond the business spaces he occupies as a hospitality service disruptor. Through biographies, he even calls upon the philosophy of those who have already exited this realm, including Dwight D. Eisenhower, Steve Jobs, Walt Disney, and Bernard Shaw.

Chesky has quotes embedded in the vast filing cabinet of his mind from the people he meets and the books he reads, and the files he pulls out are unpredictable, and often rearranged to fit his needs in a particular moment. In a *Fortune* magazine article, he reared back and delivered a new version of a quote that was originally intended as an argument against the use of nuclear weapons. "There's no learning curve for people who are in war or in startups," he said.[16]

Essentially, what Chesky is saying by using the quote is that a visionary idea can launch a company along with its inventors, leaving no time for courses in business management and administration. Chesky has a bachelor of fine arts in Industrial Design from the Rhode Island School of Design, a phenomenal school, but different from an Ivy League MBA.

In addition, he never rode through the ranks of a business in order to figure things out through a slow trajectory from bottom to top, learning about office culture and occupational interactions along the way, so his appropriation of the McNamara quote makes some sense. He had to learn the ways of leadership in a skyrocketing start-up on the fly or face the very real alternative of eventually losing control of his company and his vision.

Some handle greatness well, others fall, and Chesky, who refuses to fail, goes to the world's greatest leaders to find direction, something ordinary folks do not have the luxury of doing. However, when you run a billion-dollar digitally enabled company that stretches the planet, you can grab some time from important folks like Warran Buffett who chatted with Chesky in 2015 for four and a half hours. The accolades poured in from Buffett after the meeting.

"I think he would be doing what he's doing if he didn't get paid a dime for it," Buffett said, before adding his thoughts on Chesky's company, saying, "I wish I'd thought of it."[17]

As the success of Airbnb took shape, Chesky unabashedly asked every technology wizard on the planet to meet with him, which included Facebook's Mark Zuckerberg, Amazon's Jeff Bezos, and eBay CEO John Donahoe. Disney CEO Bob Iger taught him how to push his teams of executives to do more. Facebook COO Sheryl Sandberg gave him lessons on how to scale Airbnb efficiently on an international level. Warren Buffett established for Chesky the necessity for "pace"—an efficient one—and advised him to stay away from the noise of the world. Buffett only attends one meeting a day and reads the rest of it, according to Chesky. The ideas shared by Buffett were so profound that Chesky wrote an essay on his meeting at the airport and sent a copy to his employees.[18]

Chesky read the biographies of Steve Jobs and Walt Disney, and he uses former Intel CEO Andy Grove's book *High Output Management* as his management guide and browses through editions of the *Cornell Hospitality Quarterly* to stay up to speed on hospitality administration.[19]

Chesky calls his persistent interviewing of business role models and reading "going to the source," and he uses the collected information in what he describes as "synthesizing divergent ideas." "The most important thing I've learned how to do is learn," he told the *New York Times*. "I've had to embrace the fact that I'm constantly going to be in uncharted waters, and I'm constantly going to be doing something I've never done before. I had to learn to get comfortable in a role of ambiguity where I had to seek out advisers and learn quickly."[20]

Crisis and Consensus Threatens to Derail Airbnb

From outward appearances, one would think that Chesky, the charismatic leader of the business, draws up no mandates for his employees to follow. He smiles, he is thoughtful, he is affable, and while he is focused and intense, there isn't any negative energy peeling off of him, according to those who know him. However, you would be wrong if you think he is gullible as a manager. In the nicest way, he will slay the competition, but not his own folks. There are no complaints to be found internally.

While many of the icons of the digital era are inclined to own every aspect of their employees' life, including their heart and soul, to get ahead, Chesky has no interest in that sort of thing. He wants his employees to go home, have a life, and be a good parent, partner, person, and friend. However, let's not misinterpret him and his intentions; his operation is mandate driven, he is just nice about it. Chesky is the Mandate Driven Leader that shows it is possible that one can be a billionaire digital mogul and a decent person.

Leaders embrace the principles of Mandate Driven Leadership in many areas: strategy, product development, organizational culture, etc. Never are the principles of Mandate Driven Leadership more crucial than in time of crisis. In July 2011, Airbnb received a $1 billion valuation and $112 million in funding just as news began to circulate that a vandal and thief had systematically pillaged the home of an Airbnb host over the course of a week's stay. TechCrunch called the situation "The Moment of Truth for Airbnb."[21]

In a blog, the host "EJ" said that the visitors smashed through her locked closet door and stole her cash, jewelry, credit cards, passports, camera, iPod, laptop, and the external backup drive that she had filled with photos, journals, and her "entire life." The vandals wore her clothes, burned some of her belongings in the fireplace, and poured Comet cleaner on her kitchen counters, furniture, bed frame, desk, and printer.

"I can't stay here much longer," EJ, who has remained anonymous, said. "The feeling of having been violated is overwhelming. The apartment's energy—once light and airy—now feels thick and disquieting."[22]

Initially, the Airbnb team provided little help to the violated woman. Their policy on such matters was very clear. They did not reimburse anyone for damages that occurred at a host's home, regardless of the circumstances, and they did not offer hosts options for insurance. Their overly casual and lukewarm company response was not the reply that EJ, other hosts, or the public wanted to hear.

"Hey everyone—we were shocked when we heard about this unsettling event," Airbnb's public reply read. "We have been working closely with the authorities, and we want to reassure our community that, with the help of our security infrastructure, we were able to assist the police in their investigation, and we understand from authorities that a suspect is now in custody."[23]

As public outcry on the matter went viral, Airbnb's judgment on the matter left EJ with no alternative to fix the destruction that had occurred, and she wondered why Airbnb charged her a service fee if it did not put security measures in place to safeguard her property.

"What was the advantage of using this service over Craigslist, which is free?" she wondered, before continuing, "By hindering my ability to research the person who will rent my home, there is an implication that Airbnb.com has already done the research for me, and has eliminated the investigative work that Craigslist requires. In effect, the friendly, community-based site with its Golden Rules creates a reasonable expectation that some basic screening of its users has occurred, and speaks little to the risks involved, primarily within the very small print of the lengthy Terms of Service."[24]

Chesky hoped the matter would go away, but the more the leadership at Airbnb ignored the issue, the louder the story became. Chesky was relying on his staff to achieve a consensus decision on how to respond. They had endless debates that lasted days without conclusion. Chesky and his team could not come to an agreement on what the company should do in EJ's particular case and in cases going forward. Most Airbnb executives agreed that providing funds for the damages would set a precedent that would make Airbnb the "responsible party" in all damage situations—even the smallest—at a host's home. There were many opinions, a lot of groupthink, but none that suited Chesky.

He removed himself from the voices around him. He said he went home, fell asleep, and woke up in a state of panic, his heart racing, and he decided in those moments that company solidarity on the matter was no longer an option as far as he was concerned.

"I finally had this really dark moment, and I got to the point where I wouldn't say I stopped caring, but my priorities completely changed," Chesky told *Fortune.* "And I basically said I should stop managing for the outcome and just manage the principle."[25] While it is tempting to accept the advice of the group to instill a sense of cohesion, Mandate Driven Leaders will not sacrifice the vision. And Chesky's vision was not that of a company driven by legalese.

Chesky has stated he was too slow in acting, the entire company was flat on its feet, and its customer support wasn't near where it needed to be to solve major issues in an expedient manner. He decided to take full responsibility for the damages and the mishandled response to EJ's situation, as well as make policy changes. Most investors and internal leaders advised against his decision. They wanted him to move slower and involve "testing" into any strategy repositioning. Chesky moved forward with his plan and announced it publicly. Mandate Driven Leaders do not accept roadblocks or delays to propelling their vision to reality.

"When we learned of this our hearts sank. We felt paralyzed, and over the last four weeks, we have really screwed things up," Chesky said on Airbnb's blog. "With regards to EJ, we let her down, and for that, we are very sorry. We should have responded faster, communicated more sensitively, and taken more decisive action to make sure she felt safe and secure. But we weren't prepared for the crisis, and we dropped the ball. Now we're dealing with the consequences."[26]

Chesky mandated big changes that included amendments to their policies that no one could misconstrue as a Band-Aid. Chesky ordered $50,000 in property damage protection, created a 24-hour customer hotline, doubled the size of its support staff, and added a safety department. Airbnb also promised to implement verified user profiles that allowed hosts to view their guests before they agreed to a rental.

At that moment, Chesky's leadership style changed, and he decided that he would no longer make major decisions during times of strife through consensus.

"A consensus decision in a moment of crisis is very often going to be the middle of the road, and they're usually the worst decisions," he said. "Usually in a crisis, you have to go left or right."[27]

Chesky's mandates not only helped put the crisis behind Airbnb but it set the company on a path that was more pure to Chesky's vision and desired outcome. And, both the Airbnb staff and the public grew more confident in the Airbnb CEO. "That's when I saw what Brian was made of," Joe "Joebot" Zadeh, VP of product, told *Fortune*. "That was the turning point where I had 100 percent confidence in this company's leadership and was ready to take any challenge the world threw at us."[28] And, there would be many more that required directive stewardship.

The most recent example of a quick reaction to a building crisis came last year when the Harvard Business School released a report from a field experiment titled "Racial Discrimination in the Sharing Economy." The study concluded that black Airbnb customers with "distinctly African-American names" were 16 percent less likely to successfully book a room with an Airbnb host.

Then, a few months later, Gregory Selden, a black Airbnb user, reported on Twitter that he was turned down by a host in Philadelphia. In response to the rejection, Seldon created a fake account, impersonating a white user, and was immediately accepted as a guest. In another incident in Atlanta, black Airbnb guests were met by police officers with guns drawn after a neighbor reported them as burglars.

However, the discrimination incident that shook Airbnb into crisis mode was one in which an Airbnb host in North Carolina used racist language in a direct message to a black guest before canceling her booking with him. After he directed a racial epithet at her to explain his hatred of black people, he stated, "This is the south, darling. Find another place to rest."[29]

Immediately after the North Carolina incident, Chesky went to work and announced on Twitter, "The incident in NC was disturbing and unacceptable. Racism and discrimination have no place in Airbnb. We have permanently banned the host."

The next day, Chesky hired the former head of the legislative office of the American Civil Liberties Union in Washington. The new hire, Laura Murphy, reviewed the company's practices, and a series of changes rolled out in an effort to fight racism, as Airbnb emerged as a leader in combating discrimination in the sharing economy. Chesky established company policies that went beyond those required by federal law, put together a permanent team of researchers and scientists to identify bias and advance inclusion, and created anti-bias training for their hosts.

Beyond Philosophy, a customer service consultancy and training company, remarked in a blog, "Airbnb has done the right thing. They have faced the complaints head-on, taking a strong stand against discrimination and conducting a thorough evaluation of the company's practices. They have created new policies company-wide, which demonstrates that the company cares about their customers and is willing to change as it grows. Furthermore, they have established a way to monitor bias and complaints and continue to make changes."[30]

In interview after interview, Chesky admitted in clear speech that he had failed to safeguard against discrimination when he created Airbnb, telling *Business Insider* that the situation kept him up at night.

"As a founder, I think we were late on the issue. We were so focused on an issue of trust and keeping people safe, responding to other people's issues on trust and safety that we took our eye off the ball," Chesky said. "When we designed the platform, three white guys, there were a lot of things we didn't think about. There are racists in the world, and we need to have zero tolerance."[31]

As the crisis unfolded, Chesky sent an e-mail to his staff that said they would do more than "address the issue," which he felt was a crutch phrase used by CEOs that involves minimal action only to cover liability.

"If we try to 'address the issue,' I think we'll be on the wrong side of history," he said. "We can drive change the rest of the world will mirror."[32]

Using Directive Stewardship to Crush the Competition

Chesky moves fast these days, taking what he has learned from other Mandate Driven Leaders and acting, not waiting for a script provided by the people around him, but by improving his situations and outcomes with prudence. Airbnb had first-mover momentum, but Chesky had learned from his business mentors and teachers that first-mover advantage can mean little to nothing—where is Yahoo today? So, when competition came calling in Airbnb's space, Chesky mandated decisive action.

Wimdu was an Airbnb clone in Europe that was growing fast, and in 2011 it had received $90 million from investors, Chesky powered into Europe with a dozen offices and representatives in every global time zone, establishing services in 30 languages. Chesky also went on the attack communicating directly to hosts that Wimdu was merely an unethical clone. Wimdu never received another round of funding in the following five years, and 9flats, another home-share company, eventually acquired the company in October 2016. That firm was later sold to a subsidiary of Wyndham, which eventually spun it off to a private equity firm.[33] Clearly, Chesky's mandate driven response to this competition paid off.

Looking to the future of Airbnb, after a billion-dollar funding round in March 2017, Chesky says that not a single one of his investors have put any pressure on him to take the company public anytime soon. However, he understands the expectations that an IPO will happen in time, and he provided some perspective on when that could occur in a 2015 *Fortune* interview.

"If we decided we wanted to go public, we'd want to give ourselves a couple years to really prepare, to have that runway," he explained. "I always thought of it as a two-year project. And we won't start thinking of that for at least a year, and maybe two years."[34] At a 2017 New York Stock Exchange luncheon, he amended the plan, saying, "we're probably halfway through the project," meaning it could happen in 2019.[35]

Chesky says that remaining a private company gives them the flexibility to make big moves as Airbnb grows its brand. In this year alone, the company acquired Luxury Retreats, a high-end property rental company, and Tilt, a peer-to-peer money transfer start-up, which Airbnb will move into its ecosystem.[36]

Many Mandate Drive Leaders including Jeff Bezos, Steve Jobs, Jeff Zuckerberg, and Brian Chesky may be accused of heartlessly stomping out the competition. Perhaps. But, Mandate Driven Leaders will never allow their vision and path to the outcome to be eroded by others.

Surrounding Yourself with a Bunch of Dreamers

Chip Conley graduated from Stanford Business School and bought a seedy, rundown 1950s hotel in the Tenderloin district of San Francisco in 1987. With $1 million from investors and no experience in the hotel industry, he turned the decrepit joint in what was once the underbelly of the Golden Gate City into a destination for rock stars and other luminaries from the Red Hot Chili Peppers to David Bowie. It is a hotel where you do not get sleep, and its website provides a warning that it "isn't for everyone" and "it can be a bit noisy at times."[37]

The crafty entrepreneur then sought out other dilapidated lodging locations on his way to building a boutique hotel empire. Each of his more than 50 spaces is dedicated to a theme. For example, Conley took a typical Best Western and turned it into a Japanese pop culture paradise with anime murals and huge beanbag chairs in every room. A once unimaginative Carlton Hotel became an homage to safaris, and his Silicon Valley hotel is a "salute to invention" with a yo-yo, Etch A Sketch, Rubik's cube, and a copy of *Wired* in every room. Then after a few decades, Conley semiretired, unloading much of his stake and stepping away from the daily operations.

Looking for inspiration to build Airbnb into a complete hospitality company, Chesky sought out individuals from traditional hotels. He needed a mentor, but the big chains offered no one that fit into the Airbnb culture or got Chesky excited. His search brought him to Conley's doorstep. Chesky had read Conley's book *Peak*, a memoir that is also part application and theory that explores the idea that businesses must use Maslow's "Hierarchy of Needs" to survive.[38]

In his book, Conley explains, "Maslow believed that each of us has base needs for sleep, water, and food (physiology), and he suggested we focus in the direction of our lowest unmet needs [one] at a time. As those needs are partially fulfilled, we move up the pyramid to higher needs for physical safety, affiliation or social connection, and esteem. At the top of the period is self-actualization, a place where people have transient moments called "peak experiences." . . . "Peak experiences are transcendental moments when everything just seems to fit together perfectly. . . . I began to wonder: if humans aspire to self-actualization, why couldn't companies, which are really just a collection of people, aspire to this peak also?"[39]

The lodging sage's message spoke to Chesky in a way that other hoteliers had yet to do, and he brought Conley to Airbnb headquarters to speak to his staff. Afterward, Chesky offered Conley a full-time job, but Conley was happy being out of the hotel game and with being a bohemian world traveler. Chesky, however, had already decided for Conley; he was his man. The two met for a meal.

"I'll never forget it," Laura Hughes, Airbnb senior manager of hospitality, told *Fast Company*. "Brian was like, 'I'm going to dinner tonight with Chip, and when I come back, he's going to be an employee.'"

Conley originally agreed to consult 8 hours a week, but by the end of their outing, he committed to 15. However, once Conley was in the door, Chesky gave him more work than could be completed in a 15-hour workweek, and the writing was on the wall.

"Within a month, it was clear that nobody does anything part-time at Airbnb," Conley said.

Conley removed himself from retirement to work full-time at Airbnb as the head of global hospitality and strategy in 2013 because he liked the spirit and the attitude of the place, and the work involved, which he found rejuvenating.

"I've always liked rebellious business people, so this was a natural fit," Conley said, and then he quoted Gandhi. "First they ignore you, then they ridicule you, then they fight you, and then you win. Airbnb is the new disrupter."[40]

Chesky and Conley have a fierce relationship with serious debate, but their mutual respect holds the two together as each one clasps to their core values, which is basically a commingling of Chesky's sharing economy and Conley's ideas about modern hospitality.

"The two push back on each other a lot," says Hughes. "If Chip is proposing something that requires a lot of resources, Brian will be quick to say, 'This is not a priority.' Or Chip will say to Brian, 'This might increase conversion, but it's not supporting the hospitality experience.' They feed off each other. They're so high-energy. It's exhausting."[41]

Together with Chesky, Conley reduced the hierarchy of host requirements to nine, which are standards directed toward how complete strangers should communicate and cohabitate for a brief moment in time with the host being the ambassador of the Airbnb brand and the procurer of the host's own personal business brand.

Unlike the contentious battles that erupt between many entrepreneurial or technology visionaries and their key personnel, Chesky and Conley go out of their way to openly compliment each other. Chesky might make the final decisions on all things, and he does not make those decisions wrapped around consensus, but he has proven that Mandate Driven Leadership is powerful and successful, and can be done in an admirable way.

Once Chesky made the decision that Conley had to be part of the team, he mandated that vision to completion. Many of the Mandate Driven

Leaders profiled are adamant that a trait of Mandate Driven Leadership is to surround yourself with trusted lieutenants. The intent is not to surround yourself only with those who agree with you. A Mandate Driven Leader must have core management that agrees with the vision, will drive the vision to the outcome, and will be unrelenting in doing so. Chesky in building his core team is an adamant supporter of this principle.

"For every hire, you need a very specific thesis of what you're looking for, and it has to be simple," he told the *New York Times*. "It can't be a bunch of responsibilities; it's got to be a word or a mantra, and it has to be around the outcome or goal that I want them to achieve."[42]

In a broader sense, Chesky is looking for employees who see the world as it could look in the future, rather than the way it is currently shaped. He asks potential staff members to outline their life in three minutes so that he can determine the formative experiences and the challenges that influenced why they became their current self.

"Once I figure that out, I'm trying to understand the two or three most remarkable things you've ever done in your life. Because if you've never done anything remarkable in your life until this point, you probably never will."[43]

Mandate Driven Leaders build organizations that are rooted not in the status quo, but in disrupting the future. You can see that principle at work with Steve Jobs and Apple's "crazies" and Chesky. According to Chesky, these are the types of individuals he looks to hire: "They're dreamers, big thinkers, and they are generally trusting—they're not cynical, although they are very contrarian and they are willing to challenge the status quo. They are kids at heart—not in terms of maturity, but in terms of curiosity."[44]

Chesky and Company Culture

Chesky stays on top of the company's culture. Airbnb is his company, his brand, and provides his reputation to the world. He approves of "kooky," telling his staff in an all-hands company conference in 2015, while receiving the crowd's resounding approval, "The thing that will destroy Airbnb is if we stop being crazy."[45]

He implored them not to edit their imaginations, or think that something is impossible to negotiate or conquer. Chesky believes that nothing can destroy his company, and he passes that belief along to his employees.

Peter Thiel, who cofounded PayPal and is the founder of Clarium Capital, a Facebook board member, and a multibillionaire, invested $150 million in Airbnb, and then gave immediate and basic instructions to Chesky, saying, "Don't fuck up the culture."[46]

He went on to tell Chesky that as the business grows in size, and in order to get the best talent, he will have to include an assortment of personalities with various opinions on direction. Therefore, Chesky put maximum effort into maintaining stable company values and customs. His culture-maintaining plan also involves views from the top of the company, a continual stream of undistorted information from the Airbnb CEO himself. Chesky has an hourlong Q&A session each week with new employees and he tells his staff that they are designing the future world, and to remember they will be living in it.

In a letter, he told his employees that "culture" creates the foundation for all future innovation.

"If you break the culture, you break the machine that creates your products," he wrote. "Culture is a thousand things, a thousand times. It's living the core values when you hire, when you write an e-mail, when you are working on a project, and when you are walking in the hall. We have the power, by living the values, to build the culture. We also have the power, by breaking the values, to fuck up the culture. Each one of us has this opportunity, this burden."[47]

Crazy is part of the culture that Chesky wishes to keep intact, which is another of his rules. Maintaining the culture of his company, which in many ways is an attempt to limit company bureaucracy, is a large aspect of Chesky's game plan, as seen in the memo he sent out to his staff on October 21, 2013.

"Why is culture so important to a business? Here is a simple way to frame it," Chesky wrote. "The stronger the culture, the less corporate process a company needs. When the culture is strong, you can trust everyone to do the right thing. People can be independent and autonomous. They can be entrepreneurial. And if we have a company that is entrepreneurial in spirit, we will be able to take our next 'man on the moon' leap. Ever notice how families or tribes don't require much process? That is because there is such a strong trust and culture that it supersedes any process. In organizations (or even in a society) where culture is weak, you need an abundance of heavy, precise rules and processes. There are days when it's easy to feel the pressure of our own growth expectations. Other days when we need to ship product.

Others still where we are dealing with the latest government relations issue. It's easy to get consumed by these. And they are all very important. But compared to culture, they are relatively short-term. These problems will come and go. But culture is forever."[48]

However, for investors, Airbnb is a business, not a philosophical statement, and Chesky pushes his team to beat their rivals to innovations while maintaining a culture that is "too strange to be uniform" and "delightfully schizophrenic," Conley told *Fast Company*.[49] Those ideas are places that other companies normally do not aspire to go, but it is that mentality that keeps Airbnb's competitors off-balance and creates disruption in the hospitality industry.

Leaders like Hastings, Chesky, and others know the importance of culture to achieving vision, and they are not shy about using directive stewardship to ensure that culture is woven through the fabric of their organization.

Status Quo Fights Back Against the Vision

In 2015, the Santa Monica City Council prohibited housing rentals of less than a month. It wasn't even a close decision, issuing a vote of 7–0. The council made an exception if the primary resident was on the premises during the stay, but rentals were subjected to a 14 percent occupancy tax that hotels in the city were already paying.

The growing sharing economy is no stranger to the fight against the companies that support the status quo of an industry. Both Airbnb and Uber have had to battle local governments and local business lobbies that support competing services. At the time of the Santa Monica vote, Airbnb and hosts of other lodge-sharing entities rented 1,700 varying houses and apartments in the city. The reasoning provided by the council for the ruling was complaints from residents regarding the rotation of interlopers, who weren't always pleasant guests. The council claimed that home sharing reduced property values.

Since 2010, when New York City banned home sharing without tenant supervision for stays of less than 30 days, the climate around the Airbnb model grew more and more tempestuous as the company gained ground as a considerable threat to the hospitality industry. Therefore, in 2013, Chesky left his cozy San Francisco office and became an Airbnb ambassador in cities around the world. His hope was to cast a spell on opponents of his company, and he met with politicians, lodging and real estate leaders, and the media in cities such as New York, London, Paris, Nashville, and Philadelphia. The visits started a dialogue, they loosened and reduced tensions, and laws changed in his favor.

The Airbnb captain was even able to reach common ground with hotel chain executives, convincing them that he is a friend, not a competitor. Four of the six biggest chains have sent representatives to the Airbnb headquarters for group "immersion" meetings.

"I think we are moving away from the divisive era into the more mainstream era," Chesky told *Fortune*.[50]

The fight continues, though. The Federal Trade Commission is all over house-sharing platforms. In April 2017, three senators requested an investigation to see how Airbnb and others influence housing costs. The American Hotel and Lodging Association monitors Airbnb and has a covert plan of attack on local, state, and federal levels for systematically blocking its momentum in the hospitality market. Chesky's operation is ripe; since 2008, 150 million travelers have stayed in 3 million different host homes in nearly 200 countries.

Mandate Driven Leaders understand that often achieving their vision means disrupting the current state. This often results in the need to become an ambassador for a completely new business paradigm. For Airbnb, the disruption of the hospitality market is unprecedented as an entire industry of hotels is mounting a full-on attack. In a document obtained by the *New York Times*, the American Hotel and Lodging Association issued the following message to its staff: "Objective: Build on the successes of 2016 efforts to ensure key legislation in key markets around the country and create a receptive environment to launch a wave of strong bills at the state level while advancing a national narrative that furthers the focus on reigning commercial operators and the need for commonsense regulation on short-term rentals."[51]

The lobbyists' plan involves funding research to prove that Airbnb is nothing more than a platform for unlicensed people to run hotels out of residential buildings and in residential neighborhoods while skirting hotel tax laws and safety and security regulations. Then, the hotel organization will take those funded studies to politicians, state's attorneys, neighborhood associations, and housing groups in order to strategically reduce the number of Airbnb host locations.

The response from Chesky and his team through public affairs director Nick Papas showcases a fight for the working class against intimidating big industry oppressors: "the hotel cartel is intent on short-sheeting the middle class so they can keep price-gouging consumers," Papas told the *New York Times*. "With more than 250 government partnerships over the last year, we have shown our seriousness of purpose when it comes to putting in place fair rules."[52]

In an interview with *Fortune Live*, Chesky looked at the matter in a more practical way, saying, "We're in 34,000 cities, so actually I would say that the thing that surprises me is how many cities actually embrace us. The country of France last year legalized Airbnb, the country of Portugal did, too, the Queen of England just signed our platform into law, so I would say that the vast majority of cities have welcomed us with open arms. What I have been surprised about is that some cities haven't and those cities are closer to home. Cities like New York, where we have had lots of challenges. I am from New York, and I would have guessed that the challenges would have been in governments in countries far away from where I am born. I understand, though, I think we are a new idea."[53]

In the interview, Chesky waxed philosophical about the Internet and its way of profoundly changing the world. He believes that his disruptive lodging model will find its way into the hearts of every municipality in time, as long as he is at the realm of Airbnb.

"Every city is wrestling with this in a different way," he said. "I think where this plays out long-term is that you cannot put this idea back in the bottle. People want this globally. These things are governed at the city level, usually, not a national level, unless it is in Europe, so it is going to take a little longer than I expected. But ultimately, I think the people usually win."[54]

People usually win because Mandate Driven Leaders like Chesky are unrelenting in the actualization of their vision.

Airbnb's Leadership, Vision, and Path to the Future

As internal fighting, high turnover, angry outbursts, and tears besiege other companies, Airbnb does not seem to have those issues. For now, there seems to be balance, and it also appears that Chesky is not shy about mandating the path forward for Airbnb.

In its early days, Chesky controlled all aspects of Airbnb's operations. Nothing escaped him, from legal to finance. Chesky explained to

Fast Company, "That was the easiest way to make an impact."[55] However, since 2014, Chesky has handed daily operations over to his fellow founder Blecharczyk, but no one would know it from appearances. Chesky remains as CEO, and he is the face, the mascot, the lead strategist, and the public relations officer (even if not in name), and he will forever be the molder of culture and brand for the home-sharing company. His Mandate Driven Leadership style would require no less.

Today, Chesky devotes his energy to actions that have the greatest impact on his company, and therefore, it is imperative to keep business strategy simple. He believes that a few key moves provide the leverage to make other moves, comparing it to a game of chess. He once showed a writer a piece of paper that contained the strategy for the coming year. One standard page of paper contained four objectives for the entire coming year.

"If you can't fit it on a page, you're not simplifying it enough," he told *Fast Company*. "When you have too many initiatives, it's really hard to keep your focus."[56]

In Chesky's world, that focus must be on the nature of the customer experience, which plays the biggest role behind his Mandate Driven Leadership style. He has learned that waiting for consensus-made decisions not only leads to tepid outcomes, but it also creates chaos.

"When you first start leading people, it can be a little uncomfortable—you feel like maybe you're bossy, maybe you're mean, you might be reticent about making decisions or reluctant to give feedback," he told the *New York Times*. "But I removed all reticence whenever a crisis occurred, and I made a unilateral decision to be direct. And when I started doing that, I realized that people are thriving from this and that it's so much more helpful for people."[57]

From his early days, Chesky has worked outside the box with his questioning of the status quo; so far, that space has been highly successful for him as a Mandate Driven Leader. "Brian Chesky's audacity is fabulous," stated Jony Ive, senior VP for design at Apple. "He dares to believe that we shouldn't be strangers, that we can have a sense of true belonging whenever, wherever we travel."[58]

CHAPTER 13

MANDATE DRIVEN LEADERSHIP AND THE DIGITAL ECONOMY

At least 40% of all businesses will die in the next 10 years . . .
if they don't figure out how to change their entire company to
accommodate new technologies.

—JOHN CHAMBERS, Executive Chairman of Cisco

Powered by digital technology and the digital economy, disruption is everywhere. Every industry. Every geography. Affecting every business.

The former VP of marketing at Dell, Heather Simmons, once said, "Knowing that an asteroid is going to hit the earth is not really useful if you are not planning to launch missiles to knock it out of the sky. You have to work massively overtime on the belief that innovation or massive change is going to happen."[1] This thought is critical for leaders today because business disruption is going to continue.

Much like "out-of-the-box thinking" the phrase "digital disruption" is heavily used—however, in this case maybe not overused. You know the examples. Uber is less than 10 years old and disrupted the livery business arguably in less than 5 years from its founding. Airbnb is now the largest hospitality company in the world and does not own a single hotel. Amazon with a market valuation approaching $1 trillion has disrupted multiple industries, and it is still targeting more. Instacart hit $1 billion in valuation in 795 days. And, of course, Facebook took a mere 396 days to be valued at $1 billion and now has a valuation of $513 billion.

One aspect of the business disruption that is occurring today is what has been referred to as *disintermediation*. Disintermediation is nothing more than the elimination of the middleman, and it has been sweeping our economy, eliminating vast segments of every industry's value and supply chain.

Disintermediation is the process by which intermediaries in a supply chain—distributors, wholesalers, brokers, or agents—are removed from that chain. Instead of dealing with these middlemen, the customer deals directly with the provider of the good or service. Each of us now utilizes and values the results of disintermediation. How many times do you order Amazon for next-day delivery instead of hopping in the car and visiting numerous retailers to purchase that hard-to-find item? Who goes to the bank or writes a check anymore? Disintermediation is made possible by a new high level of market transparency and buying convenience that lets consumers pay less for items by buying directly and more conveniently from a manufacturer or some other disintermediary that has contracted the value chain.

This accelerated change and accelerated business disruption is also being powered by a truly connected world, a world where everything is collected and data recorded, a world of Big Data. This world is the Internet of Everything (IoE), and it is here. Billions of devices like refrigerators, washers, air conditioners, cars, and even industrial machines sense and predict users' needs and communicate and share information with one another automatically. This data provides business intelligence for marketing, logistics, planning, execution, and decision making. Though the IoE is already a trillion-dollar industry, Cisco predicts that the trend will quickly grow bigger: it estimates that there will be 37 billion new Internet-connected devices by 2020. Consider that the human population projection for the same period is only slightly over 8 billion.

We are on the verge of living in a thinking machine-to-machine world, one in which our devices and products themselves will anticipate and accommodate many of our needs with little or no intervention from us.

Disruption. Disintermediation. IoE. If you sit on the board of directors or are a CEO, do you really think that you don't need a Mandate Driven Leader during these times?

What business leaders must not forget is that for every disrupter that skyrockets in valuation and disrupts entire industries, a myriad number of legacy companies are disrupted right out of business as their leaders could not harness digital transformation. The once iconic Sears filed for bankruptcy in October of 2018. Blockbuster underwent a fire sale to Dish Network in

2010. Toys"R"Us filed for bankruptcy and liquidated in 2017. iHeartMedia underwent bankruptcy in March of 2018. These firms join the lists of literally thousands of newspapers, bookstores, travel agents, insurance agents, and many, many others that have been disrupted right out of business. Now more than ever, businesses need Mandate Driven Leaders because . . .

Business disruption is accelerating.

There can be no doubt that digital technology and the digital economy are driving a wave of disruption that is only accelerating. Business leaders must recognize that the speed of change is increasing and Mandate Driven Leadership is needed not only as a result of the digital disruption but as an acknowledgment of the new norm for this pace of change. A start-up today has access to world-class technology enablers that only a few years ago were available only to the largest of US businesses. Cloud-based computing and software as a service now allow entrepreneurs and established businesses to use technology on a consumption basis without the large up-front hardware or licensing fees. This allows a start-up to compete against any established business anywhere in the world if its leaders have the right vision. Technology and infrastructure are no longer a barrier to change but an accelerator to change.

These disrupters, these start-ups are a threat to every legacy business. And who do you think is leading that next wave of start-ups—someone who espouses consensus management as the leadership style needed for quick market entry and disruption? Or, a Mandate Driven Leader who has a vision for the start-up, communicates that vision clearly, and is unrelenting until the vision is achieved?

Elon Musk, the cofounder and CEO of Tesla, has had his share of negative press over the previous year. And as many reader will understand from that press, he would be categorized as a Mandate Driven Leader. Musk has told many an audience that friends, family, and business associates attempted to talk him out of both Tesla and SpaceX. He has told *USA Today* that starting SpaceX and Tesla was probably "the dumbest things to do" as far as a start-up. However, Musk has started a revolution in the car industry, proving every naysayer incorrect. Electric car sales are growing at 50+ percent a year and will increase from 3 million units in 2017 to more than 125 million units by 2030. Every automobile manufacturer is now scrambling to catch up. In typical Mandate Driven Leadership fashion, when Elon Musk was asked why he started Tesla and SpaceX if it truly was the "dumbest thing to do," he said, "he believed in the companies' abilities to change the world for the better."[2]

As we watch the vision of Elon Musk's Tesla organization come to fruition, will future innovators be studying this Mandate Driven Leader or Mark Fields? Right, most readers will have no idea who Mark Fields is. Fields spent 25 years in the Ford organization rising to the rank of CEO in 2014. As he served in that capacity for three years, sales grew modestly as market share slipped. Ford's ability to compete in the electric and autonomous automobile marketplace of the future was in doubt. It became obvious that Ford would have a difficult time competing against Tesla in the electric car market even in the short term, so investors left in droves, driving Ford's stock price down by 40 percent. Fields was forced into retirement in 2017.

For legacy businesses participating in the legacy economy, it is these start-ups, led by Mandate Driven Leaders, that are coming after you and your business and the well-being of all of your employees and their extended families. For legacy companies not just to survive but to thrive in this area of digital disruption, they need the same type of leaders as the disrupters. Legacy companies need transformational leaders who have a vision for the future state of the company and through directive leadership will become the disrupter instead of the disrupted.

Jay Samit, currently the independent vice chairman for Deloitte, has been called a serial disruptor. He is the author of *Disrupt You!* He has stated, "To thrive, all businesses must focus on the art of self-disruption. Rather than wait for the competition to steal your business, every founder and employee needs to be willing to cannibalize their existing revenue streams in order to create new ones. All disruption starts with introspection."[3] In my previous book, *Inflection Point: How the Convergence of Cloud, Mobility, Apps, and Data Will Shape the Future of Business*, I discussed how we are in the midst of one of the most profound eras of disruption seen in modern times, an inflection point.[4] Andy Grove, founder and former CEO of Intel, stated that inflection points "almost always hit the corporation in such a way that those of us in senior management are among the last ones to notice." He warned that "depending on the actions you take in responding to this challenge, you will either go on to new heights or head downward in your prosperity as a firm."[5]

I'd put forth that the reasons why senior management may be the "last ones to notice" is that many companies have the wrong senior management in place for this disruptive era. They have "run" management in place— senior managers who may be great consensus builders in identifying and establishing new, more productive ways of *doing the same business*. They may even be adequate profit and loss managers who can deliver consistent, if not weak, financial performance. And all the while these senior leaders are performing these roles, another company, possibly a start-up, is about ready to disintermediate, disrupt, or otherwise make them irrelevant.

For years, the leadership of Borders, once one of the largest bookstore chains, did not notice Amazon. Then, when it did—its leaders shrugged Amazon off as an upstart that would never be relevant. Borders declared bankruptcy in February of 2011 and was liquidated that September. Does anybody remember George L. Jones? Any great case studies of his leadership style? Hint, he was the CEO of Borders during the time Amazon ate Border's strategy. In comparison, how do you think business historians are going to treat Jeff Bezos of Amazon?

Routinely, I see business executives moving at a snail's pace in their efforts to transform to this new digital reality, and primarily it is due to leadership challenges, not technology. Some executives falsely believe they have time. They admit that digital disruption is coming, but they believe they have time for consensus building on their strategy rather than risk industry-changing decisions. These executives are wrong. Digital disruption is here now, and it is the new reality. In a recent Forbes Insights/Treasure Data survey, "One-third of executives say they are being directly affected by competition from digital and data-savvy players in their markets."[6] My guess is that the other two-thirds are so stuck in the status quo that they don't even realize it is already happening to them.

The disruption of yesterday and even today is only the beginning. We are on the cusp of an even greater round of disruption. Faster than many companies think, we will see monumental shifts in the value and supply chains in healthcare, manufacturing, insurance, finance, and consumer packaged goods. Manufacturers, wholesalers, distributors, and other intermediaries will be eliminated. More and more companies will go to market directly to the consumer or through marketplaces that bypass traditional channels. Many well-known companies will cease to exist, and others will rise.

This is not the time for business as usual. This is not the time for an incremental change. In order to succeed, companies need transformational leaders. They need visionaries who through Mandate Driven Leadership will shift a company from being the victim of today's digital disruption to harnessing it as a weapon to conquer.

CHAPTER 14

BILL GATES OF MICROSOFT: THE REVOLUTION BEGINS

People always fear change. People feared electricity when it was invented, didn't they? People feared coal, they feared gas-powered engines. . . . There will always be ignorance, and ignorance leads to fear. But with time, people will come to accept their silicon masters.

—BILL GATES, Founder of Microsoft

Microsoft was formally founded in 1975, more than 40 years ago. Bill Gates has not worked full-time at the company he founded for more than 10 years. He stepped down as chairman of the board where he was still the largest shareholder in 2014. However, no discussion about leadership styles necessary in a business environment that thrives on disruption would be complete without profiling Bill Gates.

On the evening of March 12, 1986, Microsoft CFO Frank Gaudette could not locate company cofounder Bill Gates.

It was the eve of Microsoft's public offering, and an agreement had yet to be made with Goldman Sachs regarding the management fee per share. Showing complete disdain for the excitement surrounding the IPO, Gates was not even in the country—or on land.

Before he left to parts unknown, Gates gave the order to agree to a fee of 6.13 percent or less, because Sun Microsystems had made a similar deal with its underwriter. At 6.13 percent, Goldman Sachs would receive $1.29 per share. However, the underwriter would not go any lower than $1.31.

With Gates unreachable, Gaudette agreed to the terms. Later, Gates said he would have called off the public offering had he been around, and he was very serious. Gates couldn't have cared less about the pennies involved, but the principle meant everything to him.

On March 13, 1986, Microsoft shares traded publicly on the New York Stock Exchange for the first time. The shares opened at $25.75 and closed at $27.75. From the floor of the exchange, Gaudette called COO Jon Shirley to tell him, "It's wild! I've never seen anything like it—every person here is trading Microsoft and nothing else."

By noon, the stock was moving at a thousand shares a minute, and analysts said they could not remember when a stock had traded more volume in its first day. "I'm pretty happy," Microsoft cofounder Paul Allen told the *Seattle Post-Intelligencer*. "Everybody involved in Microsoft since the beginning has looked forward to this day."[1]

Well, not everyone.

As the frenzy occurred on Wall Street, Gates was on a reading vacation off the coast of Australia. In a chartered 56-foot sailing vessel, Gates studied the Great Barrier Reef and plowed through a plethora of reading material for five days.

"I was sort of pampering myself," Gates said.[2]

A few weeks later, Microsoft stock was trading at $35.50 a share, and a year later, shares hit $90.75. When that occurred, Gates officially became a billionaire at the age of 31. No industrial tycoon, great financier, or technology mogul had ever crossed that particular frontier to riches at such an early age. However, the computer whiz and business genius has never been too concerned with his riches.

"I'm certainly well taken care of in terms of food and clothes," he told *The Telegraph*. "Money has no utility to me beyond a certain point. Its utility is entirely in building an organization and getting resources out to the poorest in the world."[3]

Bill Gates became a rich young man, and Microsoft became an icon, at the threshold of a new era that ushered in the personal computer. He combined widely known technology with the practical application of extraordinarily powerful business ideas. Gates is a master of software technology, and he is a brilliant manager who has found inspiration even in crisis, and Microsoft has seen its share of calamity.

For instance, the spread of PCs to homes accompanied and accelerated the sensational rise of the Internet. Gates got off the blocks well after the starting gun sounded, but his powerful response catapulted him to the mantle of a prophet of the revolution. Meeting the challenge of change is crucial to Gates's pragmatic approach to realizing powerful visions and being a Mandate Driven Leader. He has been a spokesperson for change, whose actions have spoken louder than words in making him both prime mover and chief figurehead of the age of information.

Today, his investments outside of Microsoft are worth $70 billion, and his shares of Microsoft top $17 billion. While he cares about his status among the wealthiest in the world, he cares very little about the wealth itself. He gives more away to charity these days than he keeps.

The Microsoft empire began from the top down through very clear mandates delivered by Bill Gates, and it stayed that way for many years as Microsoft reached impossible heights. Today, Gates's official role is that of board member and part-time technology advisor. It has been a decade since Gates left the day-to-day operation of Microsoft. However, as board member, he ensures that the brightest minds in the world are hired by Microsoft.

The Argumentative Boy Genius

William Henry Gates III was born in 1955 to a wealthy and socially connected Seattle family. Gates was the youngest of three children; he has two older sisters. His father, Bill, was a prominent Seattle lawyer and World War II veteran. His mother, Mary, was the day-to-day parent of the children, while she volunteered for various organizations and served on corporate boards.

The tight-knit family thrived on competition, including board games, cards, and Ping-Pong. They were a family of rituals as well, such as mandatory Sunday dinners and their tradition of wearing matching pajamas on Christmas Eve. The Gates's home was a peaceful and regulated household until the family's youngest member, Bill, became an adult overnight at the age of 11. It was at this time that Gates's father says his son became an increasing headache for the family.

"As a father, I never imagined that the argumentative, young boy who grew up in my house, eating my food and using my name would be my future employer," the senior Gates, who is the head of his son's philanthropic venture, the Gates Foundation, told the *Wall Street Journal*. "But that's what happened."[4]

The young Bill Gates was a diligent learner and a voracious reader, who read the entirety of the World Book Encyclopedia series, but his parents were worried about him because he enjoyed books more than he enjoyed people. His growing store of knowledge also led to many questions about international affairs, business, and the general nature of life. While his father appreciated his son's expanding intellectuality, it also created a difficult child who was willful and hard to control.

In particular, Gates had explosive arguments with his mother. Because of the tension at home, Gates's parents sent him to a child psychologist, who offered his parents the advice to ease up on their son because he would ultimately win the battle for independence. His parents did just that, and the boy received unprecedented freedoms from the age of 13.

Gates went to a private school, where he excelled at mathematics and became fascinated by personal computing, then in its formative stage. He spent nights using the free computers at the University of Washington, and he was a page in the state legislature as well as a congressional page in Washington, D.C. During his senior year, he took a break from school to work as a programmer for a power plant in southern Washington.

After graduating high school, Gates went to Harvard with the idea of studying law, but the idea never really clung to him in a lasting way. There was little doubt that he would leave Harvard without a degree. While he excelled in his computer classes at the Ivy League school, he was not a favorite of professors or his peers.

"There's one in a handful who come through in computer science that you know from the day they show up on the doorstep they will be very, very good," said professor Tom Cheatham, director of the Center for Research and Computing Technology at Harvard, in *Hard Drive*. "No doubt, he was going to go places. Gates had a bad personality and a great intellect. In a place like Harvard, where there are a lot of bright kids, when you are better than your peers some tend to be nice and others obnoxious. He was the latter."[5]

Gates played poker on some nights, but he usually worked in the Aiken Computer Center because that was when the students used the machines the least. Sometimes an exhausted Gates would sleep on the lab's worktables because he didn't have the energy to make it to his dorm room at the Currier House.

Gates dropped out of Harvard early because of his excitement over the endless possibilities of the personal computer and his growing focus on the new industry. His parents were uncertain about the choice of their independently spirited child.

"My parents weren't all that excited about their son announcing he was dropping out of a fine university to start a business in something almost nobody had heard of called 'microcomputers,'" Gates said.[6]

Breaking into the World of PCs

With an equally enthusiastic Seattle friend, Paul Allen, Gates wrote a version of the BASIC computer language in 1975 for an early PC, the MITS Altair. Immediately following this success, Gates and Allen formed Microsoft (initially Micro-Soft) in 1977, after moving to Albuquerque, New Mexico.

The initial breakthrough for the pair came in 1980 when two IBM executives visited Microsoft to commission work on BASIC for their new PC—a rush program with unprecedented tight deadlines. The crew at IBM found an engaging, bespectacled, highly intelligent, and articulate man, physically restless and with great mental agility. Gates has not changed since that time.

Microsoft sprang, not from work on BASIC, but from IBM's other needs, which included operating software for its PC. Gates boldly bid for the contract. He then approached another software company—Seattle Computer Products—and bought an operating system called Q-DOS (Quick and Dirty Operating System). Gates and Allen then modified it to suit IBM's needs, renamed it MS-DOS (Microsoft Disk Operating System), and delivered it to IBM for a relatively low price, undercutting rival software companies.

Gates's purchase of Q-DOS for only $50,000 opened the doors to billions, largely because IBM, grossly underestimating the market for its PC, signed a contract allowing Microsoft to sell the software to any other PC manufacturer. When the PC took off, astounding IBM executives by its success, Microsoft's wealthy future was assured—to the rising annoyance of IBM. The constant threat to Gates, even as his sales and profits grew astronomically with the rise of the IBM and IBM-compatible PCs, was that IBM would break the vital link with MS-DOS. Gates protected Microsoft as best he could by partnering with IBM in the development of a new operating system, OS/2. When IBM executives sought to dissolve the OS/2 partnership, Gates won a reprieve at a June 1986 lunch with CEO John Akers.

Taking over the PC Market

Little more than three years later, the war between IBM and Microsoft broke into the open. In 1990, Gates won definitively with the launch of Windows 3.0. Using the same technique—the "graphical user interface"—that had made the Apple Macintosh so popular, with its graphic icons and pull-down menus, the new product was selling a million copies a month by 1993. It gave users vastly improved access to applications, opening another door of opportunity for Gates.

Now, Microsoft could write and sell a completely new line of application programs for use with Windows. Products like Word, the word processing program, and the Excel spreadsheet were almost as dominant as MS-DOS and Windows, which still holds 90 percent of the operating system market for PCs. Gates kept piling on the pressure. Windows NT, a more powerful product aimed at the corporate market, appeared in 1993. Like the first version of Windows, NT had serious defects, but Gates's approach has always been to launch first and improve later, radically if need be.

What worked so well with Windows 3.0 also triumphed with NT. Microsoft's sales numbers soared, and up went the profits and the share price. Each advance in the stock made a new millionaire among the Microsoft ranks, but all the employee nest eggs were outweighed by the fabulous fortune created for Gates himself. His reputation as a technological genius, which is largely undeserved, and as a superb businessman, which he definitely merits, was eclipsed by his unquestionable standing as the world's richest man beginning in 1995 at the age of 39 to January 2018, when Amazon's Jeff Bezos overtook his spot. The overtaking by Bezos is largely due to the fact that Gates has given away large sums of money to charity. If not, he would still be in the top spot.

"I'm not competent to judge his technical ability," business magnate and investor Warren Buffett said, "but I regard his business savvy as extraordinary. If Bill had started a hot dog stand, he would have become the hot dog king of the world."[7]

The Internet Challenges Gates

Whether or not the adulation and success temporarily blunted Gates's vision in the mid-1990s, the company, having beaten IBM so decisively, nearly defeated itself by failing to react to the early, obvious challenge of the Internet. Since operating systems and applications could be loaded from cyberspace, Microsoft's dominance could be undermined, like IBM's before it.

By May 1995, Gates had become fully aware of the threat; he titled one of the countless memos he regularly e-mails to his employees "The Internet Tidal Wave." It gave the new technology "the highest level of importance." Billions of dollars of development capital were switched to the assault on the new market—and especially on Netscape, the company whose Internet browsers, initially given away free, had taken it from an April 1994 start-up to $5 billion of market capitalization by December of the next year. Gates had an immensely powerful weapon to deploy. The technique was to compel PC manufacturers to preload the Microsoft browser onto their machines as an allegedly integral part of Windows 95, the popular replacement for Windows 3.0.

Although commercially successful, the onslaught on Netscape made Microsoft vulnerable legally. In 1998, the US government's antitrust action went to trial, producing months of high embarrassment—and a hostile verdict—for Gates and the company.

Additionally, public sentiment had run against Gates because of his very success. Some may have simply envied his enormous fortune or resented that the multibillionaire was not spreading his wealth as generously as he could afford. Within the computer industry, Microsoft's power to crush competitors and to dominate its terms of trade with the PC manufacturers aroused more than envy. Firms were anxious about their own profits and prospects as Microsoft extended the range of its products and its ambitions.

As for PC buyers, they typically accepted the Microsoft software bundled in with their purchases as a fact, though some found it unpleasant. Many technology-savvy consumers felt that Gates was a restrictive and too powerful force, whose hold over the technology prevented important advances and trapped users into costly upgrades to a system that was inherently old-fashioned. This mood led to an open hostility that expressed itself in many ways, ranging from Internet attacks to published books, such as *Barbarians Led by Bill Gates from the Inside* by Jennifer Edstrom and Marlin Eller and *1 Microsoft Way: A Cookbook to Breaking Bill Gates Windows Monopoly Without Breaking Windows!* (with Linux CD Operating System). This book referred to a system, new at the time, that was available free over the Internet or from intermediaries who charged vastly less than Microsoft did for its own system.

Battling the Antitrust Action

Linux was seized upon by many people as the answer to their anti-Gates prayers. A significant number of corporate users also adopted Linux. This gave Gates another weapon in his battle against the antitrust authorities. He argued that Microsoft could not be described as a monopoly when the competition was more intense than ever and when customers were gaining from falling prices and greater performance. Unfortunately, this defense was not helped by taped interviews with Gates, screened at the Washington trial.

Along with other evidence, such as internal e-mails, the tapes showed Gates in an unflattering and sometimes apparently evasive light. As a consequence of the antitrust trial, Gates was forced into the public arena as never before. After a hesitant reaction, he responded with his usual determination. TV interviews showed a relaxed, smiling man, with no hint of defensiveness. Moreover, Gates and his wife decided to set up an unprecedented charitable foundation to control and distribute the bulk of their wealth, with the hope that they could do some good and swing public opinion in their favor. Gates also pushed through a major reorganization of Microsoft to delegate more of his power, while continuing to direct its huge switch of strategy to the Internet. Moreover, on one issue he remained quite determined, which was to carry on doing the job he loved in an industry that he had so long commanded.

On November 5, 1999, Judge Thomas Penfield Jackson stated that Microsoft constituted a monopoly and had taken actions to crush any opposing threats to that monopoly.[8] The court ordered a breakup of Microsoft. On appeal, the judge's decision was overturned, and later a settlement was reached, in which Microsoft was required to share its application program interfaces with third-party companies. The Department of Justice and Microsoft agreed to the obligations in regard to the suit in 2002, and it wasn't until May 12, 2011, that Gates was freed from the antitrust consent decrees, which expired. In all, antitrust action has bogged down Microsoft for 21 years. However, challenges do not trouble Bill Gates, whether it is competitive or government forces; in fact, he relishes them and mocks their chances to compete with his empire.

"Microsoft had had clear competitors in the past," he told *Infoworld*. "It's a good thing we have museums to document that."[9]

Microsoft Bureaucracy and
Top-Down Management

In the spring of 1999, Bill Gates's approach to management underwent a crucial change. Microsoft split into eight new divisions, each run by executives who, in theory, had the autonomy to manage their empires. The reorganization was required to reorient Microsoft from personal computers to all forms of information software and hardware and focus the company around the needs of customers.

"Companies fail when they become complacent and imagine they will always be successful," Gates told *BusinessWeek*. "That's even more dangerous in a world that is changing faster than ever, especially technology. So, we are always challenging ourselves: Are we making what customers want and working on the products and technologies they'll want in the future? Are we staying ahead of all our competitors? What don't our customers like about what we do, and what are we doing about it? Are we organized most effectively to achieve our goals? Even the most successful companies must constantly reinvent themselves."[10]

Until that moment in 1999, though, Gates had yet to invent the Microsoft management style, in the sense of deliberate planning. It inevitably reflected the personality of its founders, Gates in particular. He first established a working relationship with Paul Allen, and then went on to surround himself with people and systems who suited his personal style.

In the early days of Microsoft, the style had no real organization, according to Allen. "Our management style was a little loose in the beginning," he told *Fortune*. "We both took part in every decision, and it's hard to remember who did what. If there was a difference between our roles, I was probably the one always pushing a little bit in terms of new technology and new products, and Bill was more interested in doing negotiations and contracts and business deals."[11] The early division of labor is interesting in view of Gates's later reputation as the supreme geek, the man to whom technology is all.

In the early days, there were only three simple constants as far as management went with little else to provide the borders, and those included the following: technology managed toward well-defined business ends, acquiring and retaining customers, and creating and defending profit streams. Over time, the management systems on which the organization has run have evolved according to need and are not based on any theory. That's understandable when you consider that, as managers, the pair were largely self-taught, with experience being their main teacher.

"Paul and I would talk through every decision, for six or eight hours sometimes," Gates said. "We didn't have many major disagreements, but there was one tiny source of tension: I would always be calling Paul in the morning to tell him it was time to come work on this stuff. He slept even later than me."[12]

Gates and Allen were very bright computer geeks, people who could take a computer apart, write software, and understand new technology. As they developed management skills on top of their technical expertise, they sought other technical experts, some of whom, over time, would likewise evolve into managers. Hiring managers outside of the company was not Microsoft's way. Even today, the company hires people for their ability as marketers, programmers, and content providers. Microsoft management is highly professional, but it is inseparable from other professional skills—much as in the early days.

Two other lasting features of Microsoft's management style also developed during the early days. Decisions were made in very long discussions—known as "marathons"—that lasted for six to eight hours. They are still a regular occurrence today, and the pair expected others to copy their habit of working extremely hard and long. Gates has never lost the habit and has an extraordinary ability to cram a host of activities into the day, with no time wasted and with the main objective—selling more Microsoft software—never escaping from sight.

Hard work and long hours, however, do not explain how to manage a company that employs 124,000 people, as of 2017, which is up from 30,000 people in 1998 and 61,000 in 2005. Gates is evidently a highly competent manager who employs competent subordinates and deploys them effectively. However, "management" does not figure in the index of Gates's books. Nor is Gates often featured as a role model in many management studies. That is probably because Gates does not subscribe to any particular management theories or follow any role model himself, with the exception of Alfred P. Sloan, the man who made General Motors great, who died in 1966 when Gates was 11 years old.

"It's inspiring to see in Sloan's account of his career, how positive, rational, information-focused leadership can lead to extraordinary success," Gates wrote in his book *Business @ the Speed of Thought*.[13]

Gates learned about Sloan's practices while reading Sloan's business management memoir *My Years at General Motors*, which he published in 1963.[14]

Gates is especially interested in the personal attention that Sloan paid to the dealer network, and his use of a standardized accounting system that gave every dealer and every employee "categorized numbers in precisely the same way." Sloan's personal visits to dealers appealed to Gates's constant urge to sell software, which Gates imitates when he takes world tours to visit substantial business partners.

Until 1999, Gates had never publicly shown any interest in the structural principles that Sloan famously applied to turn a sprawling bunch of car companies into an organized and highly effective corporation. The reorganization, however, followed Sloan's principles to the letter, dividing the company into separate business groups and holding the leaders of the new business divisions accountable to think and act as if they were independent businesses.

At that time, the crucial issue was whether Gates could stand aside enough to allow his managers genuine independence of thought and action because decisions large and small had always funneled to the top and bottlenecked. On many occasions, this bottleneck had contributed to Microsoft's slow pace in making decisions. Compared to the hectic pace of the Internet world, Microsoft has always looked sluggish. In 1999, the reorganization aimed to free Microsoft from its bureaucratic morass and to free executives from constant top-down scrutiny that undermined the confidence of the managers below.

Today, top-down management remains basic to Microsoft's management culture, but it is not to the extreme that it was before the millennium ended, when Gates had secured a sound future for Microsoft. In those days, Gates spent 70 percent of his time reviewing teams through two or three meetings per day, according to his own estimates. It was a highly penetrating, business-oriented style. In passages from *Business @ the Speed of Thought* that are intended to show Microsoft management at its best, Gates tells how he met with headquarters colleagues to look closely at the "numbers" of all the overseas subsidiaries. He was involved in a change to the way these "financials" were reported to give him a faster, clearer picture, and how he conducted executive reviews to consider, for example, the detail of a project to identify the best US cities for a new marketing campaign.[15]

Until a customer CEO advised him to stop, Gates even passed top people's expense accounts. He knew all about the system for hiring, managing, and paying temporary staff, and so on. All this immersion in operating detail, however, is now a part of the past, but the mandates of Gates built

Microsoft's foundation for the first 15 years of operation, even when his company was at nearly 50,000 employees.

Microsoft Egalitarianism, High Performance, and Sea Change

Microsoft's egalitarianism treats all employees as equal and largely ignores all behaviors except for performance, which is highly stressed. In the book *Company Man*, journalist Anthony Sampson says that Microsoft implemented a "casual, egalitarian style."

"They're not interested in your clothes, your style, or when and how you work: you can work at home all the time," Sampson wrote. "But they're sure interested in what you produce. They review your progress twice a year, with marks from one to five. Four means exceptional; one means you're out."[16]

It seems to be a reasonable expectation, actually, and the notion fits Gates's personality, but it hid his iron fist. The definition of "production" and "performance" is troubling when the Microsoft founder defines them. You do not work for Microsoft unless you are prepared to work a 60-hour week at times, and in exceptional times, 100 hours or more.

Gates pushed these requirements through the system from the top by both being a living example of a "100-hour week" and through an abrasive style and very open intolerance of what he calls "stupid thinking." Furthermore, Gates regularly expresses his fierce criticisms of low production and performance.

Gates achieves this culture of high performance and high productivity by the way in which he has set up the structure of Microsoft, although he looks at it in a more positive light when discussing the approach.

"Our corporate culture nurtures an atmosphere in which creative thinking thrives, and employees develop to the fullest potential," he said in *Business Wisdom of the Electronic Elite*. "The way Microsoft is set up, you have all the incredible resources of a large company, yet you still have that dynamic small-group, small-company feeling where you can really make a difference. Individuals generate ideas, and Microsoft makes it possible for those ideas to become a reality. Our strategy has always been to hire strong, creative employees, and delegate responsibility and resources to them so they can get the job done."[17]

To achieve the small-company culture, Gates keeps units small. As soon as a team gets beyond a comfortable size of about 30 people, leadership divides it. Gates is a believer in controllable size and in project management, in which you place tasks under leaders who in turn subdivide the task among subordinates who work in a coordinated program to achieve the desired result. Gates then encourages constructive controversy between the divided parts of the corporation and cements the latter with a central vision as well as personal enrichment—rewarding success but swiftly penalizing failure.

The constant formation of new units is one means of gearing up for change. Gates has always seen Microsoft as an agent of transformation in society as a whole and has talked about technology changes through his life that have provided historic transitions that he finds exciting and empowering to "the human experience" and brutal to companies and institutions that don't keep pace. According to Gates, if you do not practice the change management that looks after the future, the future will not look after you, and you dare not miss the moment.

Gates has said that Microsoft is always two years away from crisis; that is, failure to react to disruption and continuous change. He has not forgotten the experience of nearly missing the explosive takeoff of the Internet, and he told *Fortune*, "That kind of crisis is going to come up every three or four years." His recipe for dealing with discontinuous change is to make sure that "today," which is every day, is not the day they miss the turn in the road. "Let's make sure we're hiring the kinds of people who can pull those things together, and let's make sure we don't get surprised," he continues.[18]

The preface of the second edition of his first book, *The Road Ahead*, gives Gates's views on change. He writes, "I work in the software industry, where change is the norm. A popular software title, whether it's an electronic encyclopedia, a word processor, or an online banking system, gets upgraded every year or two with major new features and continuous refinements. We listen to customer feedback and study new technology opportunities to determine the improvements to make."[19]

However, while some call this "discontinuity," to Gates it is continuous improvement, but the radical changes are harder to see right away, and that was the case in the early days of the Internet. "The most important and exciting part of my work as chairman is recognizing [sea changes] and articulating the opportunities they present to each person in the company," he said in *Giant Killers*.[20]

The Decisive Leadership of Gates

The key element of Gates's role in Microsoft—making all the big strategic decisions—will surely continue as long as he is alive. The *Wall Street Journal* pieced together a full account of how Gates handled the discussion on the crucial issue of whether Microsoft should continue with Windows as an entry point for the Internet. The other option was to launch a "cross-platform" replacement using Java software that would run on all computers—as many corporate customers wanted. For months, the opposing camps wrangled through e-mail conversations, exemplifying Gates's principle of letting people fight out issues.

Then, in March 1997, a meeting of top managers heard Gates deliver his verdict. He did not "discuss" the Java idea; he shot it down in flames. "In no uncertain terms, Mr. Gates had decided to protect Windows at all costs," the article concluded.[21] The 2,000 employees in the Internet group were "reassigned," and he returned the two key teams to the Windows group. This vital decision was implemented with a massive drive to take the web browser market from Netscape by bundling Microsoft's rival Explorer with Windows—a strategy that backfired in the antitrust action of 1998.

The decision severely deflated key employees, most importantly, the losing senior executive in the struggle, who had previously masterminded the enormously profitable launch of Windows 3.0. The episode demonstrated the central principles of Gates's theory and practice of management.

They are very clear that "the boss" is "the boss," and the boss is Gates. As a boss, he listens to all opposing arguments and then makes a clear, unarguable decision. The decision concentrates on solutions that will best protect and profit the company's proprietary position while offering the best trade-off between risk and return. Then, the boss makes sure that his employees observe the decision and follow it through to the end by way of relentless hours at the office and daily updates.

"Great organizations demand a high level of commitment by the people involved," Gates told *Playboy*. "That's true in any endeavor. I've never criticized a person. I have criticized ideas. If I think something's a waste of time or inappropriate, I don't wait to point it out, I say it right away. It's real time. So you might hear me say, 'That's the dumbest ideas I have ever heard,' many times during a meeting."[22]

Gates's role is not necessarily recognizing sea changes and articulating the opportunities they present, as much as exerting leadership. Spotting major trends is part of leadership, but only part. Gates will speak of an "act of leadership," meaning that he takes charge and wills what he wants to happen. However, "leadership," like "management," does not figure in Gates's writings. That is because he is not interested in the theory of leadership, only in its practice. Without this particular leader, however, the Microsoft wheel would lack its vital hub. Would it keep turning? The system easily surmounted the early retirement of Paul Allen.

"My best business decisions have had to do with picking people," Gates said in a panel discussion. "Deciding to go into business with Paul Allen is probably at the top of the list, and subsequently, hiring a friend—Steve Ballmer [Microsoft CEO from 2000–2014]—who has been my primary business partner ever since."[23]

This partnership with somebody totally trusted and totally committed, with the same vision but some difference in skills, is the only balance to the total decision power of the chief executive. "Some of the ideas you run past him," Gates continued, "you know he's going to say, 'Hey, wait a minute, have you thought about this and that?' "[24]

While the point is true and valuable, Gates's words do not suggest that he gets tremendous opposition, even from this source. He argues that he and his top managers spend time talking about succession issues, and the importance of growth in making Microsoft a significant employer in the world. However, the question must be whether the biggest job of all is not too big for anybody except Bill Gates. Through the years, Bill Gates seems to follow this line of management from his top position:

- ▶ Hire the brightest people with the greatest specific skills sets.
- ▶ Improve management information to get exactly what you need quickly.
- ▶ Treat everybody as a close colleague from whom you expect plenty.
- ▶ Keep the organization flat and use e-mail and other messaging platforms to debate issues openly.
- ▶ Watch out for radical change, and change radically to meet it.
- ▶ Keep teams small and delegate responsibility and resources to make them effective.
- ▶ When it is time to lead, make sure you lead decisively.

The "Learning" Organization or Knowledge Company

Microsoft has been credited with being a genuine example of the "learning organization." This is not a phrase used by Bill Gates, perhaps because of its vagueness. As a hard-nosed businessman, Gates is only interested in concrete results. The key to the learning organization is "knowledge management." Even in the second edition of Gates's *The Road Ahead*, there is little sign of this theme. However, his thinking has undergone a considerable change since then, and knowledge management has loomed very large in Gates's outlook.

Does Microsoft, in fact, practice what its master preaches? The company's principles and processes do embrace the five "learning disciplines" identified by Peter Senge—a professor at Massachusetts Institute of Technology and author of *The Fifth Discipline*. These disciplines are described as the basis of "learning organization work," and include all of the following:

▶ Personal Mastery. Expecting people to develop their personal capacity to meet their own objectives, and thus those of the company, which in turn is organized to encourage that personal effort.

▶ Mental Models. Developing the right "mindset" to guide actions and decisions.

▶ Shared Vision. The commitment of all members of the organization to its aims and its ways of achieving those objectives.

▶ Team Learning. Exploiting the fact that group thinking is greater than the sum of its individual parts.

▶ Systems Thinking. Acting on the understanding that actions and decisions cannot be isolated, but have ramifications throughout the organization.[25]

These five disciplines also fit the picture that Randall E. Stross paints in *The Microsoft Way* of Bill Gates as a "practical intellectual."[26] In the software industry, this is not a contradiction in terms. It requires genuine intellect to write software, but the software is useless unless it works in practice. Narrow-minded technologists have never fit Gates's broader ambitions. He is famous for using the word "bandwidth" to describe people's intellectual capacity; it is a metaphor drawn from the amount of information that a communications system can carry.

Gates believes that the greater the human "bandwidth" that he employs (in other words, the more collective intelligence Microsoft hires), the greater the strength of his company. He is less interested in the amorphous concept of a "learning organization" than in the harder notion of a "knowledge company," which stores and develops its intellectual resources and augments them by its hiring policies. The knowledge company's raw material is brainpower. You hire the best and best-trained brains, create an environment in which they can create their best work, and build systems so that the knowledge that has been created is built into the fabric and operations of the business—where it can be shared and transmitted.

Only the brightest and best of the new university graduates who approach the company are invited to enter the Microsoft campus. The headquarters site in Redmond, Washington, has been described as "organized along the lines of a university." Gates seeks not just the smart, but the "super smart." According to Stross, the super smart have all of the following attributes:

- ▶ Ability to grasp new knowledge very fast
- ▶ Ability to pose acute questions instantaneously
- ▶ Perception of connections between different areas of knowledge
- ▶ At-a-glance "linguistic" ability to interpret software code
- ▶ Obsessive concern with the problem on hand, even when away from work
- ▶ Great powers of concentration
- ▶ Photographic recall of their work[27]

All of these attributes, including the amazing recall, are personal characteristics of Gates himself. He expects them to be accompanied by an emphasis on pragmatism, verbal agility, and swift response to the challenge—qualities that also reflect Gates's own aptitudes. He believes that he was born, not made and that the success of an employee at Microsoft depends more on the hiring than on the subsequent experience. That would explain why, to quote Stross, "the best programmers are not marginally better than merely good ones. They are an order of magnitude better, measured by whatever standard: conceptual creativity, speed, the ingenuity of design, or problem-solving ability. All else being equal, the company that recruits the largest number of alphas among alphas is most likely to win the biggest sweepstakes."[28]

This theory raises a practical problem. Although Gates has indeed won the biggest prizes, the company's history has been marred by conspicuous technical failures, such as the persistent clumsiness of early MS/DOS, problems with numerous versions of Windows, the almost fatal flop of Windows NT, as well as misfires with several applications. Clearly, hiring the best brains is not enough. How they are deployed and organized is decisive in the effectiveness of their output. This is where the knowledge company, as opposed to the learning organization, makes its mark.

Here, too, the hard head of Gates as "the businessman" is at variance with the philosopher of mental bandwidth. For all the "campus" elements, Microsoft is no university but a hard-driving commercial enterprise, which, sometimes counterproductively, is only interested in hard results. In an effort to control costs, Microsoft has always deliberately sought to hire fewer people than it actually needs, following the formula "n – 1," where "n" equals the number required. While excessive headcount is to be deplored, inadequate numbers also exert a harmful effect because overwork and overstretching carry obvious risks.

Knowledge Share

Gates himself is clear that high individual intelligence is not enough "in today's dynamic markets." A company also needs a high corporate IQ, which hinges on the facility to share information widely and enable staff members "to build on each other's ideas." This is partly a matter of storing the past, and partly of exchanging current knowledge. As individuals learn, their knowledge adds to the corporate store.

What matters most is quality, not quantity; how effectively that store is mobilized by collaborative working. "The ultimate goal is to have a team develop the best ideas from throughout an organization and then act with the same unity of purpose and focus that a single, well-motivated person would bring to bear on a situation," writes Gates in *The Road Ahead*.[29] That way, the super-smart, articulate person—the Bill Gates archetype—becomes the organization itself. It is the boss's role to encourage collaboration and knowledge sharing, using not just exhortation but reward for the purpose.

Gates advocates setting up specific projects that share knowledge across the organization and making this sharing "an integral part of the work itself—not an add-on frill." Rejecting the old adage that "knowledge is power," Gates argues that "power comes not from knowledge kept, but from knowledge shared"—and managed.[30]

On this reading, knowledge management must be of extreme importance. Yet Gates seems to downplay it when he writes, "Knowledge management is a fancy term for a simple idea. You're managing data, documents, and people's efforts."[31] He goes on to explain at great length how these three processes can be deployed in the following four areas of any business: planning, customer service, training, and project collaboration.

Some of the applications—for instance, in training and customer service—are not especially high level, but they plainly serve essential purposes and answer important questions. What happens, for example, if Microsoft salespeople out in the field get queries from customers? The sales force cannot be expected to have the technical knowledge that resides in the product groups. By operating through a website called the InfoDesk, Microsoft's product people can answer 90 percent of all questions within two days. Companywide access to product knowledge is a crucial aspect of corporate IQ.

Access to training is also critical and has an obvious relationship to the effectiveness of corporate brainpower. Again, the needs can be met with high efficiency online. Microsoft employees can find the course they want, get notified when it is available, and register through a single site. In addition, the online source can provide not only training information but also the training itself, using multimedia and chat sites, for example. Online facilities at Microsoft train twice as many students as those who take physical courses. Gates regarded this as fundamental management of knowledge, which it clearly is.

What excites him more, however, is creating a "collaborative culture, reinforced by information flow, which makes it possible for smart people all over a company to be in touch with one another."[32] The technology again plays a crucial role, helping to stimulate and energize the workplace. That happens as a "critical mass of high-IQ people," working in concert, share a vital experience, and "the energy level shoots way up."[33] Gates believes that cross-stimulation breeds new ideas, raises the contribution levels of the less experienced employees, and gets the whole company working "smarter."

That does not happen by itself. Effective knowledge management is both a means and an end. Every time an internal Microsoft consultant finishes an assignment, he or she is required to send technology solutions to a central web location called InSite. However, digital technology is not the whole answer by any means. Hands-on management is required to "evangelize," recognize, reward, and review the use of information. Gates himself regularly reviews customer information provided by the sales forces, and he regards this review by superiors as possibly "the biggest incentive to keep our customer base up-to-date."[34]

The expenditure of his own time in the day-to-day business of Microsoft is justified by Gates as an investment in "intellectual capital," which he defines as "the intrinsic value of the intellectual property of your company and the knowledge your people have."[35] In the "information society," the argument that intellectual capital is the only kind that counts has become a cliché. Behind the cliché, however, lies the reality that Gates sees reshaping the world—above all, the world of business.

Thomas A. Stewart, the author of *Intellectual Capital*, has written of "the end of management as we know it."[36] Gates's efforts at Microsoft exemplify how the old-style approach to management must be changed in order to nurture the three varieties of intellectual capital, as described by Stewart, which are:

- ▶ Human. Individual powers and resources.
- ▶ Structural. Accumulated knowledge and know-how of the organization.
- ▶ Customer knowledge. Which in Stewart's view is "probably the worst managed of all intangible assets."[37]

The human aspect of intellectual capital is not only concerned with the obvious knowledge worker, such as the programmer or Gates himself, but by turning others into knowledge workers. "In the new organization, the worker is no longer a cog in the machine but is an intelligent part of the overall process," writes Stewart.[38] Computers, for example, are largely limited to the one-dimensional, repetitive work at which they excel. The excellence of human beings is needed to manage processes, rather than merely to execute tasks, and that creates knowledge workers, who use good digital information to play unique roles.

Developing, investing in, and deploying all this intellectual capital— knowledge management—surely goes beyond Gates's dismissal of the latter as "a fancy term for a simple idea." In fact, what he goes on to describe is far from simple in execution. "Your aim should be to enhance the way people work together, share ideas, sometimes wrangle, and build on one another's ideas—and then act in concert for a common purpose."[39] That goal sounds like a managerial utopia, something seen in only rare and fleeting circumstances, the heartfelt and generally frustrated desire of the CEO.

As the leader of Microsoft, Gates awards himself a specific role along the road to utopia. His challenge is "raising the corporate IQ" in four ways:

▶ Establishing an atmosphere that promotes knowledge sharing and collaboration
▶ Prioritizing the areas in which knowledge sharing is most valuable
▶ Providing digital tools that make knowledge sharing possible
▶ Rewarding people for contributing to a full flow of knowledge[40]

Bill Gates Today

Bill Gates still reads voluminously, even in odd moments, specializes in multitasking, and somehow contrives to give the running of Microsoft his full attention, while also spending much time on public relations. He appears to have no outside interests other than his family, his Porsches, his foundation, and his futuristic, technology-crammed lakeside mansion in Medina, Washington.

"Everybody is waiting for the guy to slip. He hasn't slipped, and there's very little chance that he will," said Alan Kerr of the advertising and marketing firm Ogilvy & Mather in *Bill Gates Speaks*. "Everything that he keeps in his hands will work, and he will win."[41]

Gates's philosophy and success are inseparable from the information revolution. From the start, he wanted to create "a tool for the information age that could magnify your brainpower instead of just your muscle power."[42] He sees digital tools as the means of augmenting the unique powers of the human being in the form of thinking, articulating a thought, and working together with other humans to act on thought.

In management terms, his success has been built on the proposition that information technology must and does change everything—including the ways in which companies communicate, are managed, win competitive advantage, and do business. After years devoted to advocating and enabling a revolution centering on the personal computer, his objective shifted in the mid-1990s to positioning Microsoft at the head of a new revolution founded on the Internet.

Along with the many inceptions of Windows and its applications, as well as the technology found in smart devices and the purchase of Skype, Microsoft created the XBox, a gaming console. It is the only Microsoft brand to find a physical home in people's living rooms and dorms. With 26 million boxes sold, it has become the gaming platform that developers want to be on, and the best way to play video games with friends through the social network XBox Live, which boasts 35 million members. As with other Microsoft inventions, it has had its design flaws. Repairs to systems that customers had already purchased and fixes to the consoles still in stores cost Microsoft more than $1 billion.

Microsoft's own failures have not been forgotten but stored as part of the intellectual capital. This has only come about because the company is always prepared to learn from the unfortunate past. Gates used to publish and revise annually a memo titled "The Ten Great Mistakes of Microsoft." The object was not to wallow in error but to stimulate Microsoft employees into learning the lessons. Many of the mistakes, according to Gates, came from entering markets either late or not at all.

Outsiders, however, might be more inclined to dwell on the software releases that were inadequate or faulty. In these cases, Microsoft certainly does learn from its own errors, simply because it has to correct them or lose the customers. But however much the library of knowledge about past programs builds up, however strongly the tools for software writing are standardized, however much brilliance is hired, the knowledge demands simply get more intimidating. There have been numerous times when an army of Microsoft staff struggled to get the latest version of Windows to market, writing millions of lines of code and confronting an endless procession of bugs.

As Gates well understands, the process of acquiring knowledge and applying it to new purposes never ends. Not only do the mountains to climb get progressively higher but the landscape is constantly being changed by the hosts of other brains, at other companies and universities, who are taking different lines of knowledge to different conclusions. The Gates monopoly is commercial, not technological. That is why he places so much stress on obtaining and managing knowledge about the customer. However, there is a central difficulty for Microsoft as a learning organization. It cannot know everything about all customers, nor about all information technologies.

Much of its knowledge management is dedicated to maintaining the company's proprietary position. This position is vulnerable to technological developments that are not conceived or controlled by Microsoft. In some cases, the new knowledge can be bought, by acquiring the business involved, or shared via a partnership agreement. Gates uses both approaches to deal with external intellectual challenges. However, he is defending a minority position in the market for ideas. The knowledge company can never afford to relax.

Vision Is Opportunity, and Vision Is Free

Gates regards vision as an opportunity. His intuitive belief that personal computing was the future was certainly visionary. However, as he points out, "Vision is free. And it's therefore not a competitive advantage in any way, shape, or form."[43] Unless your vision translates into a marketable product or service, it has no value. If your central vision is tightly focused on what you know and understand, you can develop enough momentum to correct your inevitable misreadings of a fast-moving future.

The core of Bill Gates's thought is an intense belief that the future is progress. In his philosophy, the meaning of human life, society, the economy, technology, and business lies in sustained, vigorous, forward movement. He applies this credo strongly to his business. He expects the technology to become obsolete and to be replaced. He expects the business to mutate as it grows. He believes that change is inherent in all organisms and that the great manager and the great business proactively turn change to their advantage.

Vision is not a prediction. Gates is prime proof of the dictum of Alan Kay, one of the great intellectual fathers of the PC, that "the best way to predict the future is to invent it." Gates made the future happen by the commercial acumen and drive he brought to the technology solutions that suited his interests. His predictive powers, however, have often failed him, most notably over the all-encompassing future of the Internet.

Gates received criticism amounting to ridicule for the omission of the Internet from the first edition of *The Road Ahead*. He was apparently blind to the fact that the information highway led through the Internet. According to Gates, Microsoft was betting that the Internet would be "important some day. But we didn't expect that within two years the Internet would captivate the whole industry and the public's imagination. Seemingly overnight people by the millions went on to the Internet."[44]

He told himself, "Yeah, I've got that on my list, so I'm okay." This was far from the truth. "There came a point when we realized it was happening faster and was a much deeper phenomenon than had been recognized in our strategy," he recalled.[45] His realization was prompted not by intellectual

arousal but by commercial necessity. Well before Gates woke up, many com-
mentators had identified the Internet as a major threat to Microsoft's brand.

A clue to understanding Gates's initial failure to grasp the overwhelming
importance of the Internet lies in an earlier lapse. In 1981, Gates affirmed,
when forecasting the future of personal computers, that "640k ought to be
enough for anybody." Today, the average nonprofessional PC comes equipped
with just fewer than 6 gigabytes of memory, and 250 to 300 gigabytes of
storage space, so that prediction now sounds ludicrous. However, Gates's
commercial interests then seemed best served by the stable development of
PC power rather than its headlong expansion. His erroneous thinking was
wishful. His complacency regarding an Internet that threatened to bypass
his quasi-monopoly of PC software was just as wishful.

By 1996, when the second edition of *The Road Ahead* was published, it
was "no exaggeration to say that virtually everything Microsoft does these
days is focused in one way or another on the Internet."[46] By 1998, Gates saw
clearly that the emerging hardware, software, and communication standards
"will reshape business and consumer behavior."[47] The time lag is especially
astonishing in the light of Gates's own later views in 1999 when he saw the
Internet as far more than a priority. It had become, in his mind and in actu-
ality, a transcendent technology. "The Internet creates a new universal space
for information sharing, collaboration, and commerce," Gates wrote in *Business @ the Speed of Thought*.[48]

This astonishing turnabout explains much about "vision" and much
about Gates himself. In *Business the Bill Gates Way*, Des Dearlove writes
that Gates regards himself as "an expert in unraveling the technological past
from the technological future." His "talent is for understanding what's just
around the corner."[49]

That description is wholly contradicted by the Internet story, when the
technological future and what was actually happening, let alone just around
the corner, eluded Gates for a significant time. The same episode also contra-
dicts Gates's own philosophy of risk-taking: "You can't look at just the past
or current state of the market. You have to also look at where it's likely to go,
and where it might go under certain circumstances, and then navigate your
company based on your best predictions. To win big, sometimes you have to
take big risks."[50]

In putting the Internet on the back burner, Gates was influenced by
the drawbacks that were prevailing at the time. The technology could not
support "video conferencing and high-bandwidth applications such as

video-on-demand—to say nothing of the needs for security, privacy, reliability, and convenience."[51] Gates also looked too long at the past, as he said, "the years of waiting for online services to catch on had made us conservative in our estimate of how soon significant numbers of people would be using interactive networks."[52]

There were also "irritating deficiencies" that caused complaint. The Internet needed faster modems, cheaper communications switches, more powerful PCs in more places, and "richer content." A true visionary, however, would have ignored these quibbles and concentrated on what the Internet really represented, which is a universal network. As the prime advocate of networking, Gates should have been better placed to spot this future (and to make it happen). The true visionary would also have been encouraged by precedent.

The lesson is that Gates relied more on his own vision than his staff of computer literate professionals and nearly the entirety of the technology world, who turned all of their attention to the World Wide Web. He didn't even look to the past for examples of what might become the future. The world had seen a previous example of a promising technology with serious limitations that seemed to restrict its value and market, but the deficiencies did not prevent rapid takeoff, and as they were remedied, the market exploded. Gates knew all about this precedent. It was the IBM and IBM-compatible PC market, the expansion of which had made him and Microsoft so rich. Extrapolation of the past into the future can be highly misleading, but looking for patterns in the past can be highly illuminating.

As Gates writes, "Ironically when a technology reaches critical mass its weaknesses and limitations almost become strengths as numerous companies, each trying to stake a claim in what quickly turns into a gold rush, step forward to fix the deficiencies."[53] That analysis is perfectly correct. It follows that the task of the visionary is to spot the buildup to critical mass before it occurs in order to stake the first claim and mine the richest seam of gold.

The Risk-Taker

Gates writes about risk; he implies that Microsoft is just such a visionary organization. He states in *Business @ the Speed of Thought*, "To be a market leader, you have to have what business writer and consultant Jim Collins calls 'big, hairy audacious goals.'"[54] Gates counts the foundation of Microsoft as just such a venture—a "big bet." Only in hindsight, he argues, does

Microsoft's success look preordained. At the time, "most people scoffed."
However, any company starting at any time in any industry is embarking on
a "hairy audacious" venture. It is only in hindsight, if the venture succeeds,
that its founders appear to have had vision.

The real problems arise when success has come and the successful market
leader is confronted with a new, disruptive technology. "Many industry leaders hesitated to move to new technologies for fear of undercutting the success
of their existing technologies," explains Gates.[55] This was the case with IBM.
That fear explains why it so underestimated the PC market and thus blinded
itself to the consequences of its naive deal with Bill Gates. As he says, the
hesitant leaders "learned a hard lesson." The hardest part of the lesson is that
they learned it too late.

Gates says, very rightly, "If you decline to take risks early, you'll decline
in the market later."[56] His policy, however, is not so audacious as he suggests.
He likes to hedge his bets, covering as wide a range as possible. This is not
quite what he says: "If you bet big, only a few of these risks have to succeed
to provide for your future."[57] In fact, the initial bet on the Internet was very
small, even though by the spring of 1991 "Microsoft was betting that the
Internet would be important someday."[58]

Microsoft was ensuring that its software could support the Internet; $100
million was being spent annually on "interactive networks of various kinds,"
although only part of that was expended on the Net. The figure soared to
billions once Gates realized that critical mass had arrived before he was ready
for it. At the time, he said, "The Internet is in an even stronger position than
the PC was 15 years ago."[59] Microsoft's position, however, was not as strong
as it was then for a variety of reasons, which include a transient failure of
vision.

Vision does not start on the far horizon or even the middle distance. It
begins right under your nose, in the proper understanding of what is going
on in the here and now. To repeat, vision to Gates is "not a competitive
advantage in any way, shape, or form." It has to be accompanied by the
action that will turn the vision into reality. That action, in turn, is impossible
unless the company has in place, or can acquire, the necessary resources,
capability, and energy. For example, when the PC market started to take off,
IBM had resources and capability in abundance, but its understanding was
erroneous, its vision defective, and its energy misplaced.

In the Gates philosophy, the concentration of organizational energy on
the object at hand is inseparable from vision. What you can do, and actually

do, has to match what you must do. Necessity does not extend to blue-sky or far-fetched ventures that will "bet the company." That is, risk total failure in the event of an error—even though Gates approvingly quotes Boeing's CEO of 1969–86, Thornton Wilson, who said, "If you want to look at it that you're betting the company, I hope we keep doing it."[60]

Boeing is also one of Gates's chosen examples of excellence in the use of the digital nervous system. The company was a bad example to pick, however, because of Boeing's record of periodic blundering, not in its bets, but in the execution of its choices. In 1998, the aircraft company plunged into losses after taking orders that could not be met with the current organization of its production machine. Heads rolled, and massive reforms were put in hand. That does not fit Gates's idea of vision.

Whatever his strategic and tactical failures, Gates has always ensured that Microsoft is able to execute the vision. That is partly because the vision is deliberately limited to what can be achieved from the existing base—to evolution, rather than revolution. In 1999, the audacious goals were to make the PC "scale in performance" beyond all existing systems. To develop computers that "see, listen, and learn", and create software to power the new personal companion devices.

These are quite plainly normal evolutions from Microsoft's existing products and capabilities, in no way representing great, daring jumps into the unknown. It would be strange to the point of absurdity if Microsoft were not pursuing the avenues it pursues, which are not so much "initiatives," but developments, and far from revolutionary. In fact, products already on the market have always performed the same functions that Gates has bettered in the end through zeal.

Gates says that Microsoft takes chances, saying things like, "one fact is clear: we have to take these risks in order to have a long-term future,"[61] but it is hardly ever the case. The risk of inertia, especially for a company with billions of dollars available, would have been far greater. It almost seems as though Gates wants to be seen as possessing precisely the type of vision— far-sighted, imaginative, bold, and quite possibly wrong—that he rejects in both word and practice.

The pragmatic way in which Gates regards vision is amply illustrated by his admissions of mistakes: "believe me, we know a lot about failures at Microsoft."[62] These failures are product failures, rather than consequences of defective vision. The first Microsoft spreadsheet flopped. So did the first database. So did the OS/2 operating system. Other failures included an office machine product and TV-style Internet shows, and Xbox (for a time). However, Gates claims that the lessons of much of this failure paid off in later products that were smash hits for Microsoft, and that is true.

The actual vision exemplified by Gates is a vision of Microsoft and what its place should be in the world of information technology. Gates expressed this vision very simply and very clearly in the early days of Microsoft in his original mission statement: "a computer on every desk and in every home, running Microsoft software."[63] Compared to nearly every other mission statement, this one has every advantage: short, sharp, to the point, and distinctive. Although Gates later dropped the last three words of his statement, getting a computer in every home and on every desk would, of course, have been meaningless to him unless Microsoft provided the software.

Subordinate visions, or strategies, flow from the overall idea. It followed that, as the profit moved downstream to the software applications that rested on the operating system, Microsoft had to join the movement. Gates took a Cosa Nostra approach to the industry. The customers were "our thing"; Microsoft should achieve the largest possible share of the applications market, emulating its achievement in operating systems. As every customer for an IBM or IBM-compatible PC was, de facto, a Microsoft customer, the vision demanded that Microsoft should seek to supply each and every software need, too.

To find the right direction for these subordinate visions, Microsoft turned to the customer. "In software, customers always want more," says Gates. "Our customers are always upping the ante, as they should."[64] The difficulty about following the customer, though, is that the customer often has to be led. Indeed, the great breakthroughs come, not from responding to customer demands, but from anticipating them. You could argue that Gates did exactly that with Windows. Before it appeared, only Apple Mac users could have envisioned it. However, too often, Microsoft has waited for the message from outside, and the wait has sometimes been too long, enabling others to steal valuable leads. Nothing in Gates's or Microsoft's history resonates with the same visionary importance as Moore's Law. In 1965, Gordon Moore, the cofounder of Intel, foresaw that the trend line for the improvement in chip performance relative to price would continue. In 1975, having been proved right, Moore pronounced what became his law, which is that chip capacity would double every 18 months with no increase in cost. This had profound implications for Intel, but Gates and Allen were quick to understand the equal impact on Microsoft.

The greater the power and speed of the computer, the more and more potent the applications it could use. To exploit this explosive potential, Gates formed a pragmatic vision around factors that included the importance of software as opposed to hardware, the role of compatibility, so that machines and programs could work together, and the need to initiate rather than follow trends.

Fear as Gates's Driving Force

The idea that Gates wants to give the appearance that the company "initiates trends" is ironic in view of the trend-following habits that Microsoft has usually demonstrated. Those habits, in turn, are curious, given a fundamental characteristic that Gates shares with his partner in the Wintel (Windows and Intel) quasi-monopoly, Andy Grove, the CEO of Intel. The latter called his 1996 book *Only the Paranoid Survive*. In his view, fear contributes powerfully to vision, just as its opposite, complacency, dulls the sight.

Gates expressed this attitude strikingly in a *Fortune* joint interview with his cofounder, Allen, saying, "The outside perception and inside perception of Microsoft are so different. The view of Microsoft inside Microsoft is always kind of an underdog thing. In the early days, that underdog, almost paranoid, view was a matter of survival. Even though, if you look back and see that our sales and profits grew by basically 50 percent a year for all these years, what I really remember is worrying all the time."[65]

Fear was the key to Gates's top-down management in the first two decades, and his shadow looming on every decision large and small even today. Gates feels he is the smartest person in the room, maybe on the planet, and he will make the final decisive decisions. Allen endorses this idea, saying that the partners could always see the "downside," even while working away to explore an upside that still dazzles Gates. "We've been climbing a steep mountain here, and you know there's still lots ahead of us," Gates says.[66] In Gates's idea of vision, you head for the highest peaks, but with the expectation that you may fall off the mountain at any time. Like any expert climber, therefore, you take every precaution to ensure that you stay firmly on the upward slope. The dangers and threats are immediate; the mountaintop is in the distance.

Considering this, Gates believes that successful companies make the future happen by first, driving the business forward vigorously. Second, concentrating on the potential of new developments, not the drawbacks. Third, never impeding progress for fear of undercutting the current business. Fourth, basing vision on a proper understanding of what is happening now. Fifth, taking all necessary action to protect the long-term future. Sixth, keeping your vision statement short, sharp, to the point, and distinctive.

And finally, run scared, while always bearing in mind the risks and threats.

WHERE DOES A LEADER GO FROM HERE?

You have to be burning with an idea, or a problem, or a wrong that you want to right. If you're not passionate enough from the start, you'll never stick it out.

—STEVE JOBS, founder of Apple

S o how does one become a Mandate Driven Leader? The first step is to remember that leadership is about moving teams, groups, and organizations toward specific outcomes. Today's leaders spend too much bandwidth, energy, and thought on process rather than outcomes. However, what we must remember is that those outcomes don't just happen as a result of barking instructions about these objectives. Successful leadership is about exhibiting behaviors that not only ensure the outcome, but inspire and enable individuals to achieve it. These behaviors result from a particular set of skills that must be learned, practiced, and developed. More importantly, they must be continually refined based on the situation and the particular talents of the leader in question. But where does one start? How does one begin the leadership journey to grow these skills?

First and foremost, each of us must take responsibility for our own leadership development. While some companies may offer outstanding leadership development programs, many do not. Those that do may offer leadership development curriculum grounded in the outdated philosophies of consensus management. Our next generation of business leaders, of disrupters, are going to need to embrace continual self-development. Henry David Thoreau stated, "You cannot dream yourself into a character; you must hammer and forge yourself one." Individuals are not destined to be great business leaders, they work hard at it, and this includes embracing self-development to hone the Mandate Driven Leadership traits necessary to ensure success.

One of the most common starting points for developing leadership skills is through attending formal training. This can include anything from corporate-sponsored multiyear professional development programs to half-day pep rallies that leave participants excited, though possibly not that well informed. Obviously, the quality of these programs can vary significantly. For a variety of reasons, such as costs and time commitments, many people driving their own leadership development end up in the half-day flavor of formal training. However, these approaches don't often get us the most bang for the buck. As such we don't really recommend investing in those unless they are closely paired with other activities or part of a broader leadership development program.

Establishing a network of formal and informal mentors is one method that is highly recommended. Earlier in this book, Brian Chesky of Airbnb described the importance of developing a network of mentors that aided in his continual development and knowledge expansion. There is no better place to learn than from a mentor who understands the path you are on. Most people consider a mentor someone they know personally that they can converse with about what they should and should not do in certain situations. The trick with this approach is that finding a mentor with the right skills and experience who has the time to work with you can be challenging. Most of those we would want to learn from are already very busy being leaders. Some people address this issue by finding a virtual mentor. For example, several people I know point to leadership guru Stephen Covey as a mentor even though they have never met him. Covey in many of his works stress that individuals without effective leadership skills can be efficient, but they will never be truly effective. For this reason, many upcoming leaders read as much of his work as possible, and they try to apply his teachings in as many different ways. This is not an ideal substitute for a true mentor, but it does lead us into our third and final category of leadership: self-development.

Perhaps the simplest way to describe this last category would be something like an independent leadership study. This means going out and consuming as much information as you can about the topic. This approach is perhaps the most consistent among great leaders. I've known and studied quite a few leaders over the course of my career, and the single most common denominator seems to be a voracious thirst for knowledge. Not just about leadership per say, bu : about any and every topic that they could apply to the teams they are trying to lead.

One of the commonalities of the leaders profiled in this book is that they read a lot. Many consume at least a book a week, even with their large responsibilities and hectic schedules. It has been said that seminal investor Warren Buffett generally takes only one meeting a day in order that he can spend the majority of the day reading and educating himself on various topics. So, your first step must be a commitment to leadership self-development including blocking out time each and every week to dedicate to that endeavor. The Endnotes and Additional Resources in this book provide a myriad number of resources for your leadership education and development.

The *MIT Sloan Management Review* article "When Consensus Hurts the Company" and its underlying research would be a great place to begin your self-development regimen. This research discusses how boards and top management teams often try to gain consensus about important decisions. The MIT research offers insights into when that's the right course, when it isn't, and how leaders can determine the best form of decision making for a given situation.

In organizations, key decisions are often made by groups—boards, senior management teams, finance committees, and so on—rather than by single individuals. Thus, an important role of the person leading a decision-making team is to know how to combine multiple opinions—in effect, to become a decision manager. The MIT research has found that how a decision is made can significantly affect the outcome of that decision. Hence, the ideas discussed in this MIT article are applicable to any setting in which one has to "decide how to decide." For the sake of clarity, we illustrate these ideas in the context of boards of directors.

The board of directors is responsible for a company's most important decisions. In turn, a key responsibility of the chairman is to lead the board so that, collectively, the board can make the best possible decisions for the company. The chairman guides the discussion among the board members and tries to get the most out of their expertise.

Imagine you are the chairman and that, after many hours of discussion about whether or not to acquire a competitor, three members strongly oppose the acquisition, while you, four board members, and the CEO support it. You need the board to make a decision now, because if your company doesn't buy this competitor soon, some other company is likely to do it. How would you combine the opinions of the nine board members to reach the best possible decision? Majority vote? Unanimous consent? Achieve a water-downed consensus?

The MIT data supports the fact that consensus level affects the type of errors made which naturally raises the question, "What is the best consensus level?" The traditional belief, particularly prevalent at the board level, is that high consensus is always good. Many groups proudly say, "All our decisions are unanimous." But the scientific evidence does not support the traditional view.

The MIT study is an example of learning that forces leaders to question status quo thinking—in this case whether unanimous decision making is beneficial. Ask yourself, how much of any given day is your calendar devoted to learning versus responding? So if you want to learn to be a leader, you first have to commit to the desire to consume information and learn more. Once you do that you'll be well on your way. Of course, then you'll need to learn how to teach others to lead.

Developing Leadership Skills in Others

While it is always great to be working on our own leadership skills, we should also think about how we teach others to lead. The reason this is so important is that another common trait of great leaders is that they pay it forward. They don't horde their knowledge, but actively share it with those who want to learn. This approach is often one of the key enablers of success for leaders of large organizations because it allows them to scale their impact beyond just those with whom they can directly interact.

The number of people that the average person can directly influence is finite. Depending upon whom you ask, that number is usually somewhere around five to seven, with extraordinary leaders being able to handle up to twice that. To be able to lead large organizations, however, leaders need to be able to influence hundreds to thousands of people. How do they do this? They lead other leaders who in turn lead others, and so on down the line. If this sounds like some kind of pyramid scheme, it kind of is. But it does not require anyone to buy a bunch of unnecessary products. What they do have to do, however, is figure out what they can do to teach others around them how to lead.

In the same way that those who want to learn to lead often consume a lot of material on how to be a leader, one of the ways some people teach others to lead is by recommending a whole bunch of material on leadership skills. Former Vice President Al Gore was known for requiring anyone who joined his cabinet to read Warren Bennis's *On Becoming a Leader*. But do these reading lists do much good? The short answer is maybe if they are part of a more comprehensive program that helps the person in question understand how to apply that knowledge. Otherwise, all you're doing is helping them fill up their bookshelf.

A great augmentation to a leadership reading list is a mentoring program. Just like in the self-directed approaches, this is where an experienced leader provides one-on-one guidance to someone trying to develop his or her skills. These relationships can be either formal or informal. The informal relationships tend to simply evolve over time, while the formal relationships have clear start dates (and sometimes end dates) and specific goals. They are often preceded by a rigorous matching process to make sure the right mentor is with the right mentee. To be most effective, however, these activities need to be part of a holistic leadership development program.

To reiterate, we are not talking about some half-day pep rally. We are talking about complete programs that include self-paced learning, reading, formal classes, and mentorship over the course of a given period of time (usually several years and ongoing). While there is no question that well-developed and well-run programs can be extremely impactful and meaningful, one of the biggest challenges for most organizations is deciding who should participate. While it would be great if anyone who wants to learn to be a better leader could participate, that wide net approach is often cost prohibitive. Most organizations have to limit participation to only those who have a high likelihood of becoming very successful leaders.

Identifying Leaders Within Your Organization

This begs the question—how do we accurately pick the people who are likely to be successful leaders? The most common approach is to pick people who have been successful as individual contributors. The paradox is that some skills, aptitudes, and attitudes that make one very successful as an individual contributor may not be the same ones that make one successful as a leader. For example, I have developed and managed many large, global sales organizations. One thing I discovered early is that the best individual salesperson does not necessarily make the best sales manager. We have to look for people who not only have done well in the past but also may do well in the future based on their traits.

Some people like to use psychometric assessments to identify those with high leadership aptitude. However, some organizations don't want to invest in the due diligence required to make sure that these tools are used in a way that differentiates without discriminating. An alternate approach is to qualitatively define the common traits of successful leaders in your organization. This can include attributes such as vision, communication, outcomes, and organizational citizenship behaviors. When these are clearly defined, it becomes easier to identify those individual contributors who might be good leaders. More importantly, it becomes easier to understand what kinds of leadership capabilities to develop. In today's business environment, Mandate Driven Leadership capabilities are what is needed. Knowing that is the vital part of teaching others how to be leaders.

Former Apple CEO John Sculley told *Business Insider* that the films about Jobs focused too much on Jobs's imperfections and missed the opportunity to explain why people love working for him as well, and the main reason was due to his passion that spilled out of him in grand fashion. "He focused his emotions entirely on the products that he was building," Sculley says. "He took on overwhelming amounts of hard work and was willing to sacrifice things in his personal life because we wanted to create products that people would love and he was very emotional about that."[1]

Steve Wilhite, Apple's VP of marketing communication in 1999–2000, said that working with Jobs was not an easy task, but he doesn't believe that he micromanaged people, and said he was inspired by him on a daily basis. "He was showing a genuine level of interest," Wilhite said in the book *Think Simple* by Ken Segall. "I've worked with iconic and amazing CEOs, but never with anyone who had the breadth of curiosity and inquisitiveness and the enthusiasm for fine detail in virtually every aspect of what we were doing. His bandwidth, his ability to grasp different concepts, his passion for delivering an off-the-charts experience, I've never experienced anything like that with any other CEO."[2]

As discussed throughout this book, different approaches to leading organizations have been tried. Sometimes there is a focus on people and process that can lead to democratic forms of leadership. Sometimes the focus on consensus gets so frustrating that true leadership moves to the background and the organization begins to default to a groupthink or laissez-faire approach. With no true leadership, chaos ensues.

Move Forward as a Mandate Driven Leader

At one time, directive leadership was the norm. Command and control leadership practiced in the military initially made its way into the corporate world. However, as our society has evolved since the industrial revolution, the directive leadership that was mainstream gave way to more participatory leadership styles. Two things happened that made the command and control approach less attractive. The first thing was that those in control gained more and more power, and some were corrupted by it. Those being led decided they didn't like this and wanted to make changes. Rather than recognizing that they simply had the wrong person leading them, they assumed it was the leadership style that was at fault and decided to wrest control from the leader and tried to rule by consensus. This makes everyone happy when things are running smoothly, but when things get messy and it becomes too difficult to make hard decisions by consensus, the group then cedes authoritarian control back to some leader. Then the whole cycle starts over again. Pick up any history book, and you can see this seesaw in leadership styles in society and business. You can often see this shifting approach in companies that have a succession of different CEOs over a short period of time.

We need a new view and discussion on leadership and what it means to be a change agent and a Mandate Driven Leader. It is not just about the role and being in charge. It is not about managing solely to an outcome. And just like we learned with our review of servant leadership, it is not solely about the selfless focus on motivating and taking care of others. In today's world, every company, every industry is at risk. The digital world is changing everything. For companies to not only survive but thrive, they need change agents—individuals with vision who through Mandate Driven Leadership can drive that vision into reality within their organizations.

For leaders who understand the difference between managing and leading, and between leading and being a change agent, great things will happen to their organizations.

So, where does a leader go from here? Throw away the teachings of old that advocate consensus-based decision making. Look at your own leadership style. Look at the leadership styles of your key management team. Using the traits discussed in this book, are they true Mandate Driven Leaders? If not, can they quickly develop into Mandate Driven Leaders? If not, replace them.

The well-being of you, your company, your employees, and their families depends on it.

ENDNOTES

CHAPTER 1

1. Alan Weber, "Consensus, Continuity, and Common Sense: An Interview with Compaq's Rod Canion," *Harvard Business Review*, July 1990.
2. Peter Drucker, *Management* (London: Collins, 2009).
3. Andrea Chang, "American Apparel's In-House Guru Shows a Lighter Side," *Los Angeles Times*, August 30, 2011.
4. William Cohen, *The Stuff of Heroes: The Eight Universal Laws of Leadership* (Atlanta: Longstreet Press, 2001).
5. Author interview with Mike Lawrie, May 21, 2018.

CHAPTER 2

1. Text of the Commencement address delivered by Steve Jobs, CEO of Apple Computer and of Pixar Animation Studios, on June 12, 2005, *Stanford News*.
2. Ibid.
3. Ibid.
4. Walter Isaacson, *Steve Jobs* (New York: Simon & Shuster, 2011).
5. David Sheff, "Playboy Interview: Steven Jobs," *Playboy*, February 1985.
6. Ibid.
7. Isaacson, *Steve Jobs*.
8. Ibid.
9. Ibid.
10. Ibid.
11. S. Wozniak and G. Smith, *iWoz: Computer Geek to Cult Icon* (New York: W.W. Norton & Company, 2007).
12. Isaacson, *Steve Jobs*.
13. Ubiquity Staff, "A Conversation with Jef Raskin," *Ubiquity*, July 2003.

14. Jef Raskin, "The Mac and Me: 15 Years of Life with the Macintosh," manuscript, 1994.

15. Brent Schlender, "Something's Rotten in Cupertino," *Fortune*, March 1997.

16. Steven Levy, *The Perfect Thing: How the iPod Shuffles Commerce, Culture, and Coolness* (New York: Simon & Shuster, 2007).

17. Isaacson, *Steve Jobs*.

18. Ken Segall, *Think Simple: How Smart Leaders Defeat Complexity* (London: Portfolio, 2016).

19. Peter Elkind, "The Trouble with Steve Jobs," *Fortune*, March 5, 2008.

20. Tom McNichol, "Be a Jerk: The Worst Business Lesson from the Steve Jobs Biography," *The Atlantic*, November 28, 2011,

21. Isaacson, *Steve Jobs*.

22. Ryan Himmel, "What Personality Traits Made Steve Jobs Successful?," *Entrepreneur*, April 18, 2013.

23. Susan Kalla, "10 Leadership Tips from Steve Jobs," *Forbes*, April 2, 2012.

CHAPTER 3

1. K. Boeke, "Sociocracy: Democracy as It Might Be," *Sociocracy*, accessed 2015, https://www.sociocracy.info/sociocracy-democracy-kees-boeke/.

2. Caitlin Morrison, "What the Analysts Are Saying About the M&S Results: 'Seismic Change' Needed After 'Humiliating' Plans Unveiled," *City A.M.*, November 8, 2016, http://www.cityam.com/253153/analysts -saying-ms-results-seismic-change-needed-after.

CHAPTER 4

1. Jeff Bezos, speech at Lake Forest College, February 26, 1998, C-Span.

2. Gerard J. Tellis, *Unrelenting Innovation: How to Create a Culture for Market Dominance* (Hoboken: John Wiley & Sons, 2013).

3. Richard L. Brandt, *One Click: Jeff Bezos and the Rise of Amazon.com* (London: Portfolio, 2012).

4. Brad Stone, *The Everything Store: Jeff Bezos and the Age of Amazon* (New York: Little, Brown and Company, 2013).

5. Julie Ray, *Turning on Bright Minds: A Parent Looks at Gifted Education in Texas* (Austin: Prologues, 1977).

6. Chip Bayers, "The Inner Bezos," *Wired*, March 1999.

7. Rebecca Johnson, "MacKenzie Bezos: Writer, Mother of Four, and High-Profile Wife," *Vogue*, February 2013.

8. "We Are What We Choose," Remarks by Jeff Bezos, as delivered to the Class of 2010, Baccalaureate, Princeton University, May 30, 2010.

9. Brandt, *One Click*.

10. Bezos, speech at Lake Forest College.

11. Bayers, "The Inner Bezos."

12. Ibid.

13. Ibid.

14. Jacqueline Doherty, "Amazon.bomb," *Barron's*, May 1999.

15. *Wired* Staff, "Bezos Blasts Low-Cash Report," *Wired*, June 28, 2000.

16. Jane Martinson, "Amazon.bomb: How the Internet's Biggest Success Story Turned Sour," *The Guardian*, May 1999.

17. *Time* magazine, Person of the Year Issue, December 27, 1999.

18. Amazon.com SEC Filings, https://www.sec.gov/cgi-bin/browse-edgar ?action=getcompany&CIK=0001018724&owner=include&count=40& hidefilings=0.

19. Ibid.

20. Jack Clark and Ashlee Vance, "How Amazon Swooped in to Own Cloud Services," *Washington Post*, June 2014.

21. Ibid.

22. Payscale Report, "The Least Loyal Employees," https://www.payscale .com/data-packages/employee-loyalty/least-loyal-employees.

23. Adam Lashinsky, "How Jeff Bezos Became a Power Beyond Amazon," *Fortune*, March 24, 2016, http://fortune.com/amazon-jeff-bezos-prime/.

24. G. Anders, "Jeff Bezos Reveals His No. 1 Leadership Secret," *Forbes*, April 4, 2012, http://www.forbes.com/forbes/2012/0423/ceo -compensation-12-amazon-technology-jeff-bezos-gets-it.html.

25. Omada King, "The Making Identity: Passwords to Personal Success and Global Transformation," Xlibris Corporation, April 9, 2013.

26. Stone, *The Everything Store*.

27. Ibid.

28. Ibid.

29. Ibid.

30. Ibid.

31. Internal e-mail from Jeff Bezos to staff, "No powerpoint presentations from now on at steam," June 9, 2004.

32. Adam Lahinsky, "Jeff Bezos: The Ultimate Disrupter," *Fortune*, November 2012.

33. "Leadership Principles," Amazon.com website, https://www.amazon .jobs/en/principles.

34. Stone, *The Everything Store.*

35. Ibid.

36. Ibid.

37. Ibid.

38. Amazon.com SEC Filing, https://www.sec.gov/Archives/edgar/data /1018724/000119312509153130/dex992.htm.

39. John Greathouse, "5 Time-Tested Success Tips from Amazon Founder Jeff Bezos," *Forbes*, April 30, 2013, http://www.forbes.com/sites /johngreathouse/2013/04/30/5-time-tested-success-tips-from-amazon -founder-jeff-bezos/#73f303c53351.

40. G. Anders, "Jeff Bezos Reveals His No. 1 Leadership Secret," *Forbes*, April 4, 2012, http://www.forbes.com/forbes/2012/0423/ceo -compensation-12-amazon-technology-jeff-bezos-gets-it.html.

41. Jillian D'Onfro, "14 Quirky Things You Didn't Know About Amazon," *Business Insider*, May 10, 2014, http://www.businessinsider.com/amazon -jeff-bezos-facts-story-history-2014-5?op=1/#azon-wasnt-the-companys -original-name-1.

42. D'Onfro, "14 Quirky Things."

43. Jodi Kantor and David Streitfeld, "Inside Amazon: Wrestling Big Ideas in a Bruising Workplace," *New York Times*, August 15, 2015, http:// www.nytimes.com/2015/08/16/technology/inside-amazon-wrestling-big -ideas-in-a-bruising-workplace.html?&_r=0.

44. Jodi Kantor, "Jeff Bezos and Amazon Employees Join Debate over Its Culture," *New York Times*, August 17, 2015, http://www.nytimes .com/2015/08/18/technology/amazon-bezos-workplace-management -practices.html.

45. Lashinsky, "How Jeff Bezos Became a Power."

46. Ibid.

47. Ibid.

48. George Anders, "Jeff Bezos's Top 10 Leadership Lessons," *Forbes*, April 23, 2012.

CHAPTER 5

1. Dr. Robert Hogan, "On Leadership: A Discussion with Dr. Robert Hogan," YouTube video, posted October 15, 2012, https://www .youtube.com/watch?v=f6orCHGppFM.

2. "The Leadership Deficit: The Problem, Its Causes, and Solutions as Identified in APQC Research Study," APQC, January 22, 2014, https://www.apqc.org/leadership-deficit-problem-its-causes-and-solutions-identified-apqc-research-study.

3. Douglas McGregor, *The Human Side of Enterprise: 25th Anniversary Printing* (New York: McGraw-Hill/Irwin, 1985).

4. Lee Thayer, *Leaders and Leadership: Searching for Wisdom in All the Right Places* (Bloomington: Xlibris Corporation, 2010).

5. Merriam-Webster.com, 2018, s.v. "benevolent," https://www.merriam-webster.com/dictionary/benevolent.

6. Susan Kalla, "10 Leadership Tips from Steve Jobs," *Forbes*, April 2, 2012.

7. Walter Isaacson, *Steve Jobs* (New York: Simon & Shuster, 2011).

8. C-Span Interview with Jeff Bezos, "Electronic Book Selling," March 18, 1999, last aired April 17, 1999.

9. Jonah Sachs, *Unsafe Thinking: How to Be Creative and Bold When You Need It Most* (New York: Random House, 2019).

10. John Bradley Jackson, *Déjà New Marketing: Increase Sales with Social Media, Search Marketing, E-mail Marketing, Blogs, and More* (Indianapolis: Dog Ear Publishing, 2010).

11. "What Really Killed the Apple III," http://www.applelogic.org/AIIIDesignBugs.html.

12. Glassdoor Employee Satisfaction Survey—Apple, https://thenextweb.com/apple/2011/08/25/97-of-apple-employees-think-steve-jobs-did-a-pretty-good-job/.

13. "The Willingness to Pursue a Long-Term Vision Was Critical to the Rise and Persistence of Amazon.com," *Washington Post*, August 5, 2013.

14. Robert M. Toguchi, *The Winning Habits of Steve Jobs* (iUniverse, 2017).

CHAPTER 6

1. Author interview with Mike Lawrie, May 21, 2018.

2. NDTV Staff, "Talking Heads: Mike Lawrie of IBM," NDTV, August 2002.

3. Steven Pearlstein, "A Turnaround Specialist Reshapes Computer Science Corps," *Washington Post*, August 1, 2015.

4. Rochelle Garner, "Siebel Systems Introduces New CEO; Mike Lawrie," CRN, May 3, 2004, https://www.crn.com/news/channel-programs /18841961/siebel-systems-introduces-new-ceo-mike-lawrie.htm.

5. Juliette Garside, "Setting Misys Apart from the IT Crowd," *The Telegraph*, September 19, 2008.

6. Vanessa Small, "News at the Top: Mike Lawrie, the Turnaround Executive," *Washington Post*, April 1, 2012.

7. Ibid.

8. Ibid.

9. Ibid.

10. Jason C.W. Hancock and Gus Zangrilli, "The Change Agent: How Mike Lawrie Transforms Cultures—and Companies," Spencer Stuart, November 2017, https://www.spencerstuart.com/research-and -insight/the-change-agent-how-mike-lawrie-transforms-cultures-and -companies.

11. Hancock and Zangrilli, "The Change Agent."

12. Ibid.

13. Pearlstein, "A Turnaround Specialist."

14. Author interview with Mike Lawrie, May 21, 2018.

15. Hancock and Zangrilli, "The Change Agent."

16. Pearlstein, "A Turnaround Specialist."

17. Author interview with Gary Stockman, April 10, 2018.

18. DXC Press Release, October 11, 2017.

19. Pearlstein, "A Turnaround Specialist."

20. Author interview with Mike Lawrie, May 21, 2018.

21. Ibid.

22. Ibid.

23. Jill R. Aitoro, "CSC Begins Rating Employees on an Extreme Bell Curve," *Washington Business Journal*, April 23, 2014.

24. Aitoro, "CSC Begins Rating Employees on an Extreme Bell Curve."

25. Author interview with Gary Stockman, April 10, 2018.

26. Author interview with Mike Lawrie, May 21, 2018.

27. Ibid.

28. Ibid.

29. Ibid.

30. Author interview with Jim Smith, March 23, 2018.

31. Author interview with Mike Lawrie, May 21, 2018.

CHAPTER 7

1. Samuel B. Griffith, *Sun Tzu: The Art of War* (London: Oxford University Press, 1963).
2. Ryan Himmel, "What Personality Traits Made Steve Jobs Successful?," *Entrepreneur*, April 18, 2013.
3. Griffith, *Sun Tzu: The Art of War*.
4. Eric Swenson, *The Five A's of Great Employees: Breakthrough Strategies for Hiring and Managing People* (Tucson: Wheatmark, Inc., 2016).
5. J. Amernic and R. Craig, "Leadership Discourse, Culture, and Corporate Ethics: CEO-speak at News Corporation," *Journal of Business Ethics* 118, no. 2 (December 2013): 379–94.
6. Walter Isaacson, *Steve Jobs* (New York: Simon & Schuster, 2011).
7. Susan Kalla, "10 Leadership Tips from Steve Jobs," *Forbes*, April 2, 2012.
8. Nick Summers, "How Pixar Gave Steve Jobs His Mojo Back," *Newsweek*, November 10, 2011.
9. Author interview with Mike Lawrie, May 21, 2018.

CHAPTER 8

1. David Kirkpatrick, *The Facebook Effect: The Inside Story of the Company That Is Connecting the World* (New York: Simon & Shuster, 2010).
2. Matt Rosoff, "Like It or Not, Mark Zuckerberg Is Now Silicon Valley's Ambassador to the Rest of the World," *Business Insider*, April 16, 2016.
3. Mark Zuckerberg, F8 Keynote Address, April 2016.
4. Somini Sengupta, "Zuckerberg Remains the Undisputed Boss at Facebook," *New York Times*, February 2, 2012.
5. Ibid.
6. Ibid.
7. Adam Lashinsky, "The Unexpected Management Genius of Facebook's Mark Zuckerberg," *Fortune*, November 10, 2016.
8. Facebook media conference call, April 4, 2018.
9. Henry Blodget, "Mark Zuckerberg on Innovation," *Business Insider*, October 1, 2009.
10. Open interview with Mark Zuckerberg, Y Combinator's Startup School, Stanford University in Palo Alto, California, April 29, 2011.
11. Jose Antonio Vargas, "The Face of Facebook," *New Yorker*, September 20, 2010.

12. Ibid.

13. Kirkpatrick, *The Facebook Effect.*

14. Vargas, "The Face of Facebook."

15. Miguel Helft, "Mark Zuckerberg's Most Valuable Friend," *New York Times*, October 2, 2010.

16. Caroline McCarthy, "Mark Zuckerberg Named *Time*'s Person of the Year," CNET, December 15, 2010.

17. Diane Sawyer, Mark Zuckerberg Interview, ABC World News, July 10, 2010.

18. Helft, "Mark Zuckerberg's Most Valuable Friend."

19. Sengupta, "Zuckerberg Remains the Undisputed Boss at Facebook."

20. Vargas, "The Face of Facebook."

21. Antonio Garcia Martinez, *Chaos Monkeys: Obscene Fortune and Random Failure in Silicon Valley* (New York: Harper, 2016).

22. Kirkpatrick, *The Facebook Effect.*

23. Ibid.

24. Alex Kantrowitz and Mat Honan, "We Talked to Mark Zuckerberg About Globalism, Protecting Users, and Fixing News," *Buzzfeed*, February 16, 2017.

25. Kara Swisher and Kurt Wagner, "Facebook's Mark Zuckerberg Wrote a 6,000 Word Letter Addressing Fake News and Saving the World," *Recode*, February 16, 2017.

26. Ibid.

27. Kantrowitz and Honan, "We Talked to Mark Zuckerberg About Globalism."

28. Swisher and Wagner, "Facebook's Mark Zuckerberg Wrote a 6,000 Word Letter."

29. Ibid.

30. Kantrowitz and Honan, "We Talked to Mark Zuckerberg About Globalism."

31. Marcia Amidon Lusted, *Mark Zuckerberg: Facebook Creator* (Minneapolis: ABDO Publishing Company, 2012).

32. Lev. Grossman, "Person of the Year 2010: Mark Zuckerberg," *Time*, December 15, 2010.

33. Charlie Rose, Mark Zuckerberg Interview, PBS, November 7, 2011.

34. Grossman, "Person of the Year 2010: Mark Zuckerberg."

CHAPTER 9

1. Harvey Mackay, "Harvey Mackay: 4 Stories with Great Management Lessons," *The Business Journals*, February 23, 2014, updated February 25, 2014, https://www.bizjournals.com/bizjournals/how-to/growth -strategies/2014/02/great-stories-great-management-lessons.html.

CHAPTER 10

1. Amy Zipkin, "Out of Africa, Onto the Web," *New York Times*, December 17, 2006.
2. Open Interview with Reed Hastings, Mobile World Congress 2017: Netflix CEO Reed Hastings Keynote, February 27, 2017.
3. Jon Xavier, " Netflix's First CEO on Reed Hastings and How the Company Really Got Started," *Inc.*, January 8, 2014.
4. Ibid.
5. Ibid.
6. Reed Hastings, "How I Did It: Reed Hastings, Netflix," *Inc.*, December 1, 2005.
7. Jim Hopkins, "Charismatic Founder Keeps Netflix Adapting," *USA Today*, April 23, 2006.
8. Reed Hastings, "How Netflix Got Started," *Fortune*, January 28, 009.
9. Zipkin, "Out of Africa, Onto the Web," Xavier, "Netflix's First CEO on Reed Hastings."
10. Xavier, "Netflix's First CEO on Reed Hastings."
11. Hastings, "How Netflix Got Started."
12. Bill Snyder, "Netflix Founder Reed Hastings: Make as Few Decisions as Possible," *Insights*, November 3. 2014.
13. Hastings, "How Netflix Got Started."
14. Hastings, "How I Did It."
15. Austin Carr, "Blockbuster CEO Jim Keyes on Competition from Apple, Netflix, Nintendo, and Redbox," *Fast Company*, June 8, 2010.
16. Hastings, "How I Did It."
17. Snyder, "Netflix Founder Reed Hastings."
18. Greg Sandoval, "Netflix's Lost Year: The Inside Story of the Price-Hike Train Wreck," CNET, July 11, 2012.
19. Chris Taylor, "Qwikster from Netflix: The Worst Product Launch Since New Coke?," *Mashable*, September 19, 2011.

20. Jason Gilbert, "Qwikster Goes Qwikly: A Look Back at a Netflix Mistake," *HuffPost*, October 10, 2011.

21. Ibid.

22. Snyder, "Netflix Founder Reed Hastings."

23. Open Q&A with Reed Hastings, *The New Yorker*'s TechFest, October 7, 2016.

24. John Lynch and Nathan McAlone, "How to Get a Job at Netflix, and What It's Like to Work There," *Business Insider,* September 18, 2018.

25. Netflix, "Reference Guide on our Freedom & Responsibility and Culture," Netflix PowerPoint Presentation 2009, https://www.slideshare.net/reed2001/culture-2009/19-19SelflessnessYou_seek_what_is_best.

26. Lynch and McAlone, "How to Get a Job at Netflix."

27. Netflix, "Reference Guide on our Freedom & Responsibility and Culture."

28. Ibid.

29. David Bond, "Reed Hastings: 'We Are Modeled on Sport,'" *Financial Times*, July 9, 2017.

30. Netflix, "Reference Guide on our Freedom & Responsibility and Culture."

31. Bond, "Reed Hastings: 'We Are Modeled on Sport.'"

32. Travis Bradberry, "Here's Why Every Employee Should Have Unlimited Vacation Days," *Entrepreneur*, January 27, 2016.

33. Hastings, "How I Did It."

CHAPTER 11

1. Dan Schawbel, "Seth Godin Urges You to Poke the Box [Exclusive Interview]," *Forbes*, March 1, 2011.

2. Author interview with Jimmy Brown, February 15, 2018.

3. "Root Cause Analysis—Challenger Explosion," ThinkReliability, https://www.thinkreliability.com/case_studies/root-cause-analysis-challenger-explosion/.

4. "The CIA's Internal Probe of the Bay of Pigs Affair," https://www.cia.gov/library/center-for-the-study-of-intelligence/csi-publications/csi-studies/studies/winter98_99/art08.html.

CHAPTER 12

1. Leigh Gallagher, "The Education of Brian Chesky," *Fortune*, June 26, 2015.

2. Leigh Gallagher, "Q&A with Brian Chesky: Disruption, Leadership, and Airbnb's Future," *Fortune*, March 27, 2017.

3. Gallagher, "The Education of Brian Chesky."

4. Adam Bryant, "Brian Chesky of Airbnb, on Scratching the Itch to Create," *New York Times*, October 11, 2014.

5. Ibid.

6. Avery Hartmans, "The Fabulous Life of Airbnb's Brian Chesky, One of the Youngest and Richest Tech Founders in America," *Business Insider*, September 5, 2017.

7. Bryant, "Brian Chesky of Airbnb, on Scratching the Itch to Create."

8. E-mail from Joe Gebbia to Brian Chesky, "Subject: subletter," September 22, 2007.

9. Bryant, "Brian Chesky of Airbnb, on Scratching the Itch to Create."

10. Drake Baer. "How LinkedIn's Reid Hoffman Jumped off a Cliff and Built an Airplane," Fast Company. May 17, 2013.

11. Gallagher, "The Education of Brian Chesky."

12. Dealroom.co, "Airbnb," https://app.dealroom.co/companies/airbnb.

13. Hartmans, "The Fabulous Life of Airbnb's Brian Chesky."

14. Gallagher, "Q&A with Brian Chesky."

15. Forbes Profiles, #568 Brian Chesky: CEO and Cofounder, AirBnB," https://www.forbes.com/profile/brian-chesky/#ae27dce44d3e.

16. Gallagher, "The Education of Brian Chesky."

17. Ibid.

18. Ibid.

19. Ibid.

20. Bryant, "Brian Chesky of Airbnb, on Scratching the Itch to Create."

21. Michael Arrington, "The Moment of Truth for Airbnb as User's Home Is Utterly Trashed," TechCrunch, July 2011.

22. AirBnb customer blog. http://ejroundtheworld.blogspot.com/2011/06/violated-travelers-lost-faith-difficult.html.

23. Brian Chesky, posting on Y Combinator, July 27, 2011, https://news.ycombinator.com/item?id=2811408.

24. AirBnb customer blog. http://ejroundtheworld.blogspot.com/2011/06/violated-travelers-lost-faith-difficult.html.

25. Gallagher, "The Education of Brian Chesky."

26. Brian Chesky, "On Safety: A Word from Airbnb," Techcrunch Blog, July 27, 2011, https://techcrunch.com/2011/07/27/on-safety-a-word-from-airbnb/.

27. Gallagher, "The Education of Brian Chesky."

28. Michael Arrington, "The Moment of Truth for Airbnb as User's Home Is Utterly Trashed," TechCrunch, July 2011.

29. Julie Bort, "Airbnb CEO Brian Chesky's Biggest Concern Is 'Discrimination We Are Having on Our Platform,'" *Business Insider*, July 12, 2016.

30. Ibid.

31. Ibid.

32. Ibid.

33. Ingrid Lunden, "Wimdu, Rocket Internet's Airbnb Clone, to Shut Down This Year 'Facing Significant Business Challenges,'" Techcrunch, September 27, 2019, https://techcrunch.com/2018/09/27/wimdu-rocket-internets-airbnb-clone-to-shut-down-this-year-facing-significant-business-challenges/.

34. Polina Marinova, "Airbnb CEO Brian Chesky: Going Public Is a 'Two-Year Project,'" *Fortune*, March 13, 2017.

35. Ibid.

36. "Airbnb > Acquisitions," Crunchbase, https://www.crunchbase.com/organization/airbnb/acquisitions/acquisitions_list.

37. Austin Carr, "Inside Airbnb's Grand Hotel Plans," *Fast Company*, March 17, 2014.

38. Ibid.

39. Ibid.

40. Ibid.

41. Ibid.

42. Bryant, "Brian Chesky of Airbnb, on Scratching the Itch to Create."

43. Ibid.

44. Ibid.

45. Gallagher, "The Education of Brian Chesky."

46. Letter from Brian Chesky to staff, October 21, 2012, https://twitter.com/bchesky/status/457953677475459072?lang=en

47. Ibid.

48. Ibid.

49. Carr, "Inside Airbnb's Grand Hotel Plans."

50. Gallagher, "The Education of Brian Chesky."

51. Katie Benner, "Inside the Hotel Industry's Plan to Combat Airbnb," *New York Times*, April 16, 2017.

52. Ibid.

53. Brian Chesky interview, Fortune Live, March 14, 2017, https://www
    .youtube.com/watch?v=GFMeuSIhIYg.
54. Benner, "Inside the Hotel Industry's Plan to Combat Airbnb."
55. Carr, "Inside Airbnb's Grand Hotel Plans."
56. Ibid.
57. Bryant, "Brian Chesky of Airbnb, on Scratching the Itch to Create."
58. Jony Ive, "Brian Chesky," April 15, 2015, *Time*, http://time.com
    /3822568/brian-chesky-2015-time-100/.

CHAPTER 13

1. Heather Simmons, *Reinventing Dell: The Innovation Imperative* (Murmurous Publishing, 2015).
2. Tom Huddleston Jr., "Elon Musk: Starting SpaceX and Tesla were 'the Dumbest Things to Do,'" CNBC, March 23, 2018.
3. Jay Samit, *Disrupt You! Master Personal Transformation, Seize Opportunity, and Thrive in the Era of Endless Innovation* (Flatiron Books, 2015).
4. Scott Stawski, *Inflection Point: How the Convergence of Cloud, Mobility, Apps, and Data Will Shape the Future of Business* (Pearson, 2015).
5. Andy Grove, Academy of Management, Annual Meeting, Keynote Address, August 9, 1998.
6. "The Reality of Digital Disruption—How to Stay Ahead," *Forbes*, July 17, 2018.

CHAPTER 14

1. Carol Smith Monkman, "Microsoft Stock Is Red Hot on First Day of Trading," *Seattle Post-Intelligencer*, March 14, 1986.
2. Ibid.
3. Neil Tweedie, "Bill Gates Interview: I Have No Use for Money. This Is God's Work," *The Telegraph*, January 18, 2013.
4. Robert Guth, "Raising Bill Gates," *Wall Street Journal*, April 25, 2009.
5. James Wallace and Jim Erickson, *Hard Drive: Bill Gates and the Making of the Microsoft Empire* (Hoboken: John Wiley & Sons, Inc, 1992).
6. Janet Lowe, *Bill Gates Speaks: Insight from the World's Greatest Entrepreneur* (Hoboken: Wiley, 1998).
7. Janet Lowe, *Warren Buffett Speaks: Wit and Wisdom from the World's Greatest Investor* (Hoboken: John Wiley & Sons, Inc, 2007).

8. Scott Stawski, *The Microsoft Monopoly Controversy: A Historical Analysis of Whether Microsoft Was an Illegal Monopoly in the 1990s* (CreateSpace, January 29, 2016).

9. Paul Krill, "Gates Undaunted by Linus," *Infoworld*, October 1, 2004.

10. Michael Moeller and Kathy Rebello, "Q&A with the Visionary-in-Chief: A Talk with Chairman Bill Gates on the World Beyond Windows," *BusinessWeek*, May 17, 1999.

11. Bro Uttal, "The Deal That Made Bill Gates, Age 30, $350 Million," *Fortune*, July 21, 1986.

12. Brent Schlender and Henry Goldblatt, "Bill Gates & Paul Allen Talk," *Fortune*, October 2, 1995.

13. Bill Gates, *Business @ the Speed of Thought: Succeeding in the Digital Economy* (Business Plus, 2000).

14. Ibid.

15. Ibid.

16. Anthony Sampson, *Company Man: The Rise and Fall of Corporate Life* (Crown Business, 1995).

17. Geoffrey James, *Business Wisdom of the Electronic Elite: 34 Winning Management Strategies from CEOs at Microsoft, COMPAQ, Sun, Hewlett Packard and Other Top Companies* (New York: Random House, 1996).

18. Brent Schlender, "The Bill and Warren Show," *Fortune*, July 20, 1998.

19. Bill Gates, *The Road Ahead* (New York: Viking Press, 1995).

20. Geoffrey James, *Giant Killers* (London: Orion, 1997).

21. David Bank, "How Microsoft Wound Up in a Civil War over Windows," *Wall Street Journal*, February 1, 1999.

22. David Rensin, "Bill Gates Interview," *Playboy*, 1994.

23. Schlender, "The Bill and Warren Show."

24. Ibid.

25. Peter M. Senge, *The Fifth Discipline* (New York: Doubleday, 2006).

26. Randall E. Stross, *The Microsoft Way* (Boston: Addison-Wesley, 1997).

27. Ibid.

28. Ibid.

29. Gates, *The Road Ahead.*

30. Gates, *Business @ the Speed of Thought.*

31. Ibid.

32. Ibid.

33. Ibid.

34. Ibid.
35. Ibid.
36. Thomas A. Stewart, *Intellectual Capital* (New York: Crown Business, 2010).
37. Ibid.
38. Ibid.
39. Gates, *Business @ the Speed of Thought.*
40. Ibid.
41. Lowe, *Bill Gates Speaks.*
42. Schlender, "The Bill and Warren Show."
43. Keith Patching, *Leadership, Character, and Strategy* (New York: Springer, 2006).
44. Schlender, "The Bill and Warren Show."
45. Ibid.
46. Gates, *The Road Ahead.*
47. Ibid.
48. Gates, *Business @ the Speed of Thought.*
49. Des Dearlove, *Big Shots: Business the Bill Gates Way*, 2nd ed. (Capstone, 2001).
50. Gates, *Business @ the Speed of Thought.*
51. Gates, *The Road Ahead.*
52. Ibid.
53. Ibid.
54. Gates, *Business @ the Speed of Thought.*
55. Ibid.
56. Ibid.
57. Ibid.
58. Gates, *The Road Ahead.*
59. Ibid.
60. Gates, *Business @ the Speed of Thought.*
61. Ibid.
62. Ibid.
63. Matt Weinberger, "Microsoft CEO Satya Nadella Says Bill Gates' original mission 'always bothered me,'" *Business Insider*, February 21, 2017.
64. Gates, *Business @ the Speed of Thought.*
65. Schlender and Goldblatt, "Bill Gates & Paul Allen Talk."
66. Ibid.

CONCLUSION

1. Natalie Walters, "Former Apple CEO John Sculley Says Steve Jobs Cried at the Office and That Is One Reason Why People Loved Working for Him," *Business Insider*, March 31, 2016.
2. Ken Segall, *Think Simple: How Smart Leaders Defeat Complexity* (Portfolio, 2016).

ADDITIONAL REFERENCES

Aitoro, Jill R., "Here's How Mike Lawrie Was Rewarded for CSC's Corporate Turnaround," *Washington Business Journal*, June 30, 2014.

Amazon Press Room, "Amazon Devices and Digital Content," Amazon .com, Inc., n.d., http://phx.corporate-ir.net/phoenix.zhtml?c=176060& p=irol-mediaKindle.

Amazon Press Room, "Biography," Amazon.com, Inc., n.d., http://phx .corporate-ir.net/phoenix.zhtml?c=97664&p=irol-govBio&ID=69376.

American Academy of Achievement, "Jeffrey P. Bezos," accessed September 30, 2013, http://www.achievement.org/autodoc/page/bez0bio-1.

Avolio, Bruce J., and Bernard M. Bass, *Developing Potential Across a Full Range of Leadership* (Mahwah, NJ: Lawrence Erlbaum Associates, 2002).

Avolio, Bruce J., *Full Range Leadership Development*, 2nd ed. (SAGE Publications Inc, 2010).

Badie, Dina, "Groupthink, Iraq, and the War on Terror: Explaining US Policy Shift Toward Iraq," *Groupthink* 6, no. 4 (2010): 277–96.

Baer, Drake, "5 Brilliant Strategies Jeff Bezos Used to Build the Amazon Empire," *Business Insider*, May 17, 2014, http://www.businessinsider .com/the-strategies-jeff-bezos-used-to-build-the-amazon-empire-2014-3.

Baer, Drake, "Malcolm Gladwell Says Entrepreneurs like Steve Jobs and IKEA Founder Ingvar Kamprad Share These 3 Personality Traits," *Business Insider*, October 10, 2014, http://www.businessinsider.com /gladwell-entrepreneur-personality-traits-2014-10.

Baer, Drake, "Why the Myers-Briggs Personality Test Is Misleading, Inaccurate, and Unscientific," *Business Insider*, June 18, 2014, http://www .businessinsider.com/myers-briggs-personality-test-is-misleading-2014-6.

Bardeh, M., and A. Shaemi, "Comparative Study of Servant Leadership Characteristics in Management Texts and Imam Ali's Tradition,"

Interdisciplinary Journal of Contemporary Research in Business 3, no. 2 (2011), 129–41.

Bateman, Thomas S., and Scott A. Snell, *Management: Leading & Collaborating in a Competitive World*, 8th ed. (Boston, MA: McGraw-Hill Irwin, 2009).

Bednarz, Ann, "In Pictures: Tech's Top-Paid CEOs," *Computer World*, 2014.

Bennis, W., *On Becoming a Leader* (Reading, MA: Addison-Wesley Publishing Company, 1989).

Bill and Melinda Gates Foundation, https://www.gatesfoundation.org/.

Blanchard, K., "Servant Leadership," *Executive Excellence*, Vol 10, no. 12.

Boyle, Matthew, "Questions for Reed Hastings," *Fortune*, May 28, 2007.

Brandt, Richard L., "Birth of Salesman," *Wall Street Journal*, October 2011.

Brennan, Chrisann, *The Bite in the Apple: A Memoir of My Life with Steve Jobs* (New York: St. Martin's Press, 2013).

Brickman, S. F., "Not-So-Artificial Intelligence," *The Crimson*, October 23, 2003.

Brown, Andrew D., Ian Colville, and Annie Pye, "Making Sense of Sensemaking in Organization Studies," *Organization Studies* 36, no. 2 (2015), 265–77.

Brown, David, "In Praise of Bad Steve," *The Atlantic*, October 6, 2011.

Bruzzese, Anita, "On the Job: Best Bosses Help You Add Skills," *USA Today*, May 5, 2013, http://www.usatoday.com/story/money/columnist /bruzzese/2013/05/05/on-the-job-good-bosses/2130779/.

Buchanan, L., and A. O'Connell, "A Brief History of Decision Making," *Harvard Business Review*, January 2006, https://hbr.org/2006/01/a-brief -history-of-decision-making.

Burgess, Reginald, *1 Microsoft Way: A Cookbook to Breaking Bill Gates Windows Monopoly Without Breaking Windows (with Linux CD Operating System)* (Amer Group Pub, 1998).

Byham, William C., and Jeff Cox, *Zapp! The Lightning of Empowerment* (New York: The Ballantine Publishing Group, 1998).

Cabrerizo, F. J., F. Chiclana, R. Al-Hmouz, A. Morfeq, A. S. Balamash, and E. Herrera-Viedma, "Fuzzy Decision Making and Consensus: Challenges," *Journal of Intelligent & Fuzzy Systems* 29, no. 3 (2015), 1109–18.

Campbell, David, *If I'm in Charge Here Why Is Everybody Laughing?* (Greensboro, NC: Center for Creative Leadership, 1980).

Chapman, J., "Anxiety and Defective Decision Making: An Elaboration of the Groupthink Model," *Management Decision* 44, no. 10 (2006), 1391–1404.

Chiclana, F., H. Fujita, E. Herrera-Viedma, J. Wu, and L. Dai, "A Minimum Adjustment Cost Feedback Mechanism Based Consensus Model for Group Decision Making Under Social Network with Distributed Linguistic Trust," *Abstract*, September 4, 2017.

Christian Science Monitor Editorial Board, "Would You Like Unlimited Days Off?," *The Christian Science Monitor*, August 22, 2013.

Cohan, Peter, "Netflix's Reed Hastings Is the Master of Adaptation," *Forbes*, October 22, 2013.

Collins, J. C., *Good to Great* (London: Random House Business, 2001).

Collins, Laura, "Desperate Plea of Amazon Founder Jeff Bezos's Ailing Biological Father," *The Daily Mail*, January 2014.

Cooperrider, D. L., and L. E. Sekerka, "Toward a Theory of Positive Organizational Change," in J. E. Cameron and R. E. Quinn, *Positive Organizational Scholarship* (San Francisco, CA: Berrett-Koehler, 2003), 225–40.

Csaszar, F. A., and A. Enrione, "When Consensus Hurts the Company," *MIT Sloan*, Spring 2015, https://sloanreview.mit.edu/article/when -consensus-hurts-the-company/.

Cuddy, Amy J.C., Matthew Kohut, and John Neffinger, "Connect, Then Lead," *Harvard Business Review* 91, no. 7 (July-August 2013), 54–61.

Dahl, Melissa, "Unlimited Vacation Policies Can Make Taking Time Off Kind of Awkward," *New York* magazine, December 10, 2014.

Das, T. K., *The Practice of Behavioral Strategy* (New York: IAP, 2015).

Davis, J. H., "Group Decision Making and Quantitative Judgments: A Consensus Model in Understanding Group Behavior," *Psychology Press* 2014, 43–68.

Davis, J. H., L. Hulbert, W. T. Au, X.P. Chen, and P. Zarnoth, "Effects of Group Size and Procedural Influence on Consensual Judgments of Quantity: The Examples of Damage Awards and Mock Civil Juries," *Journal of Personality and Social Psychology* 73, no. 4 (1997): 703.

Deutsch, Lindsay, "20 Years of Amazon: 20 Years of Major Disruptions," *USA Today*, July 14, 2015, http://www.usatoday.com/story/news/nation -now/2015/07/14/working---amazon-disruptions-timeline/30083935/.

Dilger, Daniel Eran, "iPhone Patent Wars: Xerox PARC & the Apple, Inc. Macintosh: Innovator, Duplicator & Litigator," *Appleinsider*, August 9,

2013, http://appleinsider.com/articles/13/08/10/xerox-parc-the-apple-inc
-macintosh-innovator-duplicator-litigator.

Donghong, D., L. Haiyan, S. Yi, and L. Qing, "Relationship of Servant
Leadership and Employee Loyalty: The Mediating Role of Employee Satisfaction," *I-Business* 4, no. 3 (2012), 208–15, doi:10.4236/ib.2012.43026.

Doraiswamy, Iyer Ramajanaki, "Servant or Leader? Who Will Stand up
Please?," *International Journal of Business & Social Science* 3, no. 9
(2012), 178–82.

Drucker, P. F., "What We Can Learn from Japanese Management," *Japanese Business*, 1998, 43–63.

Duhigg, Charles, "With Time Running Short, Jobs Manages His Fare-
wells," *New York Times*, October 6, 2011.

Eaton, J., "Management Communication: The Threat of Groupthink," *Corporate Communications: An International Journal* 4 (2001): 183–92.

Edstrom, Jennifer, and Marlin Eller, *Barbarians Led by Bill Gates* (Henry
Holt and Co., 1998).

Elgan, Mike, "In Defense of Steve Jobs," Cult of Mac, October 29, 2011,
http://www.cultofmac.com/126863/in-defense-of-steve-jobs/.

Elgan, Mike, "In Defense of Steve Jobs," *Cult of Mac*, October 29, 2011,
http://www.cultofmac.com/126863/in-defense-of-steve-jobs/.

Finberg, Howard, "Before the Web, There Was Viewtron," Poynter Institute, 2003.

Fisher, L. M., "Xerox Sues Apple Computer over Macintosh Copyright,"
New York Times, December 15, 1989.

Flatow, Ira (host), "A Chat with Computer Pioneer Steve Wozniak," *Talk of
the Nation: Science Friday with Ira Flatow*, NPR Radio, September 29,
2006.

Forbes, "Jeff Bezos," n.d., http://www.forbes.com/profile/jeff-bezos/.

Fox, Jeffrey J., *How to Become the CEO: The Rules for Rising to the Top of
Any Organization* (New York: Hyperion, 1998).

Fox, Justin, "Amazon's Cloud Really Is Disruptive," *Bloomberg*, April 22,
2015, https://www.bloomberg.com/view/articles/2015-04-22/amazon
-s-cloud-actually-merits-the-disruptive-tag.

Gallagher, Leigh, "Why Airbnb CEO Brian Chesky Is Among the World's
Greatest Leaders," *Fortune*, March 24, 2017.

Gardner, W. L., C. C. Cogliser, K. M. Davis, and M. P. Pickens, "Authentic Leadership: A Review of the Literature and Research Agenda," *The
Leadership Quarterly* 22, no. 6 (2011): 1120–45.

Gear, Michael Calore, "Steve Jobs' Greatest Achievements," *Wired*, October 5, 2011, http://www.wired.com/2011/10/steve-jobs-greatest -achievements/.

Greene, Robert, *The 48 Laws of Power* (New York: Penguin Books, 1998).

Greenleaf, Robert K., *Servant Leadership: A Journey into the Nature of Legitimate Power and Greatness* (Mahwah, NJ: Paulist Press, 1977).

Grove, Andrew, *Only the Paranoid Survive: How to Exploit the Crisis Points That Challenge Every Company* (Crown Business, 1999).

Haden, Jeff, "Which Successful People Share Your Personality Traits?" *Inc.*, August 4, 2014, http://www.inc.com/jeff-haden/which-successful -people-share-your-personality-traits.html.

Heath, Allister, "Group-Think and Delusion: Why VW Lost Its Bearings," *The Telegraph*, September 24, 2015, https://www.telegraph.co.uk /finance/newsbysector/industry/11889781/Group-think-and-delusion -why-VW-lost-its-bearings.html.

Hogan, Robert, and Robert B. Kaiser, "Personality," in J. C. Scott and D. H. Reynolds, *Handbook of Workplace Assessment: Evidence-Based Practices for Selecting and Developing Organizational Talent* (San Francisco: John Wiley & Sons, Inc., 2010), 81–108.

Hogan, Robert, and Robert B. Kaiser, "What We Know About Leadership," *Review of General Psychology* 9, no. 2 (2005), 169–80.

Human Synergistics, "Organizational Culture Inventory," accessed May 10,2018, https://www.humansynergistics.com/change-solutions/change -solutions-for-organizations/assessments-for-organizations/organization -culture-inventory.

Isaacson, Walter, "The Real Leadership Lessons of Steve Jobs," *Harvard Business Review*, April 2012.

Janis, L., "The Desperate Drive for Consensus at Any Cost. Classics of Organization Theory," *Groupthink* 2015, 161–68.

Janis, L., *Groupthink: Psychological Studies of Policy Decisions and Fiascoes* (Boston: Houghton Mifflin, 1982).

Janis, L., *Victims of Groupthink: A Psychological Study of Foreign Policy Decisions and Fiascoes* (NY: Houghton Mifflin Company, 1972).

Judge, Timothy A., and Ronald F. Piccolo, "Transformational and Transactional Leadership: A Meta-Analytic Test of Their Relative Validity," *Journal of Applied Psychology*, 2004.

Kaner, S., *Facilitator's Guide to Participatory Decision-Making* (John Wiley & Sons, 2014).

Kaplan, Michael, "You Have no Boss," *Fast Company*, October 31, 1997, http://www.fastcompany.com/32710/you-have-no-boss.

Keegan, John, *The Mask of Command: Alexander the Great, Wellington, Ulysses S. Grant, Hitler, and the Nature of Leadership* (New York: Penguin Books,1988).

Kelesidou, Fani, "Why One Personality Type Tends to Make the Most Money," *Motley Fool*, November 11, 2013, http://www.fool.com /investing/general/2013/11/11/why-one-personality-type-tends-to-make -more-money.aspx.

Kotterman, J., "Leadership Versus Management: What's the Difference," *The Journal for Quality & Participation* 29, no. 2 (2006): 13–17.

Krames, Jeffrey A., *Jack Welch and the 4 E's of Leadership: How to Put GE's Leadership Formula to Work in Your Organization* (New York: McGraw-Hill, 2005).

Levy, Lawrence, *My Unlikely Journey with Steve Jobs to Make Entertainment History* (Houghton Mifflin Harcourt, 2016).

Levy, Stephen, "Amazon: Reinventing the Book," *Newsweek*, November 2007.

Lew, H. J., "High-Tech Cruelty: Inside Amazon's Heartless (and Unethical) Workplace," *Ethics*, August 27, 2015, https://www.ethics.net/a/high -tech-cruelty-inside-amazon-s-heartless-and-unethical-workplace.

Lewin, Kurt, "Group Decision and Social Change," *Readings in Social Psychology* 3, no. 1 (1947): 197–211.

Love, Dylan, "16 Examples of Steve Jobs Being a Huge Jerk," *Business Insider*, October 25, 2011, http://www.businessinsider.com/steve-jobs -jerk-2011-10?op=1.

Lunenburg, F. C., "Decision Making in Organizations," *International Journal of Management, Business, and Administration* 15, no. 1 (2011): 1–9.

Malone, Michael S., *Infinite Loop: How Apple, the World's Most Insanely Great Computer Company, Went Insane* (New York: Doubleday Business, 1999).

McCrae, R. R., and P. T. Costa, "The Five-Factor Theory of Personality," in O. P. John, R. W. Robins, and L. A. Pervin, *Handbook of Personality*, 3rd ed. (New York: The Guildford Press, 2008), 159–81.

McKinsey & Company, "Organizational Health Index," accessed July 12, 2018, https://www.mckinsey.com/solutions/orgsolutions/overview /organizational-health-index.

Mitchell, E., "Participation in Unanimous Decision-Making," *The New England Monthly Meetings of Friends*, accessed 2011, http://demo.kratia.gr/wp-content/uploads/2011/10/Consensus-Decision-making.pdf.

Moniz, R. M. B. V., "Non-adjudicative Alternative Means of Dispute Resolution in Corporate Governance," doctoral dissertation, March 31, 2017.

Newcomb, Peter, and Adrienne Gaffney, "The New Establishment 2010: The Vanity Fair 100," *Vanity Fair*, October 2010.

Northouse, Peter G., *Leadership: Theory and Practice*, 8th ed. (SAGE Publications Inc., 2018).

O'Donovan, Caroline, "Unlimited Vacation Might Actually Be Bad for Workers," *BuzzFeed*, September 24, 2015.

OCAI Online, "About Organizational Culture Assessment Instrument (OACI), accessed May 11, 2018, https://www.ocai-online.com/about-the-Organizational-Culture-Assessment-Instrument-OCAI.

Organizational Culture Change, "Organizational Culture Change: Online Video Training," accessed May 10, 2018, http://organizationalculturechange.com/anecdotes/.

Ormiston, M. E., and E. M. Wong, "License to Ill: The Effects of Corporate Social Responsibility and CEO Moral Identity on Corporate Social Irresponsibility," *Personnel Psychology* 66, no. 4 (2013): 861.

Owens, B. P., A. S. Wallace, and D. A. Waldman, "Leader Narcissism and Follower Outcomes: The Counterbalancing Effect of Leader Humility," *Journal of Applied Psychology* 100, no. 4 (2015), 1203–13.

OZY Editors, "Inside the Business of Journalism," *OZY*, March 13, 2014.

Palomares, L. Martinez, and F. Herrera, "A Consensus Model to Detect and Manage Noncooperative Behaviors in Large-Scale Group Decision Making," *IEEE Transactions on Fuzzy Systems* 22, no. 3 (2014): 516–30.

Pérez, J., F. J. Cabrerizo, S. Alonso, and E. Herrera-Viedma, "A New Consensus Model for Group Decision Making Problems with Non-homogeneous Experts," *IEEE Transactions on Systems, Man, and Cybernetics: Systems* 44, no. 4 (2014): 494–98.

Pettigrew, M., *The Politics of Organizational Decision-Making* (Routledge, 2014).

Ragland, D. R., and R. J. Brand, "Type A Behavior and Mortality from Coronary Heart Disease," *New England Journal of Medicine* 318 (1988): 65–69.

Rasmus, Grace, "The 14 Strangest Steve Jobs Stories," *Mac World*, April 4, 2014, http://www.macworld.co.uk/feature/apple/14-strange-steve-jobs -anecdotes-3510030/.

Reuters News Agency, "Amazon.com. Inc. (AMZN.O)," Reuters, n.d., http://www.reuters.com/finance/stocks/companyProfile?symbol= AMZN.O.

Rhizome staff, "The Polder Model. A Brief History of Consensus Management," *Rhizomenetwork*, June 18, 2011, https://rhizomenetwork .wordpress.com/2011/06/18/a-brief-history-of-consenus-decision-making/.

Riggio, Ronald E., "The 4 Elements of Transformational Leaders," *Psychology Today*, November 15, 2014.

Rosoff, Matt, "Why Steve Jobs Was Such a Jerk to Employees," *Business Insider*, February 16, 2015, http://www.businessinsider.com/why-steve -jobs-was-such-a-jerk-to-employees-2015-2.

Ross, E. M., "*Remaking Friends: How Progressive Friends Changed Quakerism and Helped Save America* by Chuck Fager, and: *Angels of Progress: A Documentary History of the Progressive Friends: Radical Quakers in a Turbulent America* ed. by Chuck Fager (Review)," *Quaker History* 104, no. 1 (2015), 51–52.

Rupprecht, Elizabeth A., Jessica S. Waldrop, and Matthew J. Grawitch, "Initial Validation of a New Measure of Leadership," *Consulting Psychology Journal: Practice and Research* 65, no. 2 (2013), 128–48, doi:10 .1037/a0033127.

Schein, Edgar H., *Organizational Culture and Leadership*, 3rd ed. (Wiley Publishing, 2004).

Schlender, Brent, *Becoming Steve Jobs: The Evolution of a Reckless Upstart into a Visionary Leader* (Crown Business, 2007).

Sendjaya, Sen, and James C. Sarros, "Servant Leadership: Its Origin, Development, and Application in Organizations," *Journal of Leadership & Organizational Studies* 9, no. 2 (2002), 57–64.

Sharer, K., "How Should Your Leaders Behave?," *Harvard Business Review* 91, no. 10 (2013), 40.

Shaw, Colin, "Big Changes at Airbnb," *Beyond Philosophy*, September 22, 2016.

Stephens, Joe, and P. Behr, "Enron's Culture Fed its Demise," *Washington Post*, January 27, 2002, https://www.washingtonpost.com/archive /politics/2002/01/27/enrons-culture-fed-its-demise/d73cf80c-0d00 -4281-848d-968683828ef9/?utm_term=.c7ba383604b9.

Sunstein, C. R., and R. Hastie, "Wiser: Getting Beyond Groupthink to Make Groups Smarter," *Harvard Business Press*, 2015.

Swartz, Jon, "Apple Profit Up, iMac Sales Cited," *SFGATE*, January 14, 1999.

Tarantola, D., "Thinking Locally, Acting Globally?," *American Journal of Public Health* 103, no. 11 (November 2013): 1926.

Taylor III, Alexander, "Striking It Rich: A New Breed of Risk Takers Is Betting on the High-Technology Future," *Time*, February 1982.

Thomas, Owen, "Why Mark Zuckerberg Is like Hitler (and Stalin, too!)," *VentureBeat*, December 15, 2010.

Thompson, Mike, *The Anywhere Leader: How to Lead and Succeed in Any Business Environment* (San Francisco: Jossey-Bass, 2011).

Thompson, Mike, *The Organizational Champion: How to Develop Passionate Change Agents at Every Level* (New York: McGraw-Hill, 2009).

Thurston, L. D., "Business Guru Calls for More Servant Leaders," *Caribbean Business* 34, no. 44 (2006): 29.

Timm, C. M., "When Is Management by Consensus Appropriate and What Are the Alternatives," *WM'07 Conference* (Tucson, Arizona), 2007.

Urstadt, Bryant, "What Amazon Fears Most: Diapers," *Bloomberg Businessweek*, October 2010.

Vroom, V. H., and A. G. Jago, *The New Leadership: Managing Participation in Organizations* (Prentice-Hall, Inc., 1998).

Walker, Jennifer, "A New Call to Stewardship and Servant Leadership," *Nonprofit World* 21, no. 4 (2003), 25.

Wall Street Journal, "Jeff Bezos," n.d., http://topics.wsj.com/person/B/jeff -bezos/698.

Wheeler, Rob, "Amazon's Kindle Fire Is a Disruptive Innovation," *Harvard Business Review*, September 29, 2011, https://hbr.org/2011/09/amazon -kindle-fire-scare-apple.

Wolff, R. P., *In Defense of Anarchism* (Los Angeles: University of California Press, 1970).

Wolverton, Troy, "iPhone's Design, Software Transformed Phone Industry," *The Mercury News*, December 28, 2007.

Yetton, P., and P. Bottger, "The Relationships Among Group Size, Member Ability, Social Decision Schemes, and Performance," *Organizational Behavior and Human Performance* 32, no. 2 (1983): 145–59.

Zenger, Jack, "The Big Lesson About Leadership from Steve Jobs," *Forbes*, August 22, 2013.

INDEX

ABOUT THE AUTHORS

Scott **Stawski** is the Global Chief Revenue Officer for Applications and Business Process Services at DXC Technology. DXC was formed through the merger of Computer Sciences Corporation and the Enterprise Services division of Hewlett Packard Enterprise in April of 2017. With more than $21 billion in annual revenue, DXC is the world's leading independent, end-to-end IT services company, helping clients harness the power of digital innovation to enable business breakthroughs.

In his role, Scott is responsible for managing the sales and revenue generation activities for the applications services business unit globally. This business unit's portfolio consists of application development, management and transformation, and modernization to the cloud and accounts for more than $4.5 billion in annual revenue.

Prior to his current role, Scott was America's Vice President of Sales for the automotive, manufacturing, and aerospace and defense sectors. Over the preceding four years, Scott and his team have sold more than $6 billion in IT services.

Scott brings a wealth of experience in business outcome-based technology service delivery to his sales management ability. Prior to sales management, he led numerous multimillion-dollar business intelligence and digital technology solutions engagements for Global 500 companies. A trusted advisor for CEOs, CFOs, and CIOs in the Americas, Scott is a recognized expert in digital, analytics, and data management, technology strategy, outsourcing, and next-generation application transformation to the cloud.

In the fall of 2015, Scott's first book, *Inflection Point: How the Convergence of Cloud, Data, and Mobility Will Shape the Future of Business*, was published by Pearson FT Press. He is also a contributing writer for TheStreet.com and SeekingAlpha.com and is a speaker and facilitator at many of the foremost industry shows and conferences.

Prior to joining Hewlett Packard, Scott was a Senior Principal at Knightsbridge, a leading business intelligence consultancy that was acquired by Hewlett Packard. At Knightsbridge, Scott led teams developing digital and business intelligence strategies and platforms for Fortune 500 companies.

Scott is Secretary, Board Member for the Celina Economic Development Corporation where he consults on the Gigabit City initiative in North Texas. He is active with ChildFund International and Shakespeare Dallas. He is also on the Board of Advisors for Southern Methodist University's Creative Coding and Visualization Program. Scott has a Bachelor of Arts in Humanities and has a Master of Liberal Arts, Extension Studies in History from Harvard University in Cambridge.

Jimmy Brown, PhD, is a senior consulting executive with more than 20 years' experience delivering practical strategies for business performance improvement. His current efforts focus on leadership development, strategic planning, and change management. Previously Dr. Brown held senior-level consulting positions at marquee firms such as Booz Allen Hamilton, Accenture, and Hewlett Packard. In these roles, Dr. Brown has worked across several industries including healthcare (provider, payer, and bio-pharma), retail, high-tech, manufacturing, energy, and federal government (civilian and DoD). He is regularly sought out for his insights on how to apply cutting-edge theory to solve real-world business challenges.

As a complement to his consulting work, Dr. Brown is also a faculty member in the psychology and graduate management (e.g., MBA) programs of several universities, including the Grand Canyon University's College of Doctoral Studies. In these roles he both teaches courses and mentors doctoral candidates.

Dr. Brown is a frequent speaker and author on topics such as strategic planning and change management. He has presented at major conferences such as the American Society for Training and Development and the Academy of Management. His most recent books include *The 7 Assumptions That Drive Success & Happiness, Journey Management: Unleashing the Strategic Power of Change,* and *Systems Thinking Strategy: The New Way to Understand Your Business and Drive Performance.*

Dr. Brown received his Master's degree in Industrial and Organizational Psychology from the University of Tulsa, and his PhD from Benedictine University's award-winning Organizational Development program. In addition, he is a certified Professional of Human Resources (PHR) through the Society for Human Resources Management. He is an active member of the American Psychological Association, the Society for Industrial and Organizational Psychology, and the Society for Human Resources Management.